Community-University Partnerships in Practice

Edited by
Angie Hart
Elizabeth Maddison
David Wolff

D0514396

promoting adult learning

© 2007 National Institute of Adult Continuing Education (England and Wales)

21 De Montfort Street
Leicester LE1 7GE
Company registration no. 2603322
Charity registration no. 1002775
Reprinted 2008

promoting adult learning

NIACE has a broad remit to promote lifelong learning opportunities for adults. NIACE works to develop increased participation in education and training, particularly for those who do not have easy access because of class, gender, age, race, language and culture, learning difficulties or disabilities, or insufficient financial resources.

For a full catalogue of all NIACE's publications visit **www.niace.org.uk/publications**

Cataloguing in Publications Data

A CIP record for this title is available from the British Library

ISBN 978-1-86201-317-9

Cover design by Patrick Armstrong Book Production Services, London

Designed and typeset by Kerrypress, Luton

Printed and bound by Ashford Colour Press, Gosport

CONTENTS

Acknowledgements

The editors would like to thank the many contributors to this book. In particular we would like to highlight the community partners. For many, but by no means all, writing for publication has been a new experience and we are very grateful to all the community practitioners for their considerable efforts. Thanks are also due to our academic colleagues who similarly put in substantial time and energy to the project. We would also like to thank the administrative team that helped us overcome the logistical difficulties of 41 contributors jointly authoring the book. The authors are listed elsewhere but we need here to express our debt to a number of colleagues who made key contributions: Michelle Tarling, Elaine McDonnell, Paul Bramwell, Clara Heath, Flis Henwood, Elvira Mogensen and Andrew Toal.

Particular thanks go to two people without whom this book would never have been written. Angie's research assistant Chloe Gerhardt gave us patient and efficient editorial and administrative assistance. Stuart Laing made available financial assistance from the University for this volume so that we could pay community collaborators for their involvement, and more importantly has been a guiding hand in its production throughout, and a powerful advocate for community-university engagement.

Thanks are also due to the University of Brighton, the Atlantic Philanthropies (especially Michael Guinnel) and the Higher Education Funding Council for England for funding the work detailed in this volume.

We also want to acknowledge the influence of the University's previous Vice Chancellor, Professor Sir David Watson, without whom Cupp would not exist, and its current Vice Chancellor, Professor Julian Crampton, who has been a stalwart and far-sighted supporter of the work described here.

Finally, thanks are due to our families for putting up with us whilst we edited this book.

Part 1

Setting the scene

Introduction

Angie Hart, Elizabeth Maddison and David Wolff

This book, co-written by community members and academics, provides a window onto community–university engagement. In it, we describe our work at the University of Brighton and analyse the Community-University Partnership Programme (Cupp) in its wider context.

Most of the chapters discuss projects in action. These projects relate teaching and learning to the wider world, involve back-and-forth dialogue between practitioners, researchers and community members and see members of the University community take the issue of wider responsibility seriously. The first part of the book gives a rounded sense of the higher education and community context, and the core development work that has been undertaken to get the projects described here off the ground. The middle section offers an account of a number of individual projects. The final part of the book reflects on ways of evaluating community university partnership activity and sets out some of the issues we face as we develop this work for the future.

Some of the work described in this volume will seem new and innovative, yet Cupp at the University of Brighton could, many will say, be seen as the latest manifestation of a longer-standing institutional imperative. The University of Brighton itself has its origins in vocational and professional education degrees, something we say more about in Chapter 1, so it has always had a strong relationship with those working in the local community. Contemporary debates about this relationship and the role of universities are live. Aspects include the best way of managing knowledge transfer for economic growth and business development, and of stimulating public engagement more generally (Watson, 2007).

Many of the current initiatives in the UK concentrate on developing local economic capacity and on assessing local economic impact. Even in those cases where clear cultural or social benefit is the aim, university-wide structures to articulate and support such activity systemically are still relatively rare in this country, although in the US and in Australian universities they are more developed (Lerner and Simon, 1998; Maurrasse, 2001; Sunderland *et al.*, 2004). The University of Brighton is one of a few UK universities with an established institution-wide programme with a dedicated structure, and a clear focus on working locally to address capacity and regeneration, while also enhancing learning, teaching and research.

Because so few systematic community–university engagement programmes exist in the UK, there is little published about how they function, and how they achieve their maximum potential. Even within the US literature, beyond the work of Lerner and colleagues there is a dearth of material that addresses the practicalities of community–university partnership processes that draws directly on the perspectives of both the university and its community partners (Lerner and Simon, 1998).

At Brighton, we are interested in ways of making university resources accessible to communities and in ways in which universities can benefit from community resources. We want to further practice in setting up, supporting and making engagement partnerships happen. The need to inject enthusiasm and life into community–university relations and to keep them alive and kicking needs emphasising. But the work also needs conceptual bases, particularly if it is to engage senior academics and institutional leaders and managers, and attain institutional sustainability. Chapter 1 of this volume sets out some of the conceptual issues framing community–university engagement. Regarding operational delivery of Cupp, we have found the conceptual framework of 'communities of practice' particularly useful (Wenger, 1998). This is a body of work that to our knowledge has not yet featured in the literature on community-university engagement. Our own work is drawing on that theoretical debate to foster engagement and mutual benefit: the framework, as we come on to illustrate in the final part of this book, is relevant to making academic scholar-practitioner partnerships work in reality.

Although the story told here is largely one of success, this has not been without its challenges. The challenges were such that a group of us working with and through Cupp felt it worthwhile to ourselves and to others to set out a written record of how Cupp developed. This book documents that journey. Throughout the book we have tried to make clear what we have learnt from our Cupp activity to date.

When we say 'we', it is important to point out that this book has not been produced by a collective. The editors, and authors of this introduction in their various roles and commitments combine the identities of university administrator, programme director, academic, community practitioner and service user. And each of the chapters has been written in partnership for sure. As an editorial team, we gave contributors a brief – each chapter (with the exception of three chapters in Part 1), should be co-authored by university staff and community collaborators. We knew this was no easy task. Co-authorship necessarily has its challenges. To add to this, there are few texts that have previously been written jointly by university staff and community members (but see Lerner and Simon, 1998). Others have pointed out that the different practices and value systems of university academics and community collaborators when it comes to dissemination of joint work do not make for smooth collaboration (Cottrell and Parpart, 2006). We even deliberated over whether the written word was the best format through which to disseminate our work.

Our dilemma here ties into our broader deliberations about what type of knowledge is being produced, mobilised and legitimised through Cupp. There have been many attempts to classify different forms of knowledge production and mobilisation, and the debate has become fairly technical and complex. However, since knowledge production is a key function of universities, and is deeply embedded in our Cupp activity, we briefly review aspects of the debate here.

As we argue in the final chapter, academic knowledge is often described as Mode 1 knowledge. That is to say, pure, disciplinary, homogenous, expert-led, supply-driven, hierarchical, peer-reviewed and almost exclusively university-based (Gibbons *et al.*, 1994). Traditionally, Mode 1 knowledge connotes and confers prestige and legitimacy. However, knowledge thus defined does not attune well to Cupp.

A second form of knowledge suggests a better fit. Mode 2 knowledge is applied, problem-centred, transdisciplinary, heterogeneous, hybrid, demand-driven, entrepreneurial, network-embedded and often increasingly handled outside of higher education institutions (Gibbons *et al.*, 1994). This type of knowledge has not traditionally been valued by academics and by institutions of higher education (Hart and Wolff, 2006). For example, in a 2006 survey of UK scientists, 20 per cent of respondents stated that colleagues who made their work accessible to the public were less well regarded by other scientists (The Royal Society, 2006). In the US successful attempts to change promotion policies for academic staff so that community engagement is rewarded are now being documented (see for example the Community-Campus Partnerships for Health toolkit).

Since the work of Gibbons *et al.*, further levels of knowledge have been proposed, with at least two research groups putting forward different definitions of what they call Mode 3 knowledge. (Scott *et al*, 2004) propose Mode 3 knowledge as, 'dispositional and transdisciplinary knowledge' produced by individual professional practitioners through structured university work at postgraduate level (e.g. professional doctorate). Ray and Little, by contrast, tentatively offer up 'collective tacit' knowledge in Japanese workplaces as fitting the bill for Mode 3 (Ray and Little, 2001). Mode 4 has also been suggested as a conceptual category by Scott *et al.* where the purpose is explicitly or implicitly political and change-orientated (Scott *et al.*, 2004, p. 8).

None of these typologies quite fits the bill for the work we have produced for this volume. However, they do alert us to the very many ways in which knowledge is constructed and produced, and the different purposes it serves. Indeed, we can even make a case for the work of Cupp to be going in the direction of what we might call Mode 5 knowledge, which draws on aspects of 1–4 and proposes something further. In our work, from Mode 1 we take 'peer-reviewed'; from Mode 2 we take 'applied, heterogeneous, and problem-centred'; Mode 3 gives us 'transdisciplinary' and Mode 4 'change-orientated'. Mode 5 is all of these, but we add a further crucial dimension: 'co-produced by the university and community'.

Despite our very different traditions of knowledge production, in Cupp academics and community practitioners have managed to merge expertise to produce forms of knowledge together. We have a website, conferences, seminars and films (see for example www.cupp.org.uk as a general link, and more specifically www.brighton.ac.uk/cupp/projects/a2a_home.htm, for the film of one specific art project, referred to in Chapter 11).

With so much going on at the University of Brighton it is not surprising that when we mooted the idea of a 'Cupp book' there was enthusiasm for the venture, and some community colleagues were, if not quite as enthused as university staff, at least willing to give it a go. And at least some of us involved with Cupp were keen to attempt production of something relatively new in form.

With Mode 1 knowledge historically representing the most prestigious mode of university-produced knowledge, and one that academics most readily conform to, it was certainly a challenge to get something that looked more like Mode 5 off the ground. But one thing was clear to us right from the start. In producing this book, we wanted to do our best to avoid what is often the case – university staff speaking on behalf of community partners. Furthermore, we wanted to produce a book that would appeal to both university colleagues planning to work with community partners, and to community organisations and their members wanting greater involvement with academic institutions. To facilitate the process we put on writing workshops and employed a research assistant to help chapter authors, in collaboration with the editors, to structure and reference their work appropriately.

We believe we have achieved some success in meeting our aims, although we cannot say hand on heart that each chapter represents an even split between university and community partners or that the book has been produced without difficulties. Some academic partners found it difficult to stick to our brief of involving community partners, and some partners did not have the time or motivation to write about their work. Furthermore, we have, at times been criticised by community colleagues for not making the process sufficiently inclusive, and for producing a text that conforms too much to academic publication standards, and to Mode 1 knowledge. Others have shown explicit gratitude for our support and guidance through workshops and individual meetings, have been enthusiastic about being included and have felt that the book genuinely co-produces new forms of knowledge.

We have tried to engage constructively with these tensions. Reflecting back on the process, what we can say with certainty is that we stuck to our original brief. What follows are the fruits of our collective endeavour.

References

Community-Campus Partnerships for Health (CCPH). *Toolkit*, found at http://depts.washington.edu/ccph/toolkit.html, accessed 5 April 2006.

Cottrell, B. and Parpart, J. L. (2006) 'Academic-community collaboration, gender research, and development: pitfalls and possibilities', *Development in Practice*, Vol. 16, No. 1, pp. 15–26.

Gibbons, M., Limoges, C., Norwotony, H., Schwarzman, S., Scott, P. and Trow, M. (1994) *The production of knowledge: the dynamics of science and research in contemporary societies*. London: Sage.

Hart, A. and Wolff, D. (2006) 'Developing communities of practice through community–university partnerships', *Planning, Practice and Research*, Vol. 21, No. 1, pp. 121–38.

Lerner, R.M. and Simon, L.A.K. (1998) *University-community collaboration for the twenty-first century*. New York: Garland.

Maurrasse, D.J. (2001) *Beyond the campus: how colleges and universities form partnerships with their communities*. London and New York: Routledge.

Ray, T. and Little, S. (2001) 'Communication and context: collective tacit knowledge and practice in Japan's workplace *ba'*, *Creativity and Innovation Management Vol. 10, No. 3, pp. 154–64*.

Scott, D., Thorne, L., Lunt, I. and Brown, A. (2004) 'Academic, professional and hybrid forms of knowledge in higher professional development'. Paper presented to the International Sociological Association 4th Interim Conference: *Knowledge, Work and Organization*, September 2004. Available: http://www.printemps.uvsq.fr/Com_scot.html. Accessed April 2007.

Sunderland, N., Muirhead, G., Parsons, R. and Holtom, D. (2004) *The Australian consortium on Higher Education, community engagement and social responsibility*. Report. Queensland, Au: University of Queensland.

The Royal Society (2006) *Science communication: Excellence in science*. London: The Royal Society.

Watson, D. (2005) 'What have the universities ever done for us?' Talk for Higher Education Policy Institute (HEPI) seminar, House of Commons, 30 November 2005. Available: http://www.hepi.ac.uk/downloads/Whatdidtheuniversityeverdoforus-DavidWatson.pdf, accessed April 2007.

Watson, D. (2007) *Managing civic and community engagement*. Maidenhead: Open University Press.

Wenger, E. (1998) *Communities of practice: learning, meaning and identity*. Cambridge: Cambridge University Press.

Chapter 1

The Cupp model in context[1]

Stuart Laing and Elizabeth Maddison

This chapter offers an introduction to the context in which Cupp was established and now operates. In so doing, it attempts to answer two preliminary questions: what is community–university 'engagement' and why does it matter? A further and related question – 'why this particular form?' – is addressed in the next chapter. The chapter concludes by highlighting some recent changes in the institutional and policy context: some of the issues to be considered in addressing 'where next?' in that context are explored in Chapter 16.

The chapter is unashamedly written from the perspective of two senior University managers, involved in Cupp from the outset. As such, it offers a view on the institutional reasons for establishing Cupp and for supporting its development. It therefore stands back from the specificity of Cupp's evolution and the details of the projects described in the rest of the volume. We hope in so doing that it adds weight to that account by placing the institutional perspective in the context of debate about the nature and purposes of higher education.

Defining 'engagement'

Like many other UK universities, the University of Brighton has a long tradition of involvement in the life of its host towns and of making what it does accessible. It has a track-record of developing and delivering higher education that has a strong vocational and professional basis, underpinned by academic and disciplinary understanding.

For Brighton, the types of activities undertaken by the University typically have an intimate connection with the rest of the local and regional economy. The success of the University's teaching, learning and research in these areas of work can only be achieved if those connections are fostered, managed, and as far as possible, generate a degree of mutual benefit. There is a reality of mutual dependence between a university seeking to educate – and ensure a licence to practice for – hundreds of nurses and teachers each year and the in situ educational support offered by local hospitals and schools. This is not a superficial matter of simply securing a high volume of placements, necessary though that is – the students concerned increasingly do real work in real organisations as they qualify. They graduate not only with a university degree but with a professional qualification. The relationship between the University and the partner organisations involved in making this possible extends to include Continuing Professional Development (CPD), research and consultancy as well as undergraduate provision. It refreshes and ensures the currency and quality of the University's work, and underpins service delivery by the partner organisations.

Looked at from the perspective of institutional history, the resulting University (which is, as this account indicates, always evolving) is therefore deeply implicated in the economic and professional life of the region in which it operates. It follows that, in important respects, Cupp is a logical institutional imperative, one further way of maintaining and enhancing the capacity for professional and vocational formation and 'real world' relevance in its teaching, learning and research. In this context, Cupp is simply the latest way in which the University can deliver on a historic commitment in a particular local context.

But the Cupp story reflected in this book suggests that 'community-university engagement' also represents a relationship and an ambition of a different kind.

The Association of Commonwealth Universities has adopted the phrase 'the imperative of engagement' and defines it as:

> Strenuous, thoughtful, argumentative interaction with the non-university world in at least four spheres: setting universities' aims, purposes and priorities; relating teaching and learning to the wider world; the back-and-forth dialogue between researchers and practitioners; and taking on wider responsibilities as neighbours and citizens. (ACU, 2001, p. i)

It is telling that this definition is drawn from an international review: the development of university-community engagement as a formal institutional objective systematically delivered is currently somewhat more strongly developed internationally, particularly in the USA, than in the UK.[2]

In the US, a particularly strong element in the tradition, going back to the work of John Dewey, emphasises civic responsibility and capacity as a core component of an undergraduate education, arising out of the perceived intimate connection between participatory democracy and education. Service learning and work study are now relatively common, in a context where student financial support can be precarious and complex, but can often be secured in exchange for involvement in particular sorts of community-related work. It is also relatively common for universities to seek to grapple with gross disparities in power and resources and to feel a strong sense of obligation to their local communities (Maurasse, 2001). A number of federal initiatives exist as well as other initiatives involving different groupings of institutions. The thrust for many of these is to recognise the potential of universities as 'significant agents for positive change in what could be described as distressed communities' (Carriere, 2004, p. xv).

Despite this often impressive track-record, American practice and institutional priorities have been challenged, notably by Bok and Boyer, both of whom who have been influential in advocating that universities should be more engaged (Bok, 1982; Boyer, 1990). Boyer's argument is summarised thus: 'that the missions of higher education achieved their greatest fulfilment when they served larger purposes such as building a more just society' (Fisher et al., 2004, p. 14).

More recently, the Carnegie Foundation has revisited the Dewey ideals, because of concerns about the perceived decline in civic involvement and public confidence in democratic institutions; and the Kellogg Commission has reviewed engagement in land grant and state universities (Ehrlich, 2000; Colby et al., 2003; Soska and Johnson Butterfield, 2004). These reviews 'have identified civic engagement and community partnerships as critical themes for institutions of higher education (IHEs). University-community partnerships have emerged as vital for teaching, research and practice' (Johnson Butterfield and Soska, 2004, p.1). The results of civic engagement and community partnership programmes can be impressive in scale: institutions in which large numbers of students and faculty are involved in learning and research with and within the local community.

Internationally, inevitably, the picture is more mixed. Even amongst the signatory universities to the 2005 Talloires Declaration, orchestrated by Tufts University, (one of the US leaders in this field), emphases, priorities and the way the institution organises its engagement work vary. The range includes universities for whom involvement in supporting mass basic literacy is a key civic responsibility to those who prioritise linking with the school sector, to those at which nation-building and policy formation are priorities (Tufts University, 2006).

Turning to the UK, for the University of Bradford, major considerations in the direction of travel for an institution already committed to working well with its local community include the impact of the local riots in 2002. This contributed to a re-think of the University's approach, which had hitherto been characterised as one of outreach and community development. Instead, Bradford now articulates its position thus:

> Community engagement differs from other University activities involving local communities by both its goals and by the character of the relationship which the University aims to build, i.e. one of partnership and shared objectives based on mutually recognised community and university competencies (Pearce et al., 2007, p. 22).

So, whilst the answer to the definitional question nationally and globally has some common elements, it takes a particular form: and is context-dependent – arising for institutions from their individual histories and locations, and from their view about their own strategic positioning.

At one level, therefore, all this could just be left to individual institutions to work out for themselves. But we would argue that, whatever the particular form, 'engagement' needs to respect a number of key principles. As our Bradford colleagues suggest, we need to try to persuade universities and communities 'that community engagement is not just a pleasant sounding side-line but a set of strategic activities of more profound import' (Pearce *et al.*, 2007, p. 16). For the University of Brighton, as the original submission to the funders of Cupp stated, the University:

> ... wishes both to contribute to, and benefit from, greater engagement with its local and sub-regional communities, in order to contribute to social inclusion, economic growth and the quality of life, but also in order to improve the quality of the education it provides to its learners. That greater engagement will, ideally, involve greater breadth and depth than are presently achievable. (University of Brighton, 2002, p. 5)

Why 'engagement' matters

Although we have suggested here that local circumstances, including institutional history, matter to an institution's working definition of engagement, we would also argue that 'engagement' is more important than simply the sum of disparate individual responses to particular local circumstances. Engagement matters because it is part of the answer to what universities are for: this is an international and a permanent question. It concerns the nature of the 'social contract' between society and universities, manifested through the nature of knowledge in modern society – how and by whom it is defined, created, accessed, validated, transmitted and transformed (Gibbons, 2003, p. 48). In this context, Watson describes some of the 'sources of strain' for universities resulting from the changed 'size, scope and connectivity of the information and knowledge universe to which academics and their special communities of inquiry contribute' (Watson, 2003, p. 29).

Some but not all of this is captured in the distinction drawn by Gibbons and colleagues, between Mode 1 and Mode 2 knowledge, to which we refer in the introductory and final chapters of this book. More recently, applying this thinking to the idea of engagement, Gibbons argues that:

> The sites of [scientific] problem formulation and negotiation have moved from their previous domains in government, industry and universities into the agora ...the public space in which 'science meets

the public' and in which the public 'speaks back to science'... the space, *par excellence*, for the production of socially robust knowledge. (Gibbons, 2003, p. 59).

In this context, he suggests that engagement 'as a core value' will be determined by the extent to which universities invest resources in the facilitation and management of transaction spaces and support the appropriate boundary work that is necessary to generate the co-operation 'required to formulate and pursue complex problems through research' and 'make it clear that their intention is to serve the public good' (Gibbons, 2003, pp. 69–70).

To quote the Talloires Declaration, universities:

> ... carry a unique obligation to listen, understand, and contribute to social transformation and understanding. Higher education must extend itself for the good of society to embrace communities near and far. In doing so, we will promote our core missions of teaching, research and practice. (Tufts University, 2006, p. 12)

In this context, it could be said that 'engagement' is simply what universities do – or ought to do: as Gamson observes, a century after Dewey, universities need to be part of the solution, not part of the problem (Gamson, 2000, p. 367).

In the UK, we would argue that 'engagement' is a powerful way of dealing with two pressing domestic issues of current higher education (and broader social) policy – the nature of participation on the one hand and the full realisation of the 'third stream' concept on the other.[3]

The first of these pressing policy issues concerns 'widening participation' – 'widening access', 'social inclusion' or 'increasing diversity' – all terms used in the UK and internationally to denote broadly similar policy objectives.

In the UK the argument for 'widening participation' runs roughly like this, with a slightly uneasy mix of underlying social and economic imperatives. On the social side, university graduates will (as compared to a non-graduate) benefit from a 'graduate premium' – a projection of future higher earning potential related to the types of job and future career paths which are open to them (UUK, 2007). And further, graduates typically live longer, are healthier, more stable and happier than non-graduates, participate more readily in civic society and have children who do better at school (Bynner *et al.*, 2003).

It then seems a fundamental political and ethical demand that all of us – whatever our gender, race, class or disability, whatever our social origins – should have an equal opportunity to achieve this 'graduate premium'. This is a profoundly important demand – and (especially as regards social class) a profoundly difficult goal to achieve. It seems that we have become stuck: even though the higher education system has expanded so that the overall numbers of working-class students in higher education have increased, the relative chances of middle-class and working-class entrants accessing the 'graduate premium' have not changed.

If, however, we push rather harder at the idea of widening participation in higher education, of widening access to the resources which universities possess, rather than only access to existing courses, some different possibilities emerge – especially if we significantly change the angle of vision. For if it is indeed the case that engaging with higher education, with universities and their resources, does have positive effects in terms of health, stability and happiness then maybe we should imagine a set of situations where all citizens and all social groups should be able to access the intellectual capital, the resources (many of them still benefiting from public funding) and the learning networks which are at the heart of what makes a university.

In this scenario, we can imagine the possibility of 80 per cent, 85 per cent, 90 per cent participation – but not necessarily in the traditional ways of assessed course provision and formal accreditation (or even the now much less common open access adult education non-assessed class). Rather we would be speaking of forms of access which may be occasional, strategic, user-oriented – forms which may not look much like a teacher/learner relationship – diverse forms which may be akin to those designed and invented within the Cupp partnership and projects described here.

The concept of new modalities of higher education brings us straight into the second current major policy concern – that of the so-called 'third stream'. The dominant idea here is one of encouraging and persuading universities to engage with a wide range of business organisations to assist in technical innovation, the development of productive capacity and the efficient and effective management needed for organisational success – an organisational success fundamental to the strength of both the local and the national economy.

This is a project to which Brighton has had a long and effective commitment.

However, as recent attempts have been made – especially by government and the public funding agencies – to define this area of activity much more explicitly, there has been a pervasive theoretical and practical problem with the term 'community'.

Continually, there has been a degree of recognition that any conceptualisation of the 'third stream' project is incomplete without a social dimension beyond business – but equally the term 'community' has also typically seemed an afterthought, an embarrassment, since the key question has always been – how can such a sphere of non-business activity justify itself in economic terms? Therefore, in adopting either a formula or a competitive approach as the means to allocate public funding, agreement is needed on what to measure and how to assess 'delivery'. The input to business, and the measurement of the results, after all (so the argument runs) can be seen in terms of contribution to national wealth-creation – community intervention cannot.

It follows that the development of practice – and of the policy debate – in this area in the UK has tended to concentrate on relations between universities and the private sector, typically, on how to develop and support the best model of business start-up, knowledge transfer, graduate entrepreneurship, consultancy, spin-outs and the capacity of higher education to contribute to economic gain using its largely scientific and research-derived knowledge. There is an absence of established models for how to do this kind of work with the public, and particularly the community and voluntary sectors, and with social enterprises.

The term 'wealth-creation' may however bear a little examination. The origins of the word 'wealth' lie in the early modern term 'wele' meaning well-being or welfare; and in the compound word 'commonwealth' we find our two apparently opposing terms 'community' and 'wealth' fused – 'commonwealth' here meaning the common prosperity, happiness and well-being of all.

This leads us to consider the total life of all our people, of all of us – as business leaders and as paid employees, but also as parents, as carers, as active citizens, and as consumers. All these aspects of our lives have a part to play in any full sense of wealth production, of the production and maintenance of our common welfare and well-being.

Valuing 'engagement'

Thinking about why engagement matters – and deciding that it matters because it is about the full sense of wealth production – leads to a consideration of how to value it. In the UK, most analyses of the impact of higher education generally and institutions in particular – beyond understandings of individual rates of return described above – are relatively narrow in their approach. The most influential in the UK is probably that developed by the University of Strathclyde, which concentrates on assessing economic impact by valuing institutional turnover and a possible multiplier from the off-campus spending power of staff and students (UUK, 2006). The model finds that universities do indeed generate a multiplier.[4] However, this model explicitly excludes the economic (or other) impact of third-stream activity.

There are a number of other institutional attempts. A contrasting but nonetheless useful approach has been developed by the University of Cambridge, which both describes a range of activities and seeks to give some monetary value to them (University of Cambridge, 2004). Another example, arrived at by capturing a university's economic and social impact rather than engagement, is from the University of Hertfordshire, undertaken in collaboration with Welwyn Hatfield Council (PACEC, 2006). Internationally, the institutions that have signed the Talloires Declaration are now being enjoined to apply an audit instrument which requires self-scrutiny on a number of dimensions (Watson, 2007).

At this point, the University of Bradford's work is again a powerful contribution. They have developed a 'metrix' known as REAP (Pearce *et al.*, 2007, p. 4). In this metric, REAP represents reciprocity, externalities, access, and partnerships, and seeks to capture the 'public good' generated by a clear commitment to engagement. The externalities element in the Bradford tool is relevant to the conceptualisation of well-being posited above; that is to measure 'the economic value of activities of a societal nature' (Pearce *et al.*, 2007, pp. 5–6).

Pearce *et al.* (2007) stress CE in its purest form seeks to provide some benefit to the community that is not an accidental by-product in the pursuit of some other aim ... CE is not ... a 'free service' to the community ... but is based on non-market forms of reciprocity. This 'pure' idea of CE output would be therefore deeply compromised by efforts to translate it into a 'monetary value'. (pp. 5–6).

Engagement through partnership

While we would make no claims about the conceptual 'purity' of what has happened at Brighton since 2003 (there have been too many rough edges and pragmatic solutions for that) this emphasis on 'non-market forms of reciprocity' does bring us back to the instigation of Cupp.

Here, we need to remember the unusual origins of the initiative, at least from the perspective of an English university: the University was offered money, and it was offered money to experiment, with relatively few constraints. In response to hearing the then Vice-Chancellor, Professor Sir David Watson, talking about the wider role of universities on a radio programme, the Atlantic Philanthropies contacted him and asked whether he would be interested in developing his ideas with some financial backing. In the English context this is almost unheard of.

The funders seemed to recognise that, whilst the University had a relevant track record and significant commitment, the actual shape of the work to be funded would be highly developmental, was likely to involve some risk for the University and partners, and may involve some activity that would fail. Implicit in the early conversations, therefore, was a realisation that it was not possible to expect detailed outcomes to be specified in advance and that conventional metrics might not apply.

These discussions were extremely timely – as we have indicated earlier, like the sector as a whole, Brighton has been grappling for some time with ways of articulating its own response to the widening participation and 'third stream' policy issues, in the context of, but not determined by, national policy and funding parameters. The discussions with the Atlantic Philanthropies were predicated in part on the argument that existing public funding streams did not at that time recognise or support the kind of work that we believed to be necessary and desirable. Here of course we touch on the two policy issues we've just discussed: in the case of widening participation, the funding imperative under New Labour was to address social class access to existing taught courses via individual entry; in the case of the 'third stream' it was to extend the scope, volume and profitability of university-business interaction. The business plan finally submitted to the Atlantic Philanthropies noted the value of both of these, but also their limitations. It articulated a view of the relationship between the University and its communities that would achieve its objectives by:

- 'providing a structured opportunity for consolidating the identification of local community aspirations and needs in respect of the University
- capturing the activity, enthusiasm and expertise of University staff and students and community members to address those aspirations and needs
- working closely with local and regional communities to identify a joint programme of work that meets mutual needs and draws on mutual experience and expertise'. (University of Brighton, 2002, p. 6)

The bulk of this book describes how the Atlantic Philanthropies grant has, since 2003, been turned into a reality of local action, and the resulting transformation of the University's capacity to engage with its local communities, through the creation of strong and vibrant partnerships and supporting structures.

Beyond 2007

The initial grant, as noted here, reflected the University's long-standing commitment to this area of work and to a perceived gap in the available public funding streams. The period since the grant was confirmed has seen some potentially significant developments in the public policy context. In particular, the Higher Education Funding Council for England (HEFCE) has recently sought to offer a more balanced view, recognising perhaps that it has tended to concentrate in the recent past on driving universities towards a focus on wealth creation and knowledge transfer conventionally defined. Thus its current Strategic Plan for the period 2006–11 adopts as an aim 'to increase the impact of the HE knowledge base to enhance economic development and the strength and vitality of the sector' and goes on to spell out the rationale and implications of this commitment:

... supporting HEIs in their contributions to the wider social agenda – in terms of civic engagement and developing democratic values, and in supporting and helping to regenerate communities ...

we intend to articulate and then implement a strategy for the social dimension to the third stream. This strategy will describe and celebrate the diverse contributions that HE already makes in these varied arenas, and will put forward the arguments for funding, particularly public funding. (HEFCE, 2006, p. 6 and p. 27)

In support of this, HEFCE is at the time of writing working with the sector to establish a small number of Beacons of Public Engagement and to develop its social engagement policy more generally. This has included work in which Cupp has been involved, to develop some metrics and a set of good practices (see for example Nonprofit Good Practice Guide and HEFCE Beacons websites).

The University's thinking has also moved on since the Cupp grant was confirmed. Alongside the development of the Cupp organisation and the delivery of projects, the creation of Cupp has prompted further refine- ment in the University's approach to 'engagement'. The result is that the University's new Corporate Plan, for the period 2007–12, includes 'engagement' as one of its five values – 'engagement with the cultural, social and economic life of our localities, region and nation; with international imperatives; and with the practical, intellectual and ethical issues of our partner organisations' (University of Brighton, 2007). One of the six aims in the Plan is that the University will 'become recognised as a leading UK university for the quality and range of its work in economic and social engagement and productive partnerships'. Included as one of the indicators of success for this aim is that the University will conduct 'a baseline and subsequent audit of community engagement in which the data show increased levels of engagement and local benefit from University activities' (University of Brighton, 2007). In this very real sense, the Cupp story told in this volume has influenced the University's strategic thinking about its own development, and now constitutes a key vehicle for achieving some high-level ambitions.

Conclusion

To conclude, this chapter suggests that Cupp, and the engagement imperative which it signifies, is a live issue not just for Brighton and a small number of other UK universities, but for the UK sector as a whole and indeed internationally. It suggests that 'engagement' should indeed be an imperative for institutions; that engagement as understood here and as manifested through the Cupp partnership is profoundly important.

We believe that the kind of partnership working represented by Cupp contributes directly to individual and collective well-being through a series of externalities that include institutional and community capacity; contrib- utes to strengthening civil society; enhances institutional diversity and the range of those who have access to university resources; contributes to new forms of knowledge; and impacts directly on learning, teaching and research in the institution.

The chapters that follow show this in a tangible way – the excitement and challenge of making the debates introduced here work in practice.

Notes

1. Parts of this chapter appeared previously in a speech by Stuart Laing to the Cupp conference, April 2006.
2. David Watson's book *Managing Civic and Community Engagement*, offers a useful analytical comparison of the US, Australian and UK contexts through the work of three universities, Pennsylvania, Queensland and Brighton (Watson, 2007).
3. In the UK, higher education has been characterised as dealing with teaching and learning, research, and the 'third stream' or work to develop interaction with business and the community.
4. An additional 99 full-time jobs for every 100 full-time university jobs; £1.52m of additional output for every £1m of University output.

References

Association of Commonwealth Universities (ACU) (2001) *Engagement as a Core Value for the University: A Consultation Document*. London: ACU.

Bok, D.C. (1982) *Beyond the ivory tower: social responsibilities of the modern university*. Cambridge, MA: Harvard University Press.

Boyer, E.L. (1990) *Scholarship reconsidered: Priorities for the professoriate*. Menlo Park, CA: Carnegie Foundation.

Bynner, J., Dolton, P., Fensein, L., Makepiece G., Malmberg, L. and Woods, L. (2003) *Revisiting the Benefits of Education: a report by the Bedford Group for Lifecourse and Statistical Studies*. Bristol: Institute of Education, HEFCE.

Carriere, T. (2004) 'Preface', in T.M. Soska, and A.K. Johnson Butterfield (eds.), *University-community partnerships – Universities in civic engagement*. Binghamton, NY: Haworth Press.

Colby, A., Ehrlich, T., Beaumont, E., Rosner, J. and Stephens J. (2000) 'Higher education and the development of civic responsibility', in T. Ehrlich (ed.), *Civic Responsibility and Higher Education*. Westport, CT: American Council on Education and Oryx Press.

Colby, A., Ehrlich, T., Beaumont, E., Stephens, J. (2003) *Educating Citizens*. San Francisco: Carnegie Foundation for the Advancement of Teaching and Jossey-Bass.

Ehrlich, T. (2000) *Civic responsibility and Higher Education*. Westport, CT: American Council on Education and the Oryx Press.

Fisher, R., Fabricant, M. and Simmons, L. (2004) 'Understanding contemporary university-community connections: context, practice, and challenges', in T.M. Soska, and A.K. Johnson Butterfield (eds.), *University-community partnerships: Universities in civic engagement*. Binghamton, NY: Haworth Press.

Gamson, Z.F. (2000) 'Defining the civic agenda for higher education', in T. Ehrlich, (ed.), *Civic responsibility and Higher Education*, Westport, CT: American Council on Education and Oryx Press.

Gibbons, M. (2003) 'Engagement as a core value in a Mode 2 society', in S. Bjarnason, and P. Coldstream (eds.), *The idea of engagement: Universities in society*. London: Association of Commonwealth Universities.

Gibbons, M., Limoges, C., Nowotny, H., Shwartzman, S., Scott, P. and Trow, M. (1994) *The New Production of Knowledge*. London: Sage.

HEFCE (2006) *Strategic Plan, 2006–11*. Bristol: Higher Education Funding Council for England.

HEFCE website: *HEFCE Beacons for Public Engagement, Invitation to apply for funds December 2006/49*. See: http://www.hefce.ac.uk/Pubs/HEFCE/2006/06_49/ (accessed 20 January 2007).

Johnson Butterfield, A.K. and Soska, T.M. (2004) 'University-community partnerships: an introduction', in T.M. Soska, and A.K. Johnson Butterfield (eds.), *University-community partnerships: Universities in civic engagement*. Binghamton, NY: Haworth Press.

Maurrasse, D.J. (2001) *Beyond the campus: how colleges and universities form partnerships with their communities*. London and New York: Routledge.

Nonprofit Good Practice Guide website: See http://www.npgoodpractice.org/ (Accessed 17 April 2007).

PACEC (Public and Corporate Economic Consultants) (2006) *Economic and social impact of the University of Hertfordshire on Welwyn Hatfield*. Cambridge and London: PACEC.

Pearce, J., Pearson, M. with Cameron, S. (2007) *The ivory tower and beyond: Bradford University at the heart of its communities*. Bradford: University of Bradford.

Soska, T.M., and Johnson Butterfield, A.K. (eds.) (2004) *University-community partnerships: Universities in civic engagement*. Binghamton, NY: Haworth Press.

Tufts University (2006) *Strengthening the civic roles and social responsibilities of Higher Education – Building a global network, the Talloires Conference 2005*. Also at http://www.tufts.edu/talloiresnetwork/conferences.html.

Universities UK (2006) *The economic impact of UK higher education institutions – a report for universities UK by U. Kelly, D. McLelland and I. McNeal*. London: UUK and University of Strathclyde.

Universities UK (2007) *The economic benefits of a degree – research report by Price Waterhouse Coopers*. London: UUK.

University of Brighton (2002) *Proposal to the Atlantic Philanthropies*, unpublished.

University of Brighton (2007) *Corporate Plan 2007–12*.

University of Cambridge (2004) *University of Cambridge community engagement 2003–04*.

Watson, D. (2003) 'The University in the knowledge society' in S. Bjarnason, and P. Coldstream (eds.), *The idea of engagement: Universities in society*. London: Association of Commonwealth Universities.

Watson, D. (2007). *Managing civic and community engagement*. Maidenhead: Open University Press.

Chapter 2

Delivering Cupp

Susan Balloch, Dana Cohen, Angie Hart, Elizabeth Maddison,
Elaine McDonnell, Juliet Millican, Polly Rodriguez, David Wolff,
with Paul Bramwell and Stuart Laing

The previous chapter discussed 'Why Cupp?', 'Why now?' and touched on 'Why this particular form?'. This chapter explores the last of these questions in more detail. The chapter describes the evolution of the programme and analyses its main components and key processes. It is authored by the Cupp team and the author of the original bid that secured Cupp funding. It therefore offers a largely 'supply side' account of the experience of setting up and delivering Cupp – the perspective from inside the University. This is not independently evaluative nor is it designed to be: it tells a story about an innovation in conceptualisation and delivery of a service – what this team needed to do to develop the offer of funds into practical processes, systems, activities and partnerships. This chapter describes the structure and processes by which Cupp works, in three main phases, up to the time of writing.

The original bid to the funders, the Atlantic Philanthropies, in 2003, identified two main aims, to:

- ensure the University's resources (intellectual and physical) were made fully available to, informed by and exploited by its local and sub-regional communities; and to
- enhance the community's and University's capacity for engagement and mutual benefit.

In negotiating the original funding, the funders and the University were both conscious of the need for experimentation and for time for the programme to reach any kind of maturity. For the University, this was in marked contrast to many funding initiatives which expect a tight early specification, quick results, unambiguous outcomes and clear metrics; and which allow little if any room for trial and error. In this, the funding relationship has reflected the nature of the endeavour – it has been important to define Cupp 'in the doing'.

Phase 1

So, having secured the funding through an extensive and testing process of discussion with the funders, the challenge was to work out how the programme might work in practice. The preliminary task was to appoint some staff who set about an exploratory assessment. Whilst it was apparent that vibrant community–university activity already existed, it was frequently 'below the radar'. A dedicated programme would provide a means to explore this in ways not achievable through existing University structures and resources: the question to be answered was thus: 'how could such a programme best add value and bring fundamentally new capacity?'

Whilst there was interest and support for Cupp from inside the University and from representatives of local communities, there was also some suspicion and uncertainty, reflecting the mistrust that many local communities have of academics (see for example Buckeridge *et al.*, 2002). Moreover, this proposed programme had no recent UK precedent. There was no confident sense of what a 'community–university partnership project' looked like or how one might be formed. Much was known about US and Australian experiences but the contextual differences were significant: in respect of the US, the intention at Brighton was certainly not to replicate the large scale 'service learning' models. Much was known about other funding streams accessible by community and voluntary sector organisations (and by universities) but Cupp had no intention of becoming simply another 'grant giver' (although it quickly became clear that some community organisations had seen Cupp as the arrival of a new funder). Much was also known about the danger of doing 'to' rather than 'with' community partners by big organisations. So the team was clearer about what was not required than what was. The small initial Cupp team therefore embarked on an intensive process of active engagement with key University staff and with colleagues from community-based organisations, mainly from the local community and voluntary sectors. As well as gaining an operational sense of who was doing what, Cupp also needed to develop its own sophisticated and nuanced understanding of the nature of the local environment; and the possibilities, aspirations, constraints, and traditions of the University.

The second task was to tackle some key delivery issues. There were two elements here. Firstly, to really test out a model for the programme as a whole and secondly, to identify where an intervention could best contribute. To tackle these two issues, Cupp launched three pilot projects.

The third task was how to make funding decisions. Although Cupp was never intended to act as a traditional funding body seeking competitive proposals against an invitation to bid, it did have project funds firmly within its budget. How then to develop a different role in bringing together University and community partners to embark on funded activity? Placing the emphasis on mutual benefit marked out Cupp as not just another grant body to which applications could be made against criteria set by the funders. Instead, Cupp developed a brokerage role, emphasising mutual benefit from activities to partners within some broadly-defined areas of interest. The three pilot projects offered some important findings for the programme as a whole. As a result of this early work, it was agreed that: future partnership projects should focus clearly on addressing social exclusion; must connect with University expertise; and must have prospects for sustaining themselves beyond any initial funding.

To focus the programme and its delivery, four strategic themes were agreed:

1. Community research, project development and evaluation

- providing a research helpdesk service to assist community and voluntary organisations address their research support needs
- establishing capacity and coordination for funding development work for community–university projects
- releasing staff capacity for work on community projects

2. Access to education for excluded groups
- developing a clearer overall picture of which groups struggle to access Higher Education
- enabling changes to take place in relevant education systems and practices to make access easier
- addressing the needs of specific communities and groups in each project

3. Releasing student capacity for community benefit
- collecting best practice in establishing learning through community activity and to make this knowledge base available
- identifying and supporting the development work needed to stimulate further learning through community activity

4. Higher Education learning opportunities for people working in and with communities
- building on existing provision locally to provide a clear description of the range of learning opportunities required by those who work with communities
- identifying a framework that enables learners to readily identify what they need and how it relates to a pathway of learning
- developing appropriate learning opportunities for practitioners

The fourth task in the formative phase was to establish a governance structure. This too needed to reflect the collaborative and mutual nature of the endeavour. The steering group was assembled to give advice on process, decide on funding priorities, maintain an overview of activities and develop longer-term strategy. Members included:

- senior university managers (including the Vice-Chancellor)
- senior academics, the coordinator of the local Community and Voluntary Sector Forum
- the Local Authority's Neighbourhood Renewal Manager
- a community and voluntary sector training provider, the Working Together Project

The steering group was given responsibility for determining funds for projects under each of the four strategic themes, using learning gained by working on the three pilot projects. University 'champions' were identified to take responsibility for each of the four themes and to lead the conversations with community partners. Although always careful to try to manage expectations, these early conversations nonetheless generated a large number of possible projects. To maintain a manageable governance and decision-making process, Cupp therefore formed a development group to consider smaller projects and to make recommendations to the steering group for larger ones. The development group comprised the four thematic 'champions' and at least one community-based representative for each theme.

All of this could have gone badly wrong – expectations were high, but so were levels of scepticism and, in some quarters, mutual ignorance. It would have been easy to revert to a simple grant-giving function seeking influence through largesse and to some extent patronage. Not everything went smoothly and, in particular, it took time for the governance and decision-making to bed down. The fluidity referred to at the start of this chapter was not always trouble-free. For example, it is clear with hindsight that community sector and University members of the steering group had very different experiences and expectations of the way meetings would be run and decisions made. Some members from the community and voluntary sector members felt that they were there simply to rubber-stamp decisions already made by the University. Both sets of participants had much to learn about what membership of the steering group and its decisions entailed, in terms of responsibility and delivery – the University had to understand that the community sector members were not 'representative' and in turn the community sector members had to learn that senior management commitment in a university does not automatically translate into immediate action.[1]

Reflecting on why Cupp did not founder at this stage suggests that – as with any 'change' project – senior commitment and outstanding individuals running the project were critical. In addition, the Cupp team wisely worked hard to draw on work already underway between academic colleagues and those in community and voluntary organisations. And this wider group, through good will, commitment and a degree of good fortune, as well as some early indications that the thing actually worked, was able relatively quickly to find its way through the 'storming' and 'norming' phases of development. The brokerage model of project development forced the pace here. Alongside the critical bits of getting the right people in the right place at the right time, it was also vital to remain on good terms with the funder, whose staff members were challengingly supportive.

Phase 2

Encouraged by its success to date and the scale of potential activity identified, early in 2004, Cupp led a successful bid on behalf of the Universities of Brighton and Sussex for innovation funds from HEFCE to establish a 'community knowledge exchange' under the Higher Education Innovation Fund round 2 (HEIF). This added significant funds to the overall Cupp endeavour; enabled a shift in emphasis towards larger projects; and to projects that are explicitly about knowledge exchange.[2]

Phase 2 was therefore instituted with HEFCE's decision to fund the Brighton and Sussex Knowledge Exchange (BSCKE). BSCKE aims to contribute to social transformation by tackling real community problems; recognising and addressing diversity and engaging with socially-excluded groups; and facilitating the exchange and growth of knowledge across sectors. University partners provide practical support to community, voluntary, public sector and social enterprise organisations and networks, grounded in academic understanding and expertise. In their turn, community partners contribute to lasting culture change within the universities of Brighton and Sussex by bringing real issues into teaching and research. Projects funded through BSCKE typically run for about a year and run at £20–25k, a scale that enables a sustained focus on the problem at hand.

Definition of responsibilities

- **Steering group:** Programme direction, overseeing implementation and reviewing the work plan, allocating projects budget, overseeing the evaluation of Cupp, approving projects over £5,000, enabling stakeholders to participate in running of Cupp and developing long-term strategy.
- **BSCKE management group:** Approving projects, overseeing the progress of projects, assisting in the development of the BSCKE, quality assurance and ensuring generic learning for the universities and the partner organisations.
- **Development team:** Developing project proposals, approving projects under £5,000, identifying need, promoting good practice, developing supplementary funding and overseeing the progress of projects.

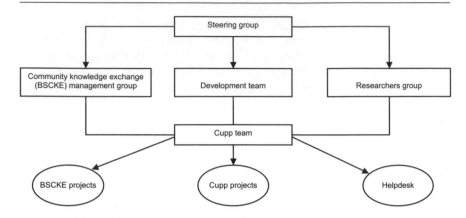

Figure 2.1   Phase 2 structure

- **Researchers group:** Ensure effective handling of helpdesk referrals, oversee the design and implementation of the helpdesk services, and help shape the future directions of the helpdesk, comment on other Cupp activities as required and to support each other and share experiences.
- **Cupp team:** Implementation of the programme.

Between its inception in August 2004 and December 2006, BSCKE has funded and supported the development of 15 knowledge-exchange projects, five more than originally proposed to the funders.[3] Predominantly this higher-than-expected activity rate has been due to BSCKE's ability to build on the groundwork done by Cupp and develop the extensive network of links with local universities and community organisations. BSCKE has built partnerships between two universities and 15 university departments spanning the disciplinary range;[4] and 50 organisations and networks from the community, voluntary, public and social enterprise sectors.[5] Knowledge exchange has been enhanced through individual projects as well as facilitated events. Over 2,000 people have been directly involved with BSCKE projects. Project learning has been disseminated through a book (Hart and Blincow, 2007), a handbook (Aumann and Hart, forthcoming 2008), academic articles, conference workshops and keynote presentations, the Cupp website and an e-list.

Drawing on lessons learnt through Cupp, underpinning the projects supported through BSCKE are a number of operating principles:

- an explicit approach to developing a learning culture, articulated within a 'communities of practice' framework (see Wenger, McDermott and Snyder, 2002, and Chapter 14 of this book). This includes:

  o the Learning Forum, providing a virtual and real space for project partners and stakeholders to discuss cross-cutting issues, develop their own model of partnership working and share good practice;

○ support for emergent communities of practice to continue beyond
   the end of individual projects, identifying ways of sustaining or
   developing these into medium-term programmes of work predicated on the continued and evolving exchange of knowledge;

• including service users in project development, management, governance and evaluation, in order to help drive up community capacity;
• supporting the intense development of skills, for example, enabling
  community and voluntary sector groups to conduct research that
  identifies need, and in turn supports funding bids and project management; and
• promoting greater linkage between day-to-day academic practice and
  local communities; and increased student opportunities to apply, test
  and develop their knowledge in real community settings analogous to
  those within which they will work after graduation.

Phase 3

By 2005 Cupp was fully-functioning, with the Knowledge Exchange as a
major component, effectively doubling the resources available for activities. However, it had also become clear through an initial external
evaluation (evaluation stage 1, see http://www.brighton.ac.uk/cupp/
aboutus/evaluation.htm) that the three layers of governance (steering
group, development group, BSCKE steering group) had become cumber-
some. Decision-making was unnecessarily time-consuming and the steering group was losing its ability to take a strategic view.
   To help thinking about the next steps and possible structure, to enable
future progress, Cupp commissioned a second-stage independent evaluation (see Chapter 15). Aided by this evaluation, the range of activities and
the ways in which Cupp sought to achieve its objectives was rethought
and the accompanying governance and decision-making arrangements
were reframed:

• Activity would be consolidated through three key 'delivery vehicles':

  ○ research (run through the research Helpdesk);

  ○ releasing student capacity (renamed 'Student Learning in the Com-
     munity' and enhanced with a new staff appointment); and

  ○ BSCKE.

• Each of these would be led by an appointed staff member (rather
  than a nominated 'champion' elsewhere in the University), charged
  with helping to identify and develop projects, and with supporting
  their subsequent progress and evaluation.

- The staff responsible for each of the three would work together to look at communities of interest that were less well served and to try to encourage proposals from or involving different areas of the University.
- They would work to leverage other funds, for example, from the Sussex Learning Network to develop work on qualifications and progression routes for those working in community practice; and to seek to base activity within the University's main academic structures.
- The development group, Cupp steering group, and the BSCKE steering group were merged into a revised steering group as a single governing body for all aspects of the programme, streamlining decision-making and enabling a greater focus on strategic development.
- A shift to seeking to add capacity to existing University activities in a number of areas, rather than developing a separate operation. In effect, this shifted the focus on some of the ways of advancing the four themes originally identified. For example, the University's widening participation function took responsibility for developing Cupp's work on access to education for excluded groups; relevant schools took on responsibility for developing opportunities for people working in and with communities, supported by a new Cupp appointee.

Alongside this evolution in ways of working, Cupp continued to reflect on the range of its work, including its coverage of 'communities of interest' and curriculum areas. A significant development from the original funding proposal was to emphasise the importance of projects oriented towards environmental sustainability, alongside those supporting the sustainability of communities, social marginalisation and disadvantage.

Project selection criteria

As a result of this review, the selection criteria set for new projects were clarified to ensure projects would:

- be targeted at tackling disadvantage or promoting sustainable development in communities local to the University;
- connect with the University, i.e. have a university partner on board and connect with its core business in some clear way; and
- have prospects for sustaining the partnership beyond Cupp funding.

Of the three main 'delivery vehicles', the research Helpdesk is described in more detail in Chapter 3. Chapters 5, 6, 7 and 8 discuss some of the projects initiated by BSCKE; and Chapters 11, 12 and 13 discuss work supported through Student Learning in the Community.

The evolved Cupp model is summarised below:

1. **Helpdesk:** advice and signposting, clarifying with community organisations how university can be accessed. Main focus on research but handling other enquiries.

2. **Consultancy:** one-to-one support, student placements. Coordinated via helpdesk and resourced through senior researchers' group, student placement officers and one-off arrangements with staff.
3. **Scoping projects:** up to £5,000 and suitable for early development of ideas for collaboration into partnership.
4. **Larger projects:** includes knowledge exchange type projects and perhaps substantial pieces of work of strategic importance that connect various university elements with community organisations to address a major problem.
5. **Learning network:** gathers learning and support project participants to develop their communities of practice. This brings together the Helpdesk research forum and BSCKE learning forum, and includes regular meeting space for project participants; online information resources; publicity; training; action learning and workshops; and dissemination events.

There are a number of key features to Cupp's work during this third phase:

- Priority continues to be given to brokerage as the most effective and appropriate way to develop projects, predicated on establishing recip-rocal relationships between the community and the University based on equal representation and seeking mutual benefit.
- There is a project-approval process via the programme's steering group; and fluidity in the roles that different people take and in the level of support that Cupp provides.
- Alongside the brokerage for particular projects, Cupp has played a more general role in helping to open up the University and make its resources more accessible. Cupp often acts as a 'point of entry', providing a way in for an outsider not wanting to enter via the formal routes of student application or course enquiry.[6]
- Cupp also plays a key role in the development of community engagement and partnership working as a concept within the UK context, for example, in assembling information about good practices in social and community engagement on behalf of HEFCE.[7]

Conclusion

This chapter has described the development of Cupp from the decision to award it funding to the time of writing. A more complex understanding of what has worked and why – including views from different perspectives – can be found in Part 5: What works.

To conclude with a sense of the scale of the undertaking, Cupp has, since 2003:

- established teaching initiatives and outreach involving 10% of overall academics and students in every Faculty of the University;
- handled 700+ community enquiries handled through Cupp's Helpdesk;
- set up a research and technical support programme attracting 800 participants;
- initiated over 70 projects with 2,500 participants;
- disseminated outputs through national and international networks, conference papers and joint publications with community partners, including this book. A major international conference event was held in April 2006 attracting 200 participants; and
- led the formation of a community engagement community of practice in the current HEFCE-sponsored third stream good practice programme.

As this chapter indicates, alongside those outputs and the processes that underpin them, Cupp has remained flexible in its thinking about the best organisational form necessary to deliver its objectives. It has been prepared to rearticulate its objectives in terms of ways of working and of conceptualising its themes. It has combined a degree of pragmatism with adherence to the original aims. It has been suitably opportunistic when reviewing funding appraisals. It has worked well alongside the University's academic and professional structures, finding ways of supporting, complementing and influencing them, and ways of shifting its relationship to them over time.

Notes

1. This part of the chapter draws heavily on reflections by Paul Bramwell, community sector member of the steering group and discussion between Paul and Professor Stuart Laing, University Chair of the group.
2. The original discussions with the funders had included the possibility of a strand to place 'associates' with community and voluntary sector organisations to work on a real 'business problem' with an academic supervisor, but this had been omitted from the final proposal in order to reduce the overall cost.
3. Details of BSCKE projects can be found at www.cupp.org.uk/projects/exchange.htm.
4. From the University of Brighton (UoB) Faculty of Arts and Architecture; UoB Faculty of Education and Sport; UoB Faculty of Health; UoB Faculty of Management and Information Sciences; UoB Faculty of Science and Engineering; UoB Administrative and Support Departments; University of Sussex Centre for Continuing Education; University Centre Hastings.

5. Including six councils, 26 community and voluntary sector organisations, four schools, one regeneration programme, four health bodies, and Brighton and Hove Police.
6. For example, Cupp has launched a Trustees project, encouraging university staff to act as trustees for voluntary organisations, matching interested people with organisations needing trustees and working alongside a voluntary organisation to provide a trustee training programme.
7. See HEFCE website at www.hefce.ac.uk for several good practice links, for example www.hefce.ac.uk/reachout/casestudies.

References

Aumann, K. and Hart, A. (2008, forthcoming) *What helps children with special needs bounce back? A parent's guide to Resilient Therapy* [Provisional title].

Buckeridge, D.L., Mason, R., Robertson, A., Frank, J., Glazier, R. (2002) 'Making health data maps: A case study of a community/university research collaboration', *Social Science and Medicine,* Vol. 55, No. 7, pp. 1,189–209.

Hart, A. and Blincow, D. with Thomas, H. (2007) *Resilient therapy*. London: Brunner-Routledge.

Watson, D. (2003) 'Universities and civic engagement: a critique and a prospectus', Keynote address for the second biennial 'Inside-out' conference on the civic role of universities: *Charting Uncertainty: capital, community and citizenship*. See Cupp website.

Wenger, E., McDermott, R., Snyder, W.M. (2002) *Cultivating communities of practice*. Boston: Harvard Business School Press.

Chapter 3

Community-university research engagement: the Cupp research Helpdesk

Polly Rodriguez with Juliet Millican

Introduction

The Helpdesk was identified as one of the central components of Cupp in its original proposal and has proved central to overall development and impact. Research support contributes to the core aims of Cupp. Equally important, having a strong research-based component to Cupp attracts individuals and groups within the University and contributes to corporate objectives and ambitions for research. This chapter explains how the Helpdesk works, its role in the overall programme and the pivotal part it plays, and analyses some of the critical success factors behind its impact.

The Helpdesk became operational six months after the funding for Cupp was confirmed and a further six months were spent in consultation with potential partners to develop a clearer idea about its scope, purpose and potential. We used this time to make sure that the Helpdesk would really be able to respond to the needs of local community and voluntary organisations, and also that it would not duplicate research training and support already on offer from local community-based training providers. Some of this time was used to explore the term 'research', as not all community groups shared the same understanding of its relevance or value, despite having utilised research tools and methods as a means of gaining information and feedback from their user groups.

The Helpdesk

The formative period for the Helpdesk culminated in the launch event in March 2004. This established that community and voluntary organisations understood the potential of the service for their organisations and the communities they served. The opportunity to work in partnership with academics and students to establish an evidence base for their services was greeted enthusiastically. Much emphasis was put on ensuring mutual benefit and a sense of equality in the relationship. However, launch participants spoke of the potential cultural divide between the University and community and voluntary organisations. There was need to find a common language, agree values, aims and objectives if the partnership was to work well. In addition, the launch underlined the importance of the Helpdesk avoiding being perceived as predominantly concerned with 'academic' interests, and enabled this perception to be addressed from the outset.

Marullo *et al.* (2003) identify five key principles of community-based research, and in many ways these are all applicable to the work of the Helpdesk. These are that research should be i) collaborative, ii) community driven, iii) guided by grounded theory iv) multi-dimensional, and v) should have methodologies that are systematic yet rigorous, flexible and influenced by context. The goal of the research process is defined ultimately in this context as effecting social change, through enhancing capacity, increasing efficiency, empowering constituents or altering structures. In setting itself up as a service, the Helpdesk has had to break down traditional perceptions of the University as 'experts' in order to promote collaborative approaches to local change.

The Helpdesk works by offering assistance in interpreting and prioritising concerns and issues which can be turned into research questions, and offers specialist skills in clarifying questions and designing research tools. It includes the capacity to train organisations to carry out their own research and also investigates the possibility of matching them up with students or academics that can carry out research with them or on their behalf.

It operates as an open access point, responding to many and varied enquiries and fielding these around the University in a considered way. Central to achieving this has been the creation of the Senior Researchers Group (SRG). The Cupp SRG was formed in September 2004 and has amongst its members a growing number of senior academics from the University of Brighton, in particular, those academics with research interests that connect with community practitioners. The SRG has enabled Cupp to manage and develop the Helpdesk and underpins the range of services on offer via the Helpdesk.

Alongside the open access point, the Helpdesk has developed a training programme of seminars and workshops, offered free to participants registering from the community and voluntary sector. An initial two-day introduction to community research was quickly booked out. This has since been followed by a series of workshops on research skills. Specific workshops include sessions on locating and analysing Great Britain Census data, an Introduction to Geographical Information Systems, and Using Excel for Statistics.

The research drop-in, held on University premises, is designed to encourage people to see the University and its facilities as a community resource. For the University there are two main barriers, physical and perceptual. Physically, the site on which Cupp is based is outside the city centre and entails a bus or a train ride. Perceptually, some of the Helpdesk users fear coming across the threshold. The University can be seen as intimidating. While people are encouraged to send in information on their research problem prior to visiting, they are also able to drop in unannounced. In reality people are often met and supported by the Helpdesk manager, who books meeting rooms, advertises the dates and times for the drop-in and introduces people to one of two senior researchers who are on hand to help. Users can use up to five sessions free with a member of the SRG, but most problems are solved within one or two meetings.

The Community Research Forum (CRF) began at the request of community members to meet up more frequently to discuss common problems in research, and as such forms a parallel group to the SRG. It provides an opportunity for particular communities of interest to share some of the latest research in their field, as well as providing an important networking opportunity for academics and students. The group meets quarterly. The Forum is a means for participants to jointly identify the research needs and priorities of an identified community. The Helpdesk then helps support a process through which the interest group can meet again outside the formality of the Forum.

The Helpdesk in context

To make the Helpdesk effective, and to help ensure it really does yield mutual benefit, some important practical and methodological issues have had to be addressed. Some of these concern the way the University operates in the broader context of UK higher education policy and pressures. Some concern issues of principle inherent in framing and doing research.

Looking first at the way the University operates, there was considerable interest from staff and students in the service the Helpdesk offered. A number of University individuals had longstanding involvement in community-based research; some in participative techniques, some in evaluations of local initiatives and interventions; and many in policy and practical issues relevant to the local communities along the southeast coast of England. For some academics, the development of the Helpdesk was therefore a refinement of ways in which they could engage in this work, and their involvement in the development of the Helpdesk has in turn helped refine how it works.

However, there are significant research pressures within UK universities. Many research-active staff members feel they have limited time to engage in activities beyond those required to meet their teaching obligations and departmental research priorities. Although there is an expectation that academic staff will take part in 'scholarly activity' and research as well as teaching, those who are working across the 'third stream' in universities frequently find that lack of time is a real barrier. There is a common view that the use of time is related directly to incentives and rewards across the sector, as well as to individual institutional priorities. Thus the argument runs that academics will prioritise research not just because of the strong 'push' factors of their own subject-based interests, but because of the strong 'pull' factor of the Research Assessment Exercise (RAE), and the high status of research recognition, for example in promotion criteria.

To address some of these issues, the Helpdesk took a significant decision to 'buy out' time from a number of experienced researchers by making small payments to their schools in return for their involvement. The SRG originally involved seven senior academics from different departments who had expressed an interest in return for a financial contribution towards their time. The SRG meets every six weeks, initially to discuss requests for support that come in through the Helpdesk and to allocate these as projects to the person most qualified, or most available. Group meetings discuss requests, pool resources and decide together how best to take things forward. Responding to requests provides academics with the opportunity to develop their advisory skills and better understand how different issues pertinent to their own work are played out on the ground.

The Helpdesk operates in contested terrain. It sets out to support research which is needed by community and voluntary sector groups, and to make available research expertise within the academy. But it also aims to do so with mutuality. Writing on Australian experience, Eversole (2004) draws attention to the differences between working with communities and making them the subjects or the objects of research. True partnerships, he argues, are based on a shared role in defining and clarifying research questions and approaches, although in some instances the university will take the lead in this. From a researcher's perspective, methodological issues are crucial to determining the impact of a programme, and sometimes too its validity; whereas for community partners, past experience, or quick solutions to pressing social problems might be more important (Riger, 2001). The Helpdesk has found that it is critical to acknowledge issues coming from the community and allow partners to have a say in deciding the methodology to be used. Community partners often know best which data collection strategies are likely to yield results and they can help to ground methodology in the realities of setting and cultural values. While they may have less technical understanding of the processes or particular methodologies, they will invariably have a greater hold of the context and of local concerns.

Community partners vary in their background and previous experiences and it is a mistake to assume that the academic content will originate from the University alone. Many partners bring vast experience in working with communities, in designing programmes and evaluating their initiatives, and look to the University more to validate than to shape their work.

The Helpdesk has also needed to be aware of the resource inequality that might influence ways of working, both physical and human. Resources that are taken for granted in the University might be scarce in

Community and Voluntary Organisations (CVOs) and in an equitable research partnership it might be more important to divide up tasks according to resource availability than to share roles at all levels. For this to happen there is a huge need to listen to concerns and to explain thinking, assumptions and context behind each group's opinions and decisions.

Impact and outcomes

One-to-one service

The SRG was reviewed by the Helpdesk in 2005. Interviews were carried out with users of the one-to-one service and members of the SRG by the Helpdesk manager. Community and statutory service users were asked to describe some of the impacts of the service on their work and organisations. The majority described both personal and professional benefits. One typical response was:

> It enabled us to question the methods and approaches that we had planned to use and gave us an insight into the most effective consultation methods.

Some explained the benefits offered by the Helpdesk service. One interviewee said:

> I could have spent ages and ages hunting for the right statistical methods, but being referred to the relevant academic within the Uni meant I could get hold of the information I was after and gain some useful tips.

Others described the impact on the perception of the quality of their work derived from working with the University, usually in terms of perceived objectivity.

Another interviewee reported that:

> To be able to say that we have been working with the University has been a great bonus for funding bids and monitoring returns, it shows that we are taking a serious approach and hopefully under-taking effective monitoring and evaluation work.

> *(All quotes from Rodriguez, 2005)*

Helpdesk facilitation

An evaluation of the Helpdesk service carried out at the end of the first year was almost unanimously positive, and showed that it had not only met but also anticipated previously unacknowledged needs. Examples include:

- a number of different organisations were able to carry out detailed evaluations of the impact of their own work to a level requested by their funders;
- evidence was compiled of residents' priorities in a community needs survey;
- an evaluation questionnaire was developed for use at a range of different events and this helped to build links with other interest groups.

Alongside specific pieces of work, evaluations of the Helpdesk indicate added value in organisational processes or reputation, for example a number of organisations commented on the level of 'professionalism' gained by working with University partners that enabled them to be seen as independent, unbiased and more reliable when working with other community groups.

Working alongside the University provided organisations with a greater level of credibility. Achieving this level of positive endorsement and impact has not always been straightforward. The early work of the Helpdesk gave rise to a number of challenges. The rapid reputation built up through early successful collaborations led people to expect considerable results, and it has not always been logistically possible for the service to respond adequately to community requests. Sometimes academics felt that enough research had already been done in a particular area and were not keen to take on a newly-specified project, at other times the needs of the group could not be matched with the academic support available. The thrust of the work is community-led, and the pool of academics that are in a position to respond to community requests is unavoidably small. While in a good partnership both sides stand to benefit from working together, at other times the priorities of the different groups are very different, and it falls to the Helpdesk to navigate this, and decide which of the agendas should take priority. Although it was set up to respond to the needs of a community, in order to respond effectively there needs to be a parallel academic group who feels they will benefit from the exchange. Each partnership is built on the notion of mutual benefit rather than commercial service provision, and will therefore only work if there is an adequate match. As the majority of requests come from the community to the University it is they who will then feel let down if this is not forthcoming.

Within the University, the impact has also been considerable. The SRG has become a key driver of academic debate and has grown to strategically influence Cupp's work. Its role has become one of strategy development rather than implementation. For example, the Group has developed an ethics process for dealing with new projects, related to the University's main research ethics policy but tailored to operate in a community context. The main principles of the ethics process are to preserve anonymity and confidentiality; to ensure no harm comes to those being researched or the researcher (minimise 'risk'); to provide referrals for any participants in the research process who may be in need; and to work to empower participants involved in the research. This process, when tested, may have important implications for the University's own ethics committees, and influences the way in which new research projects are secured and implemented.

Stoecker *et al.* (2003) emphasise the importance of 'Community-Based Research (CBR) networks' – as a ground-level infrastructure of solid relationships able to provide support to communities. It is these internal relationships and ties that have the potential over time to influence major policy change. Faculty staff who have no opportunity for community research in their own institutions can be drawn in to other networks and bring with them important experience.

Although the Helpdesk has to date been largely a responsive service it has inevitably been shaped by the availability of expertise as well as by the requests received. More recently, it has explored whether expertise could be called in, or developed in line with new requests, with discussions underway about how community needs might be able to influence academic provision. For example, can the community initiate or influence a particular academic direction, such as housing, or black and minority ethnic (BME) work, that is currently under-represented within the University, by bringing together academics from outside the institution, encouraging areas of new research, or influencing research questions? A strong research forum, acting as a network of senior researchers can begin to present the case for this on the community's behalf.

Strand *et al.* (2003) point out that while we most often think about the potential for CBR to affect social change in the community there are also opportunities for huge changes within colleges and universities. Through CBR programmes such as the Cupp Helpdesk, or broader networks such as the CRF and SRG, new approaches to defining and acquiring knowledge can begin to influence the structures and policies of institutions.

The Helpdesk and the SRG have become an important focal point for debates about disciplinarity. The need to allocate enquiries amongst the academic team has required discussion about the limits of discipline areas, with many particular research problems needing to be informed by approaches from a range of disciplines. Building a reciprocal relationship has involved openness to working in an interdisciplinary fashion and appreciating and respecting the knowledge and skills capacities that different partners bring. Sometimes two or more researchers have decided to work together with a particular organisation, and the group has been a good initiator of interdisciplinary work. The SRG has been mindful of not absorbing any one question too far into a particular disciplinary approach, but of using its own expertise to respond in the most appropriate way possible. The most important element of the Group is the trusting relationships that have built up between researchers, and the value of dialogue between disciplines and approaches.

Critical success factors

The Helpdesk has been a successful innovation. Reflection on why this is so suggests the following critical success factors:

- It adopted a prudent and careful developmental process that sought both to identify possibilities and to manage expectations. The Suarez-Balcazar *et al.* model for community–university research collaborations is helpful here. They identify three phases in the development and sustainability of such partnerships: gaining entry into the community; developing and sustaining collaboration; and recognising outcomes and benefits. They stress the importance of relationship-building and the development of trust and mutual respect. They point to the different communication styles of different partners, to the need for respect for diversity and the different cultures of the two organisations (Suarez-Balcazar *et al.*, 2005). This model can be applied both to the structure of the Helpdesk and to the processes used in individual research projects.
- Much time has been invested in building up trust and mutual understanding. The Helpdesk has worked hard to balance the needs and perceptions of academic professional advancement with those of the CVOs and of the community as a whole. To do so, it has been vital to discuss different goals and expectations from the outset and feedback to the coordinating group the decisions that have been made.
- The Helpdesk has enabled each partner to learn from the other in a reciprocal arrangement. The Helpdesk has emphasised communicating research results so that those who are implicated in them can gain access to outcomes. Research can help define who a community is, what constitutes its membership, who needs to know what. Where universities are involved in doing this, they can also play an important role in ensuring equitable access to information (Eversole, 2004).
- The success of this kind of partnership depends in part on the skills of the different people facilitating them. Selecting people who can communicate well is as important as their academic background, and staff members have been brought in from different schools within the university on the basis of their experience and their enthusiasm.
- The Helpdesk has been mindful of the different operating contexts in partner organisations. For example, aware of high turnover in parts of the voluntary and community sector, the Helpdesk has offered training to multiple staff members in organisations, to try to make training effective in the longer term by ensuring skills can be nurtured within organisations.

The value and impact/s of the service have been captured in monitoring and evaluation reports (Rodriguez, 2005). These reports have provided strong evidence of the Helpdesk contribution towards helping local community, voluntary and statutory sector organisations build capacity and aid the development of more sustainable services, as well as showing the benefits for individual academics and the academic development of the University.

References

Brighton and Hove City Council (2005), *Brighton and Hove Community Safety Plan 2005–2008*. Brighton: Brighton and Hove City Council.

Buckeridge, D.L., Mason, R., Robertson, A., Frank, J., Glazier, R., Purdon, L., (2002) 'Making health data maps: A case study of community university research collaboration', *Social Science and Medicine*, Vol. 55, No. 7, pp. 1,189–206.

Eversole R. (2004) *Regional social research and community university engagement*. Conference Proceedings: University regional and rural engagement, Charles Sturt University New South Wales 14–16 July.

Marullo, S., Cooke, D., Willis, J., Rollins, A., Burke, J., Bonilla, P., Waldref, V. (2003) 'Community-Based Research assessments: Some principles and practices', *Michigan Journal of Community Service Learning*, Summer, pp. 57–68.

Riger, S. (2001) 'Working together: Challenges in collaborative research', in M. Sullivan and J.G. Kelly (eds.) *Collaborative research: University and community partnership* (pp. 25–44). Washington, DC: American Public Health Association.

Rodriguez, P. (2005) Cupp's Senior Researchers Group and the one to one research support service, monitoring and evaluation report , September 2004 – August 2005. Brighton: University of Brighton.

Stoecker, R., Ambler, S.H., Cutforth, N., Donohue, P., Dougherty, D., Marully, S., Nelson, K.S., Stutts, N. (2003) 'Community-Based Research networks: Development and lessons learned in an emerging field', *Michigan Journal of Community Service Learning*, Summer, pp. 44–56.

Strand, K., Marullo, S., Cutforth, N., Stoecker, R., Donohue, P. (2003) 'Principles of best practice for Community-Based Research', *Michigan Journal of Community Service Learning*, Summer, pp. 5–15.

Suarez-Balcazar, Y., Harper, G.W., and Lewis, R. (2005) 'An interactive and contextual model of community–university collaborations for research and action', *Health Education and Behaviour*, Vol. 32, No. 1, pp. 84–101.

Chapter 4

Riding tandem

Kim Aumann, Jenny Broome-Smith and Ros Cook

Introduction

This is the story of two organisations, the University of Brighton and Amaze. We use the metaphor of 'riding tandem' to tell this story, since we have found it useful in thinking about work undertaken together. These two organisations rode tandem to develop a range of projects that share their skill and expertise, and achieved something more than if they had ridden alone. Seen through the eyes of Amaze, the voluntary sector organisation involved in the partnership, it reflects on the impact of university partnership working on one small organisation, contrasts the before and after effects, and identifies the major learning points along the way.

What we are

Amaze is a charity that offers independent information, advice and support to parents of children with special needs and disabilities aged 0 to 19 years. We offer direct services for parents such as a helpline, handbooks and fact sheets, one-to-one help with education and benefits issues, workshops and parent-support courses. We are a parent-led organisation and believe the views of parents should be central to the decisions made about their child, so we aim to make sure parents' voices are heard. We work to encourage good communication and partnership between individual parents and service providers. But we also try to influence how services operate for all disabled children and families, working alongside colleagues across the sectors towards the ideal of integrated, seamless services. We run the Compass, Brighton's database of children with special needs, and the data we draw from this informs our contribution to the planning and development of services.

Making links

Some years before we wanted to get a piece of work evaluated and approached the University of Brighton hoping that this might be a suitable research project. But we found they were only interested if we could fund it. More recently, we were asked by the University to find parents to act as a user focus group to inform their course design. The way they went about it raised concerns for us about whether we had a shared view about good user involvement. In both these cases, what was on offer was not about partnership. The Community-University Partnership Programme (Cupp) seems to promise something different.

Our first contact with Cupp at the University of Brighton was in response to their email to community and voluntary sector groups across the city. This one captured our attention. Why so? Amaze wants to use an evidence-base approach to making its work more effective. We had already identified a need to find out more about quantitative research and statistical significance in relation to the Compass database. While we knew we didn't have the right set of skills to analyse the data rigorously, we also knew researchers could probably point us to the right people to help build our skills. We thought the Compass was likely to be something that would appeal to academics because it provides rich data on the circumstances of local families with disabled children. Here was a chance to sharpen our thinking in order to ask the right evaluative questions, improve our skill to assess our work and develop our talent to better scrutinise existing research findings. There is much greater emphasis from funders to demonstrate an evidence base before they will consider project proposals and they require systematic evaluation of the projects they fund. But this was not our primary motivation. We simply did not want to waste our time doing things that were unlikely to work.

Why did it work?

Our partnership with the University has worked extraordinarily well. We were aware that the University would, initially at least, be the power partner in any project, because it brought both its research expertise and funding to the table. But we were a mature voluntary sector organisation with relatively sophisticated problem-solving skills. With our understanding and insights into life at the coalface, we felt we would be able to offer fresh takes on the work. So we were confident we could soon grow into a more equal partner.

What crystallised our commitment was successfully finding a university partner who shared our passion to make things better for children with special needs and their families. In our experience, quality partnerships rely on finding the right match. We had tentative contacts with other academics that we didn't pursue further. In retrospect, we think this was because a necessary spark between us just didn't happen. Chemistry really matters!

Here is a list to get a flavour of what we did and what we think we have gained from our partnership:

Drawing on academic expertise

- Discussions with statisticians about developing the Compass led to increased clarity about what we need to do next to develop this work.
- Advice on research methodology gave us the extra skills necessary to evaluate Leave it Out. This was a pilot project testing materials in primary schools aimed at raising the profile of the relationship between bullying and special needs.

Leading on new projects

- We wanted to bid to design and implement a parent-support course called 'Insiders' guide to bringing up children with special needs'. We included in the bid funds to commission the University to evaluate the work. The bid was successful and we now have a model of parent-support courses that we know are effective and we can refine and develop further. Plus we gained direct experience of commissioning and working with independent researchers.

Developing projects together

- We worked with our University partner to test a new methodology being developed with practitioners to build the resilience of disadvantaged children. This particular project is discussed in more depth in Chapter 14. Because of our long-standing relationship and credibility with parents we were able to secure their involvement in a series of workshops to test the materials. Their input helped refine the methodology and make it more accessible. By working collaboratively on this particular project, the quality of solutions has been improved.

Training and learning

- Staff members have attended a range of University of Brighton workshops.
- One of us attended a workshop one year and taught on it the next.
- Reporting on project findings to national and international audiences has provided opportunities to develop writing and presentation skills.

Accessing university resources

- We have used the university library extensively and have access to abundant databases to search the most up-to-date publications.
- We have accessed affordable software for statistical analysis and maintaining bibliographies.
- We have drawn on the University's networks to extend our contacts.

Ups and downs

The experience of riding tandem with the University has been a positive one. For us, the benefits far outweighed the disadvantages. But we would also like to offer a few lessons on the ups and downs.

Lesson One: Pedal power

One of the most encouraging lessons was the speed and power achieved as a result of working together, although this did not come about straight away. The positive energy we were able to generate to get work done, expand our thinking and meet deadlines seemed much larger than if we had gone it alone. On one occasion, calling on our University partner's expertise to reference the evidence-base and research methodology, enabled us to finalise an application ahead of schedule.

Another time, we had misgivings about sharing our data. We had reservations about submitting Compass data to the City Council's demographic mapping tool. We couldn't see how the way it 'anonymised' data points could safeguard against the identification of some children, and we had promised families registering on the Compass that they would never be individually identified. Our city partners couldn't understand our reluctance to trust in a widely-used method until an expert at the University of Brighton confirmed that, for this kind of data, the method was indeed limited. In this case, drawing on the University's authority helped us uphold the integrity of our organisation.

While joint work can maximise outputs, joint working in two different settings in quite different ways makes communication difficult. Sometimes it felt like we were talking two dialects within the same language. As a result the volume of emails and phone calls and level of explanation was higher than it would otherwise have been.

Joint working opens you up to criticism, so you have to want to acquire a critical friend and offer the same in return. It seemed to us that academics and voluntary sector workers share in common a culture that values and encourages independent thought and opinion. By working with the University we had the rare opportunity to open our work to scrutiny without fear of making ourselves vulnerable or jeopardising funding. At the same time, we learnt about academic practice. It felt as though showing our 'warts and all' helped to generate a space of genuine enquiry.

We doubt we would have been able to allocate as much time and resource to working with the University without one of us being freed from her regular workload, to pursue new avenues. Stepping back from the usual and having time to reflect on the organisation's strategic and operational activity contributed to creating the conditions to think more laterally and participate fully.

Lesson Two: Sharing the steering

We didn't know any other local organisation that had travelled this path before us. However, we quickly discovered that we could find our own route and that university partnerships could meld themselves around the needs, interests and hopes of partners. This developed rather organically for us. We swiftly developed an easy rapport and dialogue with our partners. We had a trusting relationship within months of our first contact. Trying to pinpoint how this was achieved is tricky. Did we just strike lucky? Or is it to do with compatible working styles, good people skills, similar interests and hopes?

We are confident that sharing an interest in the subject or the methodology makes all the difference. For example, when embarking on the knowledge exchange project, we were impressed by our University partner's interest to make Resilient Therapy, which is a new methodology for supporting disadvantaged children, accessible to parents. Her eagerness to link the theory and research to improving people's real lives and practically tackling disadvantage warmed our hearts. Much of our contact was with an academic who is also a practitioner and a parent and so it is difficult to be sure that these multiple roles have not in fact been the necessary ingredient. We suspect a social or moral commitment to improve the lot of disadvantaged groups might be the real glue for effective partnerships with voluntary sector organisations.

At first, the University partner led lots of the time but as we got more confident about what we had to offer, we took the lead too. The Resilient Therapy workshops we ran for parents began with the University partner up front and us in an observer role, but by the second round of workshops, we were co-delivering. You may feel less confident and want to negotiate a partnership where you take more of a back seat but trust your own knowledge, as the process of building a partnership forces the articulation of voluntary sector organisation expertise. This all fell into place for us but we are aware of how easy it can be to make assumptions – for academics to assume voluntary organisations don't have the sufficient capability to share leadership, and for voluntary sector organisations to underestimate what expertise they have to offer.

The community university partnership went well for us without the need for contracts and formalised agreements, but what if it had gone wrong? When we invited parents to Resilient Therapy workshops we were trading on the trust parents have in our organisation. If our University partner had not worked sensitively with parents and for example not respected confidentiality, it's us that parents would blame and it is our organisation that would be compromised. Consider the terms of the relationship, clarify expectations and agree who is responsible if things go wrong. While not wanting to stereotype, academics are autonomous individuals who are likely to shy away from prescription and we agree that bureaucratic procedures are not the stuff of creativity and innovation. But working in the community exposing inequalities and challenging power bases is an edgy arena. Things will go wrong and the terms of the partnership will at times be challenged. If and when it does, we suspect the dice are loaded in the university's favour because voluntary organisations have no ranks to close, cannot waste time on unsuccessful project work, are dependent on monitoring and evaluating their work and cannot afford to lose access to university expertise.

We each embark on the journey from different starting positions. Universities have an imperative to write and publish findings, which is not often the case for voluntary sector organisations. For universities, this work is their bread and butter while for voluntary sector organisations it is often a venture involving risk. It would probably help to clarify responsibilities, actions and timescales at the outset and review things along the way.

Joint working sparks unanticipated developments. But whereas voluntary sector workers are usually driven by the need to solve specific problems, academics are trained to formulate and test new theories. As the voluntary sector partner it is important to be open to new possibilities, as these can provide you with new ways to attack your problem. But, at the same time, you need to keep a strong focus on your major goals, so that you can resist the possibility of getting side-tracked down paths that just aren't relevant enough to your mission. If your organisation has the capacity, it's great to have a contingency plan in place to capitalise on the productive spin-offs. And if you are lucky enough to decide to use it, make sure you finish the original project before being seduced into starting new work. Academics may argue the finer points of their particular field over many years, whereas voluntary sector organisations generally have less-rounded, but more pressing, objectives.

Lesson Three: Shifting gear

University partnerships can offer access to a range of knowledge banks, not always known at the outset. Only by taking the journey will you discover the riches. You can really improve the quality of your thinking and practice because of access to the additional knowledge and skills held within universities. Although sometimes a step removed from the real world of social disadvantage, universities can help make connections with broader research and debate, such as:

- Increasing skills by using specialist IT applications, learning research skills and tools for measuring and evaluating, attending thematic lectures and study courses. Now when we see that black and minority ethnic (BME) children on the Compass are less likely to access play and leisure facilities, our first question is, is this statistically significant? And when we are looking at a new area of work, we start by doing a literature review. Look carefully at courses and ask searching questions about whether they are pitched at a level that will be useful to you. It may not be as sophisticated as you expect.

- Universities have an imperative to produce new knowledge, write and publish ideas and findings, but this is not often a voluntary sector organisation priority. If this is what you want, universities are a good place to learn and improve your talent to articulate what you know about your community. We would like our work to contribute to the national agenda on disabled children and the experience of writing with the university partners has equipped us to do this on our own.
- Sharpening voluntary sector organisations' skills at negotiating in another sector. It's a chance to critique another setting and culture and take from it what you want.
- Providing access to communities of practice, new ways of thinking, the chance to embark on formal learning and the opportunity to conduct dedicated research.

Be careful that the momentum of new partnership work doesn't take you on a separate route to that of the organisation. The more you invest in a master plan, the better. For example, as an umbrella organisation representing the interests of disabled children from a parent perspective, we are frequently presented with invitations to participate in new initiatives. We are familiar with and experienced at checking these opportunities against our strategic priorities to decide whether or not to get involved. Community-university partnership work ought to be seen in the same light, particularly as universities appear less constrained by their choice of projects. Applying some checks and balances without stifling the creativity takes careful management but is important when the activity is not a core one.

Lesson Four: Ring the bell

It's important to communicate widely and often. Some stakeholders are likely to be sceptical and struggle to see the difference working with universities will make to the quality of people's lives. Explaining the partnership and keeping people updated needs to be routine. And spreading involvement around helps avoid locating the learning in an individual.

In retrospect we wish we had done more to communicate the work at every organisational level. Our stakeholders want us to do hands-on work with parents and may mistrust a university partnership because they assume it will be rarefied and impractical. You need to be ready to explain what difference it will make to people's lives. For example, when we embarked on the knowledge exchange project and invited parents to take part in workshops about Resilient Therapy, we relied on the rest of the team to promote the benefits to parents so they would come along. Our staff members know that parents' time and energy is precious. The team needed to believe that parents would get something of value from the experience.

We suggest you sort a system for updating everyone at the outset so that the learning is spread. It's worth thinking strategically about who in your organisation gets to be involved. The type of project will determine who gets to be involved. So considering the match and thinking about who can offer a degree of autonomy and authority to the partnership will help. Being entrepreneurial can leave others out and unthinkingly locating the work in just one person has its drawbacks. But we suspect instructing individuals to take part would be misguided, as being innovative probably relies on individuals freely choosing to take part.

Lesson Five: Front rack, back rack and panniers too!

Creatively seeking out and strapping resources together can reveal surprises and is likely to need practitioners with a degree of autonomy to operate in this way. Successful partnerships require people able and willing to be entrepreneurs. This might sound rather grandiose but in our experience the energy and drive partnerships are capable of generating is dependent to some degree on having an opportunistic eye.

Being ready to grab resources and run with initiatives without having to check back with your board of trustees keeps the momentum going and avoids stifling the innovative process through bureaucratic delay. It's possible that partnerships work best when personnel involved have enough organisational authority to exploit the opportunities that relationships throw up.

You have to want to seize the day but you also have to be able to prioritise and consider your capacity to undertake the work. Universities are great spaces for fostering lateral thinking and may want to develop lots of projects simultaneously. You can get the best out of community-university partnerships if you are able to learn quickly and work even faster. And it makes sense to try to identify what the partnership needs, and clarify your capacity sooner rather than later.

Working with the University has brought us access to a range of resources including their library and online databases, training courses, specialist computer software, people who have research and writing expertise, and on-tap advice. We have been surprised at the extent of the University's network and how often our partners were able to lead us to someone 'in the know'.

We were initially taken aback by the high level of university costs. If you're considering a joint funding bid the project needs to be of a size to incorporate these costs. But it did prompt us to consider whether our own formula was sufficiently realistic and was another example of the fresh thinking that happens when you step outside your own sector and enter another.

In summary

Riding in tandem more or less summarises our experience of being a partner in the community–university partnership programme. We have built strong and friendly links with the University that will last far beyond the length of current projects. We had the right match of partners, and shared a passion and drive that made all the extra time and work involved worthwhile. We have expanded our knowledge base and built our capacity to support parents, despite the peculiar mismatch of expertise that exists between us. The absence of bureaucratic and administrative hurdles has enabled growth and while we did not set out expecting to have so much involvement, the enthusiasm generated by the partnership has made the growth very fluid. We have explored new ways of thinking about supporting children and families and applied this to our practice, which would not have happened otherwise. Our organisation has changed so that research and evidenced-based work is now routine. And we have been enthused and rejuvenated by the experience. The adrenalin is pumping. We are embarking on more.

Part 2

From research to practice

Introduction

The next four chapters concentrate on examples of evidence-informed practice developed via Cupp-sponsored collaborative research projects. They offer some answers to the question of how best to develop practice in and with the community, or parts of it, by relevant research. The principle elaborated here is that to identify 'what works' it is best to work with the practitioners and individuals directly involved. The chapters suggest that the nature and impact of 'practice improvement' needs to be informed by a more inclusive research process.

Chapter 5 describes collaborative research to improve service provision and community capacity for homeless lesbian, gay, bisexual and transgender (LGBT) youth. This research involved Hove YMCA and the University and succeeded in reaching a population that remains socially excluded and whose needs remain poorly understood. This chapter illustrates a number of ways in which the collaborative nature of the research project can influence service provision by being more effective in identifying the needs of those otherwise underprovided for.

Chapter 6 examines substance misuse – how to make better use of evidence-based practice for teaching, research and professional practice supporting those working with addicts. The chapter describes work undertaken by the University and Drug and Alcohol Action Teams (DAATs) in East and West Sussex and Brighton and Hove. The partnership pre-dated the project and includes a professional course at the University for those working in the field. So, in that context, what more could be achieved? The answer from this project is 'quite a lot' – including substantive improvements in the knowledge base and better ways of involving practitioners in critically developing evidence of 'what works'.

Chapter 7 explores a project to develop a 'community of practice' to support Neighbourhood Renewal. The starting-point was a recognition that effective Neighbourhood Renewal – despite considerable investment – was being hampered by the inability to learn from one intervention to another. The chapter describes the use of 'action learning' to achieve this objective.

Chapter 8 describes the historical process involved in developing a service responsive to helping refugees access higher education. This has involved two local universities, post-16 education providers, as well as services that work with refugees and asylum seekers. It shows how the roles have changed and expanded over time, and describes a project that now encompasses both action research and wide participation in the governance structures of the partnership.

Taken together, these chapters show the benefits of research partnerships that:

- get closer to 'service users' often excluded from service design and delivery;
- improve the capacity of the 'community of interest' as well as the community organisation;
- involve service professionals in the research thereby improving their knowledge base and the quality of their professional practice;
- has additional weight because of the credibility of university involvement in the research;
- provide the basis for an ongoing relationship and further collaborative work between the partners to mutual benefit;
- draw on the particular strengths of each partner.

As Haynes, Britt and Gill observe, quoting Miller *et al.*, in introducing Chapter 6, while evidence-based practices may have some 'natural benefits', they have not been widely adopted in community practice. These four chapters show the benefits of so doing, and how an initiative such as Cupp can help provide, as Haynes *et al.* comment, the necessary 'good face-to-face discussion and critical reflection about knowledge-based practice, in a safe and supported environment' to support an evidence-based culture.

Chapter 5

Researching the needs of homeless LGBT youth: Hove YMCA and Cupp in a very civil partnership

Mark Cull and Hazel Platzer

Introduction

The research project discussed in this chapter was a qualitative study of the needs and experiences of homeless lesbian, gay, bisexual and trans-gender (LGBT) youth (Cull *et al.*, 2006); the research was collaborative in partnership between Hove YMCA and the University of Brighton. Successful university community partnerships are characterised by the sharing of power through building trust, a culture of mutual learning, sharing skills and resources, and the transfer of skills (Strand *et al.*, 2003; Suarez-Balcazar, 2005). This project sought to work in such a collaborative way to identify the needs of LGBT homeless youth, in order to influence service providers to effect social change and build capacity within the community in relation to research skills.

The partnership working between the University and Hove YMCA allowed us to use a research design which accessed a vulnerable and hard-to-reach population; we did this by recruiting research participants through a voluntary sector youth advice service which was accessible to LGBT youth. Typically academic research on this population fails to recruit a robust sample of the most socially-excluded members of hidden populations whereas in this study a diverse group of socially-excluded LGBT youth was obtained. Further funding was obtained from Cupp to extend the project to investigate the views of service providers about homeless LGBT youth. This enabled us, as a research team, to engage with local service providers and involve them in developing services in line with our research findings. Whilst this approach led to a greater application of research findings than is perhaps typical of an academically-led research project with less community involvement, we recognise that the sustainability of the partnership was limited by the contract research culture of the university. The project was short-term and the University's involvement was largely curtailed by the end of the researcher's contract; however, the researcher was given an honorary fellowship at the end of the project which potentially provides a mechanism for the development of future joint-funding bids with the partners to develop further work.

Researching the hidden and hard-to-reach

The difficulties of researching hidden populations on sensitive topics are well documented (see for example O'Connor and Molloy, 2001; Platzer, 2006; Prendergast et al., 2001; Lee, 1993; Dunne et al., 2002; Gold, 2005; Shelter and Stonewall Housing). Gaining entry to community organisations has been identified as a major barrier to community–university engagement (Suarez-Balcazar, 2005), but this initial hurdle was sidestepped through the community partner initially approaching the University partner. As a result, this research project was set up in such a way that the challenges normally facing academic researchers when trying to recruit LGBT participants into a research study were overcome with relative ease. The University was initially commissioned by Hove YMCA to carry out the research thus side-stepping any issues regarding gate keepers as Hove YMCA provided a housing advice service and other services to young people. This service was already monitoring sexual and gender identity following the best practice guidance from Shelter and Stonewall enabling the research team to invite young LGBT accessing their service to participate in the research. The research team also recognised that although a diverse sample could be, and was, obtained by recruiting young people through their service, there was still a possibility that the most vulnerable young people who were not accessing services would not be recruited into the study. The research team therefore also conducted street outreach to recruit homeless young people into the study.

These recruitment strategies were successful in generating a diverse sample of homeless LGBT youth which included some young people who were disengaged from services and some young people who had not accessed support from LGBT communities. This enabled us to research and understand the vulnerability of homeless LGBT youth and deepen existing knowledge about the relationship between sexual identities, transgender identity and homelessness. We found a link between homophobic bullying in schools, lack of appropriate sex education and lack of support for LGBT youth in schools and later vulnerability to homelessness. We also found that where families and young people accessed mental health services their needs in relation to sexual identity and transgender identity were not recognised; this meant that early work which may have prevented homelessness did not take place. Nearly all of the young LGBT people we interviewed had mental health problems and they also had difficulty in accessing services which took account of the way that homophobia, transphobia, and isolation had impacted on their mental health. We also found that once young people had become homeless, the effects of homophobia, transphobia and isolation continued within housing and homelessness services. We recommended that preventative work needs to take place in schools and in mental health services to reduce the risk of family breakdown and to reduce the incidence of homophobic bullying in order to prevent homelessness; we also recommended that specific services need to be developed for homeless LGBT youth so that they can access peer support and specialised support from housing and homelessness staff which would help them to overcome the disadvantage that had led to their homelessness. A key feature of these recommendations was that LGBT youth need a safe space in which they can develop their life skills in an environment where they are not threatened by homophobia and transphobia; LGBT specific accommodation would enable young people to fully participate in, and engage with, services that are designed to provide support.

A further advantage to the way that the research and recruitment was set up, was that young people participating in the research were able to access services and support from Hove YMCA in relation to their homelessness and associated needs. It is often the case that academic researchers working alone cannot set up sufficient support structures to ensure the safety and well-being of research participants; ironically, the needs of the most vulnerable may then not be identified through research because of ethical considerations about harming research participants and therefore excluding them from the research process.

Building research capacity and developing an effective partnership

A key feature of Cupp is to build research capacity in community partners. This is achieved through the university and community partners working closely together with a mutual sharing and development of expertise. The way in which this occurred on the LGBT youth homelessness project is best illustrated by way of a conversation between the partners: Hazel the University partner and Mark the community partner. The context for this conversation is that Mark originally obtained funding from a number of bodies and commissioned the University to undertake the research. Additional Cupp funding extended the project to including data collection with service providers, and getting the community partner more involved in the research process which included Mark enrolling at the University in a Masters-level module on research methods. We also worked with other partners, such as the local authority and the local LGBT community forum (Spectrum), to discuss and disseminate the research findings with a view to influencing service delivery and local strategic policy. This last aim was very important to both of us as, in common with successful partnerships (Strand *et al.*, 2003), we shared a passion to do a piece of research which would make a real difference to vulnerable people's lives:

> **Hazel:** To what extent do you feel you've developed your capacity to undertake research?

Mark: The Cupp funding gave me more time to really get involved in the research and to take the module which gave me more of a theoretical understanding of what we were doing. You also gave me feedback about the research interviews that I did – there were lots of things that hadn't occurred to me and so I've developed my interviewing skills.

Hazel: So what difference has the partnership working made?

Mark: When we first commissioned the research I thought you'd just do the research and hand me a report but you've been much more involved than I had expected in terms of taking the research findings back into the community and to local service providers. I didn't have the confidence to present the findings before, but because we did it together, I've become less nervous about it. I'm now much more able to get my points across to people who influence service provision.

Hazel: Have there been any other spin-offs?

Mark: Well, the whole of our organisation is now more connected to the University and thinking about how the University can help us with other research and evaluation needs.

A key to developing effective partnerships between universities and communities, is that, as part of a necessary process of empowerment, learning should be mutual and skills should be complementary. We have so far seen only one side of this equation with Mark identifying how he developed his research skills and the confidence to present those findings to policy makers. In order to build trust and a truly collaborative relationship between partners, this should be a two-way process (Strand *et al.*, 2003). Again a conversation between the partners helps to illuminate what took place:

Mark: What did you do in this project that you couldn't have done on your own?

Hazel: I would never have done the street outreach to find research participants in public sex environments who weren't accessing services. You had the skills, as a youth worker and an advice worker, to engage people in that way and the safety net of a service to refer them to, so that we didn't just grab some data and leave them on the streets. We did the outreach together and that helped me to develop confidence and skills in that area.

Mark: Do you think this research will make more of a difference to young LGBT people compared to your previous work?

Hazel: In the past I've done sound pieces of academic research but was not always convinced that it was going to make a difference unless I could collaborate with people in practice settings. With this project you were connected in to all the service providers and had access to policy makers because of your practice base. That enabled us to get service providers on board and really think about the significance of the research findings for their practice, so that has been really encouraging in terms of making a difference to vulnerable people's lives.

The benefits of collaborative research between community and university partners have been identified by Strand *et al.* (2003) as a process of democratisation and civic engagement where community-based organisations enhance their ability to act strategically influencing policy makers and decision makers; this occurs when collaborative research improves the credibility of community-based organisations and enables them to engage policy makers with compelling information.

Influencing local policy and service provision

Mark observed that frontline service providers lack credibility with the local authority. This was borne out by our observations at a consultation event which we participated in. The local authority were consulting the LGBT community about housing needs: when Mark's colleagues related the experiences of homeless LGBT youth who they had supported and provided advice to, local authority workers were dismissive of these accounts implying that they were anecdotal. When we presented similar material within the context of our research study, there was a sense that our findings were given more status and credibility giving us hope that the voices of marginalised and vulnerable youth were more likely to be heard and taken seriously.

For Hazel, as an academic, this stage of the research project, where we disseminated our findings with policy makers and service providers was the most exciting part of the project and one of the major benefits of partnership working. All too often a rigorous piece of research can have little impact on practice; however Mark as the community partner was networked into local services and centrally involved in consultation events being staged around local strategic developments in relation to housing and homelessness and a re-structuring of Children's and Young People's Services into a new city-wide Children and Young People's Trust. Mark was able to ensure that the University partner was brought into this process and we worked together to feed our research findings into these processes at every opportunity.

We presented our preliminary findings to service providers through direct contacts or by participating at community events hosted by the local LGBT community forum. This raised interest and awareness about the research amongst service providers and helped to build a head of steam before we publicly launched the final report. Coincidentally, the report was being concluded whilst the local authority was developing its first youth homeless strategy. We met with the manager responsible for this new policy and although some of the data was fairly damning, he was open to hearing what we had found. This manager was a guest speaker at the launch event and spoke about how the research had helped to inform the new strategy and demonstrated a commitment to the needs of homeless LGBT youth.

To coincide with the publication of the report and to generate wider awareness of the research, Hazel gave local radio interviews, whilst Mark was interviewed for the local daily newspaper and a national youth magazine. Publicity was also generated through both local and national gay media.

The launch, and the activity leading up to it, was a major part of the partnership work; it was strategically planned to bring all the major stakeholders together and the process increased the accountability of local service providers and those in a position to plan local service provision. Mark had made a short film with three of the research participants specifically for the launch event. Their moving accounts of their life experiences helped to humanise the research data and added to people's gained awareness and commitment to the report recommendations.

Feedback from the launch provided strong indications that the project had a significant impact on the awareness of local providers about previously unmet needs in a vulnerable population, and that they were now committed to developing services to meet those needs. The local Primary Care Trust released funds for a local LGBT youth group to provide training to mainstream service providers, and some organisations that had not been monitoring the sexual identity of their service users committed to developing this. Service providers who attended the launch also disseminated the research findings to colleagues within their organisations; for instance the findings were cascaded down in relation to specific services such as to the teenage pregnancy unit and upwards to directors involved in the current review of Children's Services.

We also heard in the feedback how the research and its launch had strengthened the resolve of key people in statutory agencies to pursue this aspect of their equalities agenda – whereas before many of them had felt they were working in isolation, the event brought such people together leading to a shared and therefore strengthened commitment within their organisations. The Cupp Director said that the launch event had been exemplary. He commented that often research findings and recommendations can be seen as threatening to the very audience that you wish to influence. He said that the way the research had been conducted, by consulting and including stakeholders through the process, had encouraged a large, participative and engaged audience at the event.

A local Member of Parliament had attended the launch event and was particularly concerned about young people's experiences of homophobic bullying in schools. He gave a commitment to following this particular area of the research up with the Government minister responsible for

Education and Skills. As the research report is nationally relevant, Hove YMCA was keen for it to be disseminated as widely as possible and Mark has continued to send the report to MPs, government departments and follow up with local stakeholders. The national body, YMCA England, was able to support this process through generating national media interest and promoting the research through the YMCA network in the UK. The report was also published on several websites to increase readership and ease access.

One of the community events that we spoke at, an LGBT housing forum, led to the development of a LGBT housing and support working group. This group was established to act as a consultee on a range of council policy development work, including the Council's housing strategy, homelessness strategy, youth homelessness strategy, sheltered housing strategy, and community safety strategy – and inform discussions on training, consultation, and inclusivity in council service provision for LGBT people. Both Hazel and Mark were invited to join this group. The Council have since committed to developing a specific LGBT housing strategy and our research should greatly inform the new strategy. A fortnight after the publication of our report, a consultation event for the new youth homelessness strategy was held by the local authority. The research was referred to twice in the opening presentation, affirming the importance Brighton and Hove City Council are placing on the report.

Conclusion

This partnership enabled us to conduct a piece of research which identified the needs of a hidden and hard-to-reach group of homeless LGBT youth. The partnership enabled us to reach a very vulnerable and marginalised group whose needs were poorly understood. The partnership working also enabled us to place that information clearly in a policy-making and service-delivery arena and we managed, in doing that, to shift the understanding of service providers about the needs of this group. Before, this group were seen as homeless youth who happened to be LGBT and there was little understanding of the relationships between sexual identity, transgender identity, homophobia, transphobia and home-lessness. In carrying out this in-depth study with vulnerable people we were able to illuminate those relationships and further mental and sexual health vulnerabilities. We were also able to draw attention to the need for preventative work in schools and families and the need for specific services once LGBT youth had become homeless. We are confident that this research will influence local service provision, and Hove YMCA will continue to promote and advocate for the research recommendations to be delivered within Brighton and Hove. We are also confident that the research will have a wider influence on service provision and national policy.

References

Cull, M., Platzer, H.K. and Balloch, S. (2006) *Out on my own – Understanding the experiences and needs of homeless lesbian, gay, bisexual and transgender youth.* Brighton: Health and Social Policy Research Centre, University of Brighton.

Dunne, G.A., Prendergast, S. and Telford, D. (2002) Young, gay, homeless and invisible: a growing population? *Culture, Health and Sexuality,* Vol. 4, pp. 103–115.

Gold, D. (2005) *Sexual exclusion: issues and best practice in lesbian, gay and bisexual housing and homelessness.* London: Stonewall Housing in association with Shelter.

Lee, R.M. (1993) *Doing research on sensitive topics.* Sage: London.

O'Connor, W. and Molloy, D. (2001) *'Hidden in plain sight': homelessness amongst lesbian and gay youth.* London: National Centre for Social Research.

Platzer, H.K. (2006) *Positioning identities: lesbians' and gay men's experiences in mental health care.* Edmonton, Alberta: Qual Institute Press.

Prendergast, S., Dunne, G.A. and Telford, D. (2001) 'A story of "difference", a different story: young homeless lesbian, gay and bisexual people', *International Journal of Sociology and Social Policy,* Vol. 21, pp. 64–91.

Shelter and Stonewall Housing *Monitoring of client sexuality: Guidance on implementation. Promoting good practice in lesbian, gay and bisexual housing.* See: http://england.shelter.org.uk/ and http://www.stonewallhousing.org/good_practice.html

Strand, K.M.S., Cutforth, N., Stoecker, R., Donohue, P. (2003) *Community-based research and higher education – principles and practices.* San Francisco: Jossey-Bass.

Suarez-Balcazar, Y., Harper, G.W., and Lewis, R. (2005) 'An interactive and contextual model of community–university collaborations for research and action', *Health Education and Behaviour,* Vol. 32, No. 1, pp. 84–101.

Chapter 6

Substance misuse teaching and research – using knowledge and evidence for community benefit

Philip Haynes, Daren Britt, Stuart Gill

Introduction

> Whatever natural benefits there are for using evidence-based prac-
> tices have usually been insufficient to bring about their adoption in
> community practice. Nonetheless, it is clear that, unlike other health
> care providers, substance abuse practitioners will be increasingly
> required to learn and adopt evidence-based practices. (Miller *et al.*,
> 2006, p.35)

The substance misuse treatment community in the UK is a diverse
community which includes professionals and volunteers with a wide range
of professional experiences, training and knowledge. However, whilst
encompassing experience, evidence and knowledge from multiple sources
and backgrounds it has been noted that the community often fails to
utilise or disseminate evidence and knowledge to influence practice (Miller
et al., 2006).

This chapter has arisen from research undertaken by the University of
Brighton with the Drug and Alcohol Action Teams (DAATs) of East
Sussex, West Sussex and Brighton and Hove. The research undertaken by
this community–university partnership utilised both quantitative and qualitative methods to identify how the substance misuse practitioner community can make sense of knowledge and evidence-based practice.

The research was designed and implemented within a pre-existing
partnership between the University and the DAATs. A first partnership
was set up in 2002 to examine professional training for substance misuse
workers and included local government DAATs. The partnership continues through 2003–2007 and manages a part-time professional course
based at the University. Members of partner organisations are seconded
into the learning and teaching delivery team.

Key to contextualisation is recognition of the complexity and diversity
of the knowledge and evidence sources represented within the field. This
chapter explores the definitions of knowledge and evidence-based practice
emerging from the higher education research and teaching communities
and examines their relevance to the diverse and multi-professional,
multi-sector community of substance misuse treatment workers.

The results of the new research are discussed with reference to two key aspects of knowledge management: facilitating communities of practice and implementing knowledge and information repositories (like websites and libraries). The chapter draws conclusions on how a stronger partnership between the University sector and practitioners can be developed to enhance knowledge and evidence-based practice that is of real value to service users. The need for brokerage and facilitation across boundaries, with the goal of creating opportunities for practitioners to share their voices within the evidence-base, is argued.

A complex context: The multiple knowledge sources of the substance misuse field

It is first necessary to identify the key professional and interest groups who have contested knowledge and practice in the substance misuse sector. The historical development of these groups illustrates how knowledge and practice has become contested, and how this contest has grown in its complexity in recent decades. This allows us to understand organisational cultural background and to evaluate some of the key issues about how the groups can work together. It is argued in this chapter that in the contemporary policy environment, universities can take a mediating role in these 'knowledge contests' by helping to facilitate an awareness of the full range of information and knowledge available and encouraging practitioners to have space to reflect critically on all that is available.

Public health and public control

The modern substance misuse treatment sector has its roots in the first part of the last century. After the First World War there was a national concern that the trauma of war and larger scale movements of people would fuel an increase in serious drug dependency amongst the masses. A key debate developed between the Ministry of Health and the Home Office at this time (Berridge, 1984). The history of the debate between these two ministries identifies a tension that remains central to contemporary policy, namely to what extent substance use can be addressed as a health issue, versus the extent to which substance misuse becomes an issue of public safety and security.

The Dangerous Drugs Act of 1920 initially allowed the Ministry of Health, and medical professionals to manage addiction and control the use of drugs. They argued that different drugs could be used for different reasons and doctors, as medical professionals, were best suited to make the decision about when supply of a drug was appropriate. This included prescribing routine amounts of addictive drugs, like opiates, to someone

with drug dependency so that administration was controlled and monitored and they could carry on other aspects of their lives relatively
normally.

The Home Office wanted the prohibition of addictive drugs, and their
limited licence and prescribing for medical emergencies. The move to
more comprehensive prohibition was achieved with the 1971 Misuse of
Drugs Act. Support for this change of focus was enabled by the
perception, during the 1960s, of the arrival of larger quantities of drugs
in the community, and indications that large numbers of young people
were becoming interested in drug experimentation. The 1971 Act categorised a whole range of substances that could potentially be abused and to
some extent gave the Home Office more direct control of when and
where doctors could prescribe addictive substances.

Contemporary policy has followed the trend established in 1971, with
the Home Office assuming greater responsibility for the management and
direction of drug policy. Most recently, in 1998, the Labour Government
produced its ten-year strategy 'Tackling Drugs to Build a Better Britain'
(UKADCU, 1998). The circumstances saw the Home Office take responsibility for the delivery of the strategy. Significantly the strategy, and its
update in 2002, draws directly on evidence linking substance use and its
negative impact (often through crime) on communities and individuals[1].
Treatment has become one of four strands within the policy, treatment
being seen as a means of reducing drug-related crime, with other strands
focusing on reduction of availability, drug prevention amongst young
people, and reducing drug-related crime (Home Office, 2006).

The refocus on reducing crime has led to the creation of a range of
legislation since 1998, all with implications for the treatment of substance
misusers, and their experience of the judicial system. The creation of the
Drugs Intervention Programme in 2003 was accompanied by funding
specifically aimed at identifying drug offenders and providing drug
treatment programmes. It could be argued that treatment as a means of
reducing crime has taken primacy over treatment as a means of addressing ill-health.

Medical research and social science research

During the period between 1920 and 1971 drug and alcohol treatment
received few resources, and research was under-developed with research
primarily undertaken by medically-oriented academics. However, during
the 1970s substance misuse was linked with a range of growing social
problems, e.g. rising divorce rates, unemployment, mental ill health,
homelessness, and crime. This complex entanglement of social problems
brought with it new professional interests and approaches. The growing
influence of social science (sociology, psychology, criminology, etc.) in
higher education in the late 1960s and 1970s meant that academic

disciplines, in addition to medical science, began to influence the research and teaching of those dealing with substance misuse problems.

In the higher education sector research funding tended to go to the big medical departments with an addiction interest, for example the London medical schools, and the Institute of Psychiatry. Alternative, non-medical research struggled to find research funding; the main exception to this rule being Home Office funding of criminological research. A consequence of this has been the dominance, within addiction research, of quantitative research studies wedded to the methods of large scale studies and statistical analysis. This is perhaps exemplified by the National Treatment Outcome Research Study (NTORS), championed as a 'watershed for addiction treatment in Britain; no research before and perhaps none to come will be more crucial' (Ashton, 1999, p. 18)[2].

There has been a tradition for qualitative, ethnographic research within the field, primarily instigated in the US during the mid-twentieth century by the sociologists of the Chicago School. More recently there has been a debate, and a drive, to value the role of qualitative research (from across the social sciences) alongside the more traditional positivist approach. This debate has been led by the International Journal of Drug Policy which has an editorial commitment to increasingly '... place weight on original research papers, qualitative and quantitative' (Rhodes and Stimson, 2006, p. 377). To date, however, it is still difficult for small-scale qualitative research to find funding from substance misuse research funders, unless specifically commissioned by the National Treatment Agency, or regional Drug and Alcohol Action Teams. In both cases the preference is still for statistical, outcome/output focused research which is related to performance monitoring.

Statutory agencies and voluntary agencies

Treatment services, in this field, tend to be delivered by a mixture of statutory and/or voluntary agencies. This unique mixture has arisen, in no small part, from the complex historical development of treatment and the significant role that voluntary bodies have had in championing the needs of substance users in the face of neglect and disinterest from statutory bodies. From the early part of the twentieth century voluntary and lay bodies played a key role as the agents of treatment delivery, treatment programmes and approaches, such as the new residential rehabilitation movement. Also the anonymous fellowships (Alcoholics Anonymous and Narcotics Anonymous), were formed by recovering users who drew on their own experiences to inform treatment content. Religious groups had a strong interest in promoting alternatives, both moral and social, to drug and alcohol addiction; and treatment approaches with a religious focus had (and continue to have) significant influence.

Multi-disciplinary approaches to treatment only arose during the later part of the twentieth century, encouraged by the new professions of clinical psychology, psychiatric nursing, social work and counselling. These tended to be linked firmly to statutory health and local government services. However engagement and integration with pre-existing community/user-based initiatives and self-help groups, such as the anonymous fellowships, did not necessarily follow.

By the end of the 1970s it was possible to observe a diverse sector with many different players and interest groups. Substance misusers could potentially pick and choose the treatments and services that seemed most appropriate to them at any one time in their life. But beneath this mix were fundamental tensions and limitations. Resources were still largely controlled by the dominant professional established groups; in particular psychiatry. Voluntary sector services were often dependent on non-recurring grant funding and never sure if they could survive from one year to the next. Services were inconsistent in their geographical coverage. There was no sophisticated resource allocation model to determine an individual's access to services. There were fundamental disagreements between differing professional, academic, and lay interpretations of addiction and its treatment.

Partnerships, knowledge and the 'evidence-base'

Partnership became a central component of substance policy with the publication of 'Tackling Drugs Together' (Home Office, 1995), which instituted a partnership approach to drug problems where local authority and local health agencies would work formally together through multi-agency Drug Action Teams (DATs) to scope local need and support and eventually fund some local treatment services. These partnership groups were to include a wide range of professionals and agency interests, including education, the police and voluntary groups. This policy was also backed by the New Labour administrations after 1997; New Labour did allocate more resources to the DATs, so that treatment services, especially in the voluntary sector could expand and develop a more comprehensive range of levels and options. The incorporation of alcohol into the local agenda has led to the renaming of DATs as Drug and Alcohol Action Teams (DAATs).

In terms of the implications that the partnership approach has to knowledge and evidence this policy drive towards localisation has led to the development of strong local partnership approaches and has enabled previously ignored groups (e.g. service users) to challenge the medical and law enforcement orthodoxy in new and creative ways (even though the majority of public funding is still implicitly linked to these two orthodoxies).

The growth of localised interventions accompanied by an increase in more direct multi-professional delivery teams (both actual and virtual) has led to a more widely disseminated pool of experienced practitioners in substance misuse. There has been an emerging willingness to seek out more local centres of professional development and learning relevant to substance misuse workers that reflects the diversity of new service provision, and which seeks to address and challenge existing medical and law orthodoxies. This has led to an emerging variety of provision for development and learning that encompasses the further education and higher education sectors and work-based learning. It has also highlighted the need to engage with the management of knowledge and the, sometimes competing, systems that key partners bring with them to the partnerships.

Academic and professional voices

Evidence-based practice was first built on a narrow scientific paradigm. Arguably, this paradigm should give more accountability to the public and users about what kinds of interventions are most likely to help them, and what they should expect as manifestations of 'good practice'. Universities have been central to the development of evidence-based practice and universities (like Brighton) with a strong tradition of professional education, are committed to exploring how to apply evidence-based practice in a way that is helpful to the local community of practitioners and service users. Professionals can be suspicious that limits in the evidence methodologies used can tie them to fixed outputs, and limit their creativity and ability to respond flexibly to diverse situations. There has been some frustration in the substance misuse community about the dominance of a medical, scientific tradition and a feeling that more qualitative and practitioner- and user-based accounts, or 'stories' (as described in the knowledge management literature) need to be encouraged.

The knowledge management literature highlights distinctions (first proposed by Polanyi, 1983) between represented (or explicit) knowledge and embodied (or tacit) knowledge (Nonaka and Takeuchi, 1995). Represented knowledge is typically that which can be stored and codified in paper or electronic form, whereas embodied knowledge is more personal, involving beliefs, values and experience (Gamble and Blackwell, 2001; Firestone and McElroy, 2003). A particular challenge is represented here in addressing both forms of knowledge within the multi-professional and multi-agency substance misuse field.

Higher education, further education, and new opportunities for knowledge dissemination

The localisation of policy and practice opened some new opportunities for higher education to become involved. New universities, (the old polytechnics), were particularly well placed to become involved with such partnerships given their strong local identity and regional focus. It should be acknowledged that some traditional and 1960s universities also like to take this 'local' role and are geographically and institutionally well placed to do so. Some DAATs have directly and indirectly (by channelling money from central government) commissioned university staff to undertake training and research that has a strong local focus and evaluates local services. The sums of money involved are small by local government and university standards and not mainstream activity. They are dwarfed by a few mega national grants of Higher Education Funding Council for England (HEFCE) Research Assessment Exercise (RAE) monies that still allow a few medical schools to focus on their key interests in substance misuse. Nevertheless the new policy approach does represent a new and significant engagement between higher education and substance misuse treatment communities in the local Sussex county area and this has also been true for some other local areas in the country.

It is relevant to note at this point a national initiative led by the National Treatment Agency for substance misuse (NTA) which together with the sector skills councils in this field has introduced the Drug and Alcohol National Occupational Standards (DANOS). These form a set of competencies for the field that are now incorporated into awards such as the Health and Social Care National Vocational Qualifications (NVQs), and can be used in a variety of ways, for example to provide a framework for job descriptions in the field. A competency in this sense can be defined as a specific set of knowledge and skills that represent best practice.

The role of DANOS competencies (which all have discrete knowledge components) in developing knowledge and practice in the community, form an important part of the assessed outcome for the University of Brighton Diploma award established by the DAAT and university partnership (referred to below). This serves as an example of how knowledge and the acquisition and application of knowledge as evidence underpins local practice.

The significance of knowledge management to practice

No one, single model of evidence can be said to influence practice, but rather several emerging models appear significant. This signifies the need to develop a pluralistic framework or taxonomy to assess effectiveness and quality (Davies and Macdonald, 1998). Macdonald (1999) has identified the importance of understanding the use of evidence in practice, after evidence has been systematically collected and rated. She identifies the important processes of dissemination and organisational change, the latter to develop evidence-based culture. Similarly, in a review of the impact of evidence-based practice in health care, Davies and Nutley (1999, p. 15) conclude: 'changing professional practice has not been easy ...prompting smooth and efficient change in the right direction, even in the face of overwhelming evidence of the need for that change, remains a major challenge.' Webb (2001, p. 57), provoked a debate in social work given his comment that: 'the tendency to separate processes into facts and values implicit in evidence-based procedures undermines professional judgement and discretion.' From our own experience student evaluation feedback from the professional part-time course confirmed to us that many practitioners felt that separate research into practice outputs (using traditional scientific method that was removed from the daily observations of practitioners) was of little value to them.

There is a danger that classical management approaches to knowledge when applied in the public sector put too much emphasis on knowledge repositories and the powerful potential of information technology (IT) systems to develop complex databases of case studies and practice examples. By knowledge repositories we mean large organisational data-bases or inter-organisational databases that are accessible to a particular community of practice or associated staff group. There are important associated issues and questions about whether IT is the best method for disseminating ideas of practice, and how practitioners will contribute and use such a repository, and how the information will be managed, stored, catalogued and ranked (Haynes, 2005; Bundred, 2006). Knowledge management in the public services needs to focus more on encouraging practice to be shared and reflected on in practice communities and knowledge networks (Hartley and Benington, 2006).

What sort of knowledge is relevant to these practice communities and knowledge networks? The fact that discrete knowledge is required to complement the skills required for best practice in substance misuse through DANOS has been mentioned. Here a distinction emerges between the collection of data and information required to support the classical management approaches whereby policy makers, managers and commissioners of services gather information on 'what works', usually against performance targets. Then there is knowledge about individual practice that can be shared, as well as useful knowledge sources for sustaining and enhancing practice. How can substance misuse practitioners be helped to know what they know and what they need to know? This question is important now, not in a philosophical or rhetorical sense, but in a practical sense, as practitioners are required to demonstrate their competencies against DANOS.

The Brighton and Sussex Community Knowledge Exchange research project

One of the first national examples of DAAT and university partnership was the setting up of the Diploma in Substance Misuse Intervention Studies Strategies at the University of Brighton. This followed extensive negotiations between the three Sussex DAATs (Brighton and Hove, West Sussex and East Sussex) and the University of Brighton, resulting in the signing of a contract between the parties where the University would deliver a part-time training course, running for a full year, over a number of years. All the places on the course were purchased in advance by the DAATs and this gave the university the security of income needed to commit resources to establishing the course. In addition the contract committed the DAATs to each providing a part-time professional tutor and user representative who could assist the University with delivering the course. The contract is overseen by a steering committee that includes DAAT senior managers, course tutors, a user representative and relevant university staff. The first two years of the course proved to be highly successful in that an external examiner and the students rated the learning experience highly. A further contract was signed allowing the university to commit funds to a part-time lecturer in substance misuse.

It is from within this context that a Brighton and Sussex Community Knowledge Exchange (BSCKE) research project developed. Prior experience from the University of Brighton Diploma indicated that the part-time professional students, whilst varied in their original backgrounds, tended to give primacy to embodied knowledge and struggled when engaged with represented knowledge. Information technology mechanisms for the dissemination of knowledge and practice proved particularly challenging and attempts to engage the students in online communities and learning met with strong opposition and consistently poor feedback. With the support of BSCKE we wanted to investigate 'where do our practitioners gain their knowledge?' and 'how can we support their development as practitioners?' These questions became central concerns for the BSCKE project.

The BSCKE research tool and process

The 'Substance Misuse Practitioners Knowledge and Evidence Base Questionnaire' (SMPQ) research tool was developed to enable the identification of all Sussex practitioners' current methods of accessing practice-based knowledge and evidence. The research tool was piloted utilising students on the Progression Award in Community Justice at a local FE college, and then disseminated through participants drawn from substance misuse specialist organisations throughout Sussex. In total 400 questionnaires were sent out, and 81 (20 per cent) were returned.

The development of the research tool proved to be a long and complex process. It quickly became apparent that the research tool would need to be greatly simplified. Consequently we realised a more generalised survey, seeking to capture the wide and intermittent sources and access that workers had to knowledge and evidence sources, might prove more effective and beneficial.

Participant recruitment

Participants for this project were recruited with support from the relevant DAATs. It was decided that there needed to be the collation of an up-to-date contact list which covered all three DAAT regions; this complete list would then be handed over to the DAAT partners.

The timeframe available for the recruitment process was short with organisational managers frequently unavailable, or unable to return calls. Similarly the project researcher was employed part-time and was therefore often unavailable to answer returned calls. Given the low recruitment at this stage it was decided to extend the recruitment period, and extend the deadline for completed questionnaires accordingly.

The key questions for the project to address were:

1. How do workers understand the concept of 'evidence' and 'knowledge' and relate it to practice?
2. How do workers obtain relevant information and what preferences do they have for obtaining information? To what extent are workers able to make systematic use of resources?
3. Do workers have a preference for a specific knowledge-management method?
4. How do workers interact with information and make use of it in practice?
5. Is it helpful to teach workers how to rank evidence and to perceive types of evidence?
6. What is the role for e-learning in critical reflection and practice development?
7. Do workers have access to web materials and find them easy to use?
8. How do workers work in partnership to develop and use the evidence and is there a similar or different perspective when representing different agencies?

Overall the results showed the rising importance of IT as a method of dissemination of knowledge and evidence to the activity of specialist drug misuse work. There was also significant involvement in ongoing training and professional courses. Perhaps the most surprising finding was the lack of a consistent professional supportive network for all workers, where workers could meet face-to-face, to share ideas and practice developments.

When respondents were asked to rate which source of knowledge they found 'most useful', websites and email distribution were very likely to be seen as most useful (94 per cent/80 per cent). Next were periodicals, and then conferences and local group meetings. However local group meetings were the method of knowledge acquisition that most people wanted more information on.

Conclusions

The partnership between the University and the local practitioner community has established an important process for ensuring that knowledge and evidence are delivered and supported with learning methods that are actually useful to those in practice.

The lure of IT has certainly reached drug workers. The evidence that the sector is able to use IT to abstract relevant information is encouraging, although it is important to acknowledge that the knowledge management literature questions the ability of IT repositories to solve the difficulties of institutionalising an evidence-based practice culture. Finding information is different to knowing how to use it in practice. In a diverse professional field, like drug and substance misuse, it is vital that practitioners are empowered to critically reflect on information and knowledge 'usefulness' and that they are doing this with like-minded professionals.

The BSCKE project has worked to produce a website framework and structure that consolidates the research findings about what websites are most useful to workers in the field and encourages them to share and experience such online information. A multi-agency group will continue to manage and oversee the future evolution of the website.

An evidence-based culture needs good face-to-face discussion and critical reflection about knowledge-based practice, in a safe and supported environment. Knowledge management research and writing suggests the importance of informal opportunities for workers to reflect on their practice in face-to-face and small-group circumstances. This is likely to be particularly important given the demise of one-to-one professional and clinical supervision in some agencies. It would appear from recent research that the rapid growth of services in this field is not supported by a strong and wide ranging informal professional support network, where practitioners have the chance to reflect and develop the information and knowledge they have required.

Some of this reflective process may be happening in the large number of courses and training days attended, but there is also a danger that these activities are quite functional and not necessarily flexible to support workers in their day-to-day reflections. The partnership experience of running a professional training course has shown us that it is not difficult to find information and knowledge content to present to workers, but that it is much more difficult to give them the confidence to critically engage with new ways of working in their own practice.

Notes

1. 'A stronger focus on education, prevention, enforcement and treatment to prevent and tackle problematic drug use. The 250,000 class A drug users with the most severe problems who account for 99% of the

costs of drug misuse in England and Wales and do most harm to themselves, their families and communities' (Home Office, 2002, p. 4).

2. This is a longitudinal study utilising data from 1,075 clients, engaged with treatment, and exploring the impact of treatment via a range of social and psychological health measures (Gossop et al., 2003).

References

Ashton, M. (1999) 'NTORS: The most crucial test yet for addiction treatment in Britain', Drug and Alcohol Findings, Vol. 2, p. 18.

Berridge, V. (1984) 'Drugs and social policy: The establishment of drug control in Britain 1900–1930', British Journal of Addiction, Vol. 79, pp. 17–29.

Bundred, S. (2006) 'Solutions to silos: Joining up knowledge', Public Money and Management, Vol. 26, No. 2, pp. 125–131.

Davies, H.T.O. and Nutley, S.M. (1999) 'The rise and rise of evidence in health care', Public Money and Management, Vol. 19, No. 1, pp. 25–32.

Davies, J.K. and Macdonald, G. (1998) Quality, evidence and effectiveness in Health Promotion; Striving for certainties. London: Routledge.

Firestone, J.M. and McElroy, M.W. (2003) Key issues in the new knowledge management. Oxford: Butterworth-Heinemann.

Gamble, P. and Blackwell, J. (2001) Knowledge management: A state of the art guide. London: Kogan Page.

Gossop, M., Marsden, J., Stewart, D. and Kidd, T. (2003) 'The National Treatment Outcome Research Study (NTORS): 4–5 year follow-up results', Addiction, Vol. 98, pp. 291–303.

Hartley, J. and Benington, J. (2006) 'Copy and paste, or graft and transplant? Knowledge sharing through inter-organizational networks', Public Money and Management, Vol. 2, No. 6, pp. 101–08.

Haynes, P. (2005) 'Demystifying knowledge management for the public services', Public Money and Management, Vol. 25, No. 2, pp. 131–35.

Home Office (1995) Tackling drugs together: A strategy for England 1995–1998 (White Paper). London: HMSO.

Home Office (2002) Updated Drug Strategy. London: The Home Office Drug Strategy Directorate.

Home Office (2006) Tackling Drugs Misuse. www.homeoffice.gov.uk Available from http://www.homeoffice.gov.uk/drugs/drugs-misuse/ [accessed 25 October 2006]

Macdonald, G. (1999) 'Social work and its evaluation', in F. Williams, J. Popay and A. Oakley (eds.) Welfare Research: A critical Review, pp. 89–103. London: UCL Press.

Miller, W.R., Sorensen, J.L., Selzer, J.A., Brigham, G.S. (2006) 'Disseminating evidence-based practices in substance abuse treatment: A review with suggestions', Journal of Substance Abuse Treatment, Vol. 31, pp. 25–39.

Nonaka, I. and Takeuchi, H. (1995) *The knowledge-creating company: How Japanese companies create the dynamics of innovation.* New York: Oxford University Press.

Polanyi, M. (1983) *The tacit dimension.* Gloucester. Mass: Peter Smith.

Rhodes, T. and Stimson G.V. (2006) 'Science, action and the International Journal of Drug Policy', *International Journal of Drug Policy*, Vol. 17, pp. 377–78.

UKADCU (1998) *Tackling drugs to build a better Britain: the government's 10-year strategy for tackling drug misuse* (United Kingdom Anti-Drugs Co-ordinating Unit). London: The Stationery Office.

Webb, S. (2001) 'Some considerations on the validity of evidence-based practice in social work', *The British Journal of Social Work*, Vol. 31, No. 1, pp. 57–79.

Learning together – community and university collaboration to evaluate Neighbourhood Renewal projects

Dee MacDonald, Carol Mullineux, Sarah Hardman, Susan Balloch

Introduction

> We consider that access to information about sustainable communities needs to be made available to a wide audience to enable them to contribute to delivering such communities. (Egan, 2004, p. 14)

The evaluation we describe in this chapter arose out of frustration with trying to identify meaningful case studies that highlighted key issues faced by community projects in Neighbourhood Renewal (NR). We wanted to know how these had been addressed and, critically why certain interventions had or had not been successful. Without this level of detail, the case studies available at the time did not enable other community projects to translate the learning and to benefit as a result.

Both partners, a research fellow within the Health and Social Policy Research Centre at the University of Brighton, and the Neighbourhood Renewal coordinator for Brighton and Hove, were involved in ALTogether, a local Learning and Skills Council funded action learning programme for those working in NR. The ALTogether programme provided the opportunity to identify six individual projects that were interrelated but also very diverse in terms of the community groups and organisations involved, and their NR themes (Community Safety, Education, Employment, Health, Housing and Liveability). Funding for the project was gained through the Brighton and Sussex Community Knowledge Exchange (BSCKE) programme (see Chapter 2), whose ethos of shared learning fitted particularly well with the aims and ambitions of this project.

Figure 7.1 illustrates a 'learning relationship framework' showing the six levels of impact and shared learning that were anticipated at the project proposal stage.

With reference to Pawson and Tilley's (1997) evaluation framework focusing on context, mechanism and outcome, this chapter will provide an overview of the research project itself, and discussion of the types and levels of resultant impact on both the community and University.

As a result of the six case studies, common themes were drawn out and recommendations made about how issues might be addressed or positive learning shared. An outline of each case study is provided in Box 7.1.

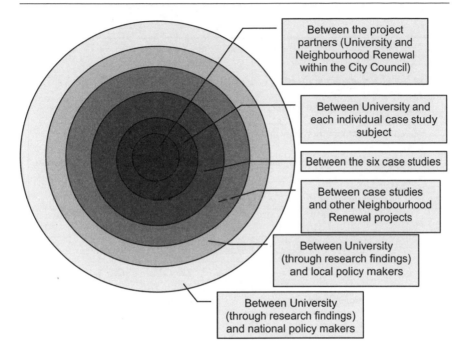

Between the project partners (University and Neighbourhood Renewal within the City Council)

Between University and each individual case study subject

Between the six case studies

Between case studies and other Neighbourhood Renewal projects

Between University (through research findings) and local policy makers

Between University (through research findings) and national policy makers

Figure 7.1 Learning relation framework

There was a clear intention that participation in the research process should 'add value' to the case study projects. The understanding of adding value assumed enabling, supporting or leading to the organisation, project or individual achieving a positive outcome (as defined by any or all of the stakeholders involved) that can be attributed at least in part to the community–university partnership. To this end, we based our research on action-research methods, described further below.

Our discussion of the impact or added value of our own community-university partnership has drawn on Pawson and Tilley's (1997) framework for 'realistic' evaluation which we thought could be helpful. However, in the case of our research we identified three difficulties with their approach which we explain below. Pawson and Tilley describe the basic realist formula in terms of project *outcomes* resulting from *mechanisms* operating in particular *contexts*.

> What is under test in realist evaluation are theories of how programmes work ...the design of evaluation should produce ever more detailed answers to the question of why a programme works, for whom and in what circumstances. (Pawson and Tilley, 1997, p. xvi)

Just as the research took a 'case study' approach, identifying the contextual detail of what works in NR in particular circumstances, we will take

The Hangleton and Knoll Project

A community development project undertaking a community survey in partnership with the local community association

The Whitehawk Inn

Atraining organisation seeking greater involvement of local people in th e organisation through volunteering.

Engage

A Christian community development project providing support to those engaging with their communities in the form of action learning opportunities.

The Carers Centre in partnership with East Brighton New Deal for Communities 'eb4U'

An outreach project identifying 'hidden carers' in East Brighton.

Sussex Community Internet Project (SCIP)

An infrastructure organisation providing ICT support and training to community and voluntary organisations looking at the impact of its web design training.

Sussex Police

A project seeking to establish local police surgeries in central Brighton.

Box 7.1 Case studies

a similar approach in our discussion of the impact of the project on both the university and its community partners.

Our own desired outcome was that the collaboration would 'add value', via learning achieved, to those involved at a variety of levels (see Figure 7.1). Use of Pawson and Tilley's (1997) framework to explore the context and the approach (mechanism) taken and the impact our collaboration actually had in terms of opportunities for adding value for both university and local authority partners and the six case studies themselves raised the following issues. Firstly, on reflection we found that the boundaries between what can be defined as 'context', 'mechanism' or 'outcomes' are often blurred. This is particularly the case when trying to define 'context' and 'mechanism' as, over time, the latter becomes part of the context. Similarly, over time, an outcome can become either part of the context or a mechanism.

In order to achieve the added value intended, the approach taken was based on action research methods which allowed us to work with projects informing their development through shared learning and supporting change. 'Action researchers are intent on describing, interpreting and explaining events (enquiry) while they seek to change them (action) for the better (purpose)' (McNiff *et al.*, 1996, p. 13).

This is often described in terms of a cycle encompassing the following: planning, taking action, observing results of action and reflecting on such to inform future planning. Because all the projects we had identified for the research were based on effecting change, and because it was our intention that the research should positively support such change, this approach seemed the most appropriate.

Secondly, as Figure 7.2 shows, action research is not a linear process. One of the problems with using Pawson and Tilley's framework is that it suggests a linear approach to research. In the long term, this may be less than helpful.

Thirdly, we would note that evaluations inevitably take place in a political context, something overlooked in Pawson and Tilley's realistic approach (Taylor and Balloch, 2005). Evaluators intrude into territory already structured by power relationships and to these the evaluators add their own, new dimension. These case studies were all situated within the local Neighbourhood Renewal programme, based on nationally-defined principles of combating social exclusion and supporting citizenship. Each also had its own internal structure of power and authority and lines of accountability. It was important from the beginning that the University researchers were not only aware of these but sensitive to the power dynamics that they themselves might generate, particularly if they appeared to be threatening the status quo, challenging behaviour or simply using assumed authority. The strategies deployed to minimise this interference included university researchers taking time to understand the context in which they were working, checking their own behaviour and reflecting on their impact.

In any small-scale evaluation project ethical issues need particular attention. Among these, protecting the confidentiality and anonymity of participants is difficult, particularly in an action research setting. The researcher's role often becomes one of mediator between different opinions and trajectories. Within these projects it was, therefore, particularly important to build up trust so that views could be shared openly between stakeholders in a friendly atmosphere, with participants not worrying about the identification of their views to each other. In reporting the findings from action research to the outside world, trust continues to be an important issue. Stakeholders' agreement on a final report is vital. In a small project, reporting to its wider community, individuals' identities must either be totally protected, even if with difficulty, or only divulged in a positive way with their complete agreement. These principles were observed throughout the life of the project.

Context

Primavera (2004), comments on the propensity of community–university collaborations to surface in a relatively informal way, as a result of existing relationships. In our case, the recognition of shared frustrations emerged through the partners' joint work on the ALTogether programme. Both partners had been involved in developing and overseeing the programme which provided the space for getting to know each other, understanding each other's perspective and developing trust, key elements in the development of collaboration between two organisations with different cultures.

The nature of the developing relationship between the two partner organisations, i.e. the NR team within the City Council and a research centre within the University, was new and exciting. Previously, partners were more used to working in a business-oriented way which typically centred on commissioning research. NR funding has clear priorities relating to delivery and often does not stretch to such exploratory, localised research. Both partners appreciated the freedom associated with designing a research proposal which addressed gaps in evidence which did not necessarily fit neatly with funding streams working to tight targets or outcomes. The flexibility associated with the BSCKE funding allowed for the development of the partnership and a deepening of understanding of each other's organisations and desired outcomes.

Partners worked together to identify the six case studies which would represent a diverse mix of projects, organisations and NR themes. A key advantage to sourcing projects via the ALTogether programme was that all were at a similar stage of development, i.e. embryonic. It was important that the aims of the research were clearly articulated to the individuals concerned.

Once projects agreed to participate, the dynamics of the original partnership changed as there were now, in effect, seven community partners (the six projects and the NR team). Much time and effort was put into working with project leads to ensure a shared understanding of the aims, the key one being that participation in the research process would add value to their individual projects whilst at the same time producing a weight of evidence which could be used to influence policy. Of course, the overall aim of influencing local, regional and national policy would, it was anticipated, ultimately have a positive impact on the projects themselves.

A second researcher was brought in, employed by the University, but based within the NR team in the Local Authority. Selection criteria for this post included experience of working within both the public and voluntary/community sectors, bringing an additional perspective. Such a partnership between the University and the Local Authority would strengthen the existing relationships and widen the 'reach' of the university to the broader community.

In embarking upon the project, researchers and case study leads became part of a wider learning community, or a 'community of practice' (Wenger *et al.*, 2002), comprising those working in NR across Brighton and Hove. Members of this community included local residents and neighbourhood projects working on the ground, infrastructure organisations, the NR team, the Local Strategic Partnership and associated structures for representation as well as service providers and funders.

A division of expertise and knowledge existed within this community of practice. Interactions with some of the members of this community of practice, through the research process, provided opportunities for cross-fertilisation of different interpretations and expertise and contributed towards a shared understanding of why certain interventions had or had not been successful.

Approach/mechanism

Action research

Action research is an iterative process involving researchers and practitioners acting together on a particular cycle of activities, including problem diagnosis, action intervention, and reflective learning. (Avison *et al.*, 1999, p. 94)

A very practical form of research, action research can encompass a variety of research methods, making it particularly attractive to those working in communities and lending itself to active participation by a wide range of people. For us this meant the research ran in parallel with the projects and their development. This approach was adopted because whilst we were interested in the learning for NR, we were also very keen that the research should inform individual project development where appropriate.

In the early stages, it was not always easy to explain the benefits of the research and its approach to the case study project leaders. An obvious benefit was the element of free evaluation that would be produced for each project. However, some projects raised concerns such as the amount of time they might need to dedicate to the research when faced with so many competing demands. In reality, the range of positive outcomes experienced by the projects was far wider than simply a free evaluation, as is illustrated in our later discussion of outcomes. The relevance of the central tools of action research, i.e. reflection and planning, to our particular work are looked at below.

Reflection and planning

Project leads became increasingly aware of the benefits of the research process via regular review meetings which provided an opportunity for findings to be reported and reflected on. It could be argued either that this changed the context of research or was in fact a desirable outcome! Researchers took on the role of 'critical friend' to projects and the review meetings enabled feedback of emerging findings to be shared as quickly as possible. Project leads found these meetings provided a useful space for them to step back from their own project and reflect on successes and challenges as the researchers took a supportive and questioning approach. Similarly, regular review meetings with the NR coordinator (the community partner) proved invaluable, making use of the knowledge she brought regarding the NR context, both within Brighton and Hove and at a national level. Such knowledge provided a framework for analysing emerging research findings and advising on the appropriateness/ workability of the final recommendations.

For the NR coordinator, these regular meetings enabled an ongoing involvement in the project and meant that emerging issues, ideas and findings could inform the work that was being developed in a wider context within the NR community of practice. This process of exchange fits within the innermost circle of our 'learning relationship' framework.

Feedback events involving all stakeholders that had taken part in the research were planned for each case study. This provided useful opportunities for research findings, recommendations and possible future action to be discussed and agreed as well as providing a valuable networking and social opportunity for projects and their stakeholders.

Outcomes

The sections below look at outcomes from the various perspectives. We refer back to Figure 7.1 which illustrated the various levels at which we anticipated impact and shared learning would emerge. We have illustrated throughout the chapter how learning was shared between the various partners.

Case study project leads

The action research approach produced a range of outcomes for the individual case study projects, demonstrating the 'added value' hoped for by the research team. In most cases, the benefits of reflection and planning that the action research process required added greatly to the development of their projects and reinforced the learning that was taking place on the ALTogether programme, equipping people with a range of tools and increased networks to inform future ways of working. In one case, the process reminded a worker of the value of research, in particular the value of seeking out existing research related to their area of interest. The project lead, a graduate herself, commented that the involvement of the university researchers highlighted the importance of seeking evidence from other sources which could inform her work and recognised that the local university could be utilised more (e.g. library resources) in achieving this. The close working relationship between the university and the individual projects ensured the organisations and their wide range of stakeholders became familiar with and were supported to explore the various ways in which they could choose to interact with the university in the future. These opportunities for interaction included making use of Cupp services or potentially hosting students on work or research placements. Whilst projects might have been aware of such opportunities through general publicity, it was via personal contact with the researchers that projects were motivated to take action.

The overt aim of the researchers to ensure that as wide a range of stakeholders as possible were involved in the research process in each case proved beneficial. The process provided space and time for those involved in projects, either centrally or at the margins, to come together and corroborate or challenge research recommendations in a learning environment. In the current policy climate which prioritises user involvement, the validation of recommendations by users will increase their currency when projects are seeking to influence relevant policy and funders. This is a key intended outcome of our research.

In the case of the Whitehawk Inn, the feedback event provided an opportunity for trustees and volunteers to get to know each other, and to understand better their respective roles within the organisation. In Hangleton, an informal lunch brought local residents and the community development worker together, in some instances for the first time. In addition to sharing learning within individual case study projects, researchers were also able to ensure that learning emerging could be shared between case studies, via the review process.

As mentioned earlier, the contribution of researchers to organisations' planning meetings provided useful evidence on which to base strategic decisions. In the case of the hidden carers' project, the research led directly to three examples of added value, one of them a successful funding bid for an additional member of staff, which would enable the project to meet the needs of more carers.

At a more collective level, the composite work provided a weight of evidence to potentially influence local, regional and national policy on a number of issues common to all the projects, for example funding and participation. These will be longer-term outcomes that we will be working towards throughout the dissemination stage and beyond. At the time of writing, there were encouraging signs that this goal would be achieved as the major funder supporting the ALTogether programme indicated an intention to highlight findings to regional government with a view to influencing related decisions.

Neighbourhood Renewal team

The research process deepened the relationship between the NR team and the University. The team was used to working collaboratively but as a whole unit engaging with external partners. The close working relationship that evolved between the NR team and the university as a result of their shared member of staff led to reflection within the NR team on potential relationships that could be developed with other partner organisations. In addition, despite the NR team's awareness of resources within the University, the working relationship that emerged as a result of this research encouraged members of the team to seek the collaboration of other University staff in order to take forward other areas of the team's work.

As the research developed, the NR team were able to draw parallels with other projects and to look for collaborative approaches to addressing these. The NR community support worker, whose role included facilitating the sharing of learning and good practice within the NR community, was informed by the research in two ways: firstly in terms of examples of learning that could be shared and, secondly, through examples of issues that groups were raising where hearing about the experiences of others would be of benefit. The fact that a researcher was physically based within the team facilitated this exchange of information to a greater extent than if the researcher had been 'remote'.

The researcher based within the NR team encouraged the team to work in a more reflective way, informed by locally-based research. Findings from this research supplemented other evidence collected by the NR team to highlight core issues related to NR such as funding and participation. It was hoped that enhancing the profile of Brighton and Hove through dissemination of the research could enable the NR team to be viewed as a 'trailblazer' by regional government and possibly lead to opportunities to pilot new initiatives. This in turn would then have a trickle-down effect on individual community projects.

The University

The outcomes for the university of such collaborative work were diverse. There were those that are common to a lot of university research, i.e.

publications, contributions to conferences and teaching, along with those particular to this type of partnership work, e.g. opening up opportunities for courses and curricula to be contributed to by those working locally in the field.

Undoubtedly, the building of relationships with a wide range of local organisations increased opportunities for further research and highlighted the value of working collaboratively with community partners. Also, new relationships laid down firm foundations for future partnership working, for example via Cupp projects or via the placement of students on work/research practice.

Dissemination events provided further opportunities to widen the community of practice circle by engaging with another layer of people who related to the work in a variety of ways. Further networking occurred and the University's relationship with community partners was deepened. The range of outcomes demonstrates the scope of the impact of such a partnership and the many ways in which all partners gain through participation in such a 'community of practice'. Outcomes overall fall broadly into four categories: those that relate to relationship building; those to do with learning and, more traditionally, those linked to the production of evidence. The fourth intended outcome, relating to policy change, will take longer to emerge. When taken together, they present a compelling case for such collaborative work, conducted within a 'community of practice' with a commitment to shared learning for all concerned.

Discussion

Negotiating roles and relationships

We have stated that our aim, or desired outcome, was to inform the development of the projects through shared learning. Each of the projects existed in the first place to effect changes in certain contexts. The aim of 'adding value' to projects had implications for the role that researchers took on. The similarity between action research and project development work, outlined by McNiff (1992), resonates with our own experience. We found that the close relationship we cultivated with projects resulted in us taking on multiple roles. At different times with the various projects our roles became that of adviser, observer, development worker or even mentor (in a case where a project lead was line managed and supported 'remotely').

On a practical level at times this led to some slight confusion. When we suggested to those involved in the Hangleton community survey that they might benefit from the research support available through Cupp it raised an obvious question, 'but surely *you* are researchers too so why can't *you* help us?'. In this case we had felt it was more appropriate to observe the process of a voluntary organisation planning a survey and the support they were able to access rather than influence this process. A similar issue emerged at the community fun day held in a local park. Should the researchers actually help facilitate the questionnaire or observe the process of others carrying out the community survey? Often the decision was taken to get involved and take a very hands-on approach and in doing so the role became more like that of community development worker than independent researcher. Pragmatic decisions, such as helping the project staff to ensure as many of their questionnaires as possible were completed on the day, felt appropriate as it clearly added value to the project development, one of our stated aims. It also contributed to our own research in that it deepened our understanding of the journey the project was taking and issues/decisions it faced.

A focus group with stakeholders from the Whitehawk Inn, a training centre based within a recognised area of deprivation, provided an opportunity to work with them to clarify their aims and define their 'next steps' in terms of increasing involvement of local people within the organisation. Researchers took on the role of facilitator/development worker, introducing models of user involvement (from both within the literature and our own experience within the community/voluntary sector) as a framework for encouraging discussion.

As researchers we were often included within the projects as honorary staff members. Projects were keen to receive findings as work progressed and at fairly early stages we were asked to feed back emerging evidence. While such requests did require unforeseen periods of analysis (and researcher's time) during the fieldwork, they illustrate the way in which the projects had begun to identify how the research support attached to their project could usefully 'add value' for them and the importance of such 'early wins' for the projects in building trust/cementing the partnership with the University (Suarez-Balcazar et al., 2005). In this way, the projects were extending and defining the impact of the research beyond being passive recipients of a research report at the end of a research process.

Despite some confusion, flexibility and discussion around roles was a positive experience, bringing together community and University partners. Negotiating the roles was further complicated in that the research associate employed by the University had herself come from a community development and voluntary sector background, with experience of development work and project evaluation. Similarly, the BSCKE funder/manager had a history of working in that sector. Differing backgrounds and preferred approaches led to negotiations between researchers, community–university partners and the funder around use of language, methods, roles and presentation of findings. This proved a really positive experience, providing checks either to question or confirm the appropriateness of the approach taken and going someway to overcome 'the tendencies that many of us have to stereotype academics and community partners respectively' (Hart and Wolff, 2006, p. 132).

Working across the community/university boundary

While community organisations mostly carry out research either to inform practice or to evaluate their delivery in order to achieve funding, a purist might argue that university research is driven primarily by the desire to inform and extend theory.

> A typical university approach is to study the situation, read the relevant literature, and develop an impact model of how various factors influence one another. In contrast, communities are more likely to develop a plan of action based on current local practice, implement the plan, and then revise the plan based on the resulting outcome. (Todd *et al.*, 1998, p. 247)

Of course in reality universities and communities do come together to develop evidence-based practice, and we aimed to develop this model through the action research approach that we took. So, for example, with SCIP, through the research and our interviews with various stakeholders we were able to develop a model that demonstrated the factors influencing the sustainability of their web design courses. By feeding into staff planning meetings this understanding directly contributed to the organisation's decision-making. Underpinning our approach to the project was commitment to ensuring a close relationship between development of theory and practice, with each feeding into and informing the other.

There were some anxieties associated with working across the university-community boundary. On the one hand working in this hybrid space resulted in researchers' concerns about the 'pitch' of the work, the methodology and whether it would be valued academically (judged on the basis of the quality of the research). Equally, previous experience of the sector contributed to researchers wondering whether some findings would appear too 'obvious' to many within the community and voluntary organisations (who often evaluate their own practice in order to inform their own work).

This issue was particularly acute at the dissemination stage where decisions needed to be made regarding how we presented the research findings given the wide range of audiences interested in the work. Taking a learning approach and recognising that this learning was the result of working collaboratively within a 'community of practice' helped to bridge the gap, rather than setting up the University and community agendas/ expectations as 'us' and 'them'. It was also important that we looked, with the community and voluntary organisations involved, at the longer-term impact that could be achieved through taking findings from individual projects to contribute to a body of evidence that could affect policies developed at a national, regional or local level which might later be imposed on those same individual organisations.

Dissemination of research findings included running a workshop at the Community and Voluntary Sector Forum's quarterly conference. Our aim was both to feed back learning that had emerged during the research as well as seeking agreement about what the recommendations should be. Presenting research findings to the Forum illustrates the learning which occurred within our 'community of practice'.

Workshop participants were drawn into the NR 'community of practice' and shared their experiences and the particular expertise they brought, which in some cases resonated with core research findings (contributing to agreed expertise/good practice), and in some cases led them to question or qualify them. This experience was felt to be extremely effective in ensuring that all concerned could bring their experience and knowledge to bear, contributing to a more developed understanding of what works and what doesn't in relation to NR processes.

The action learning process equipped projects with tools to use in the cyclical mechanism of reflection, planning, action and observation within their working practice. It was anticipated that the research would continue to evolve and to impact on those involved, perpetuating the cycle illustrated below, but with the projects rather than researchers as the driving force.

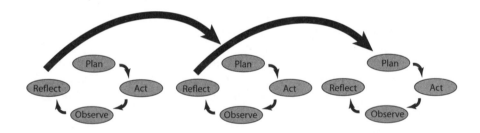

Figure 7.2   Cycle of action research
Source: Adapted from McNiff et al., 1996.

Conclusion

A key aspect of our partnership work was to add value to the organisations with whom we worked (in terms of assisting their projects' development and accumulating a body of evidence in relation to a range of policies). The outcomes described above clearly indicate that this was achieved for both community partners and the University itself. However, the experience has raised the issue of sustainability of such collaborations. The work was funded via BSCKE, a time- and budget-limited initiative. We would argue that such collaborations, whilst showing distinct short-term benefits for all concerned, can only be truly sustained and built upon if there is a long-term commitment within higher education to prioritise such community engagement and value and use outcomes it produces as an element of its core business. Community/voluntary organisations can certainly benefit from input from outside organisations who can offer technical expertise, support, opportunities for networking and sharing information and learning. Experience of initiatives such as the Joseph Rowntree Neighbourhood Programme suggests that 'light touch' support can add significant value. However there are still numerous challenges to address in offering these resources. This chapter demonstrates that universities are in a good position to offer such support, as our project did, with all concerned reaping rewards.

References

Avison, D., Lau, F., Myers, M. and Nielsen, P.A. (1999) 'Action Research to make academic research relevant, researchers should try out their theories with practitioners in real situations and real organisations', *Communications of the ACM*, Vol. 42, No. 4, pp. 94–7.

Egan, J. (2004) *The Egan review: Skills for sustainable communities, (Recommendation 19)*. London: Office of the Deputy Prime Minister.

Hart, A. and Wolff, D. (2006) 'Developing local "communities of practice" through local community–university partnerships', *Planning, Practice and Research*, Vol. 21, No. 1, pp. 121–138.

MacDonald, D., Mullineux, C., Hardman, S. and Balloch, S. (2006) *Both sides of the coin: Neighbourhood renewal in context*. Brighton: Health and Social Policy Research Centre, University of Brighton.

McNiff, J. (1992) *Action research: Principles and practice*. London: Routledge.

McNiff, J., Lomax, P. and Whitehead, J. (1996) *You and your action research project*. London: Routledge.

Pawson, R. and Tilley, N. (1997) *Realistic evaluation*. London: Sage.

Primavera, J. (2004) 'You can't get there from here: identifying process routes to replication. *American Journal of Community Psychology*, Vol. 33, No. 3/4, pp. 181–91.

Suarez-Balcazar, Y., Harper, G.W., and Lewis, R. (2005) 'An interactive and contextual model of community–university collaborations for research and action', *Health Education and Behaviour*, Vol. 32, No. 1, pp. 84–101.

Taylor, D. and Balloch, S. (2005) *The politics of evaluation: Policy implementation and practice*. Bristol: The Policy Press.

Todd, C.M., Ebata, A.T. and Hughes, R. (1998) 'Making university and community collaborations work', in R.M. Lerner and L.A.K. Simon (eds.), *University-community collaboration for the twenty-first century: outreach scholarship for youth and families*, pp. 231–54. New York: Garland.

Wenger, E., McDermott, R. and Snyder, W.M. (2002) *Cultivating communities of practice: a guide to managing knowledge*. Boston, Mass: Harvard Business School Press.

Wilson, M., Wilde. P., Purdue, D. and Taylor, M. (2005) *Lending a hand: The value of 'light touch' support in empowering communities.* York: Joseph Rowntree Foundation.

Chapter 8

Addressing the barriers to accessing higher education: Supporting refugees into HE through community–university engagement

Nicky Conlan, Stephen Silverwood and Cherie Woolmer

Partnership working is not the solution to every problem but it is possible to use it to help [us] explore different approaches to similar difficulties.

(Stuart, 2002, p. 59)

Introduction

This chapter presents the development of a project between two local universities in Sussex, Refugee Community Organisations (RCOs) and the services that work in partnership with them to enable refugees to access higher education in the UK. The authors discuss the limitations imposed by current Home Office policy on immigration and integration as well as UK widening participation policy and explain how they have sought to overcome these limitations.

Policy overview

From the beginning of large-scale immigration to Britain, there has been little thought given in policy terms to long-term settlement or integration; Windrush-era migrants were not even expected to become permanent residents.

Recent years have seen an attempt to catch up, with a series of policy initiatives and perennial immigration Acts informed by an ongoing process of research, consultation and the publication of strategic documents. It is the experience of the authors that these documents are deeply unsatisfying to migrant communities and the services that work with them, presenting a nearsighted, top-down model of asylum. This is because they have consistently failed to address the central issues of segregation that arise in the asylum process and the ongoing denial of access to public services.

On the whole, much of recent immigration policy neglects to address the barriers faced by individuals with refugee status who wish to gain recognition of, usually, high level qualifications and significant levels of professional expertise. There have been waves of Home Office policy over the past seven years. Accompanying policy documents make little or no reference to the role higher education can play in helping to tackle and/or remove these barriers.

To begin with, they overlooked higher education entirely, confining themselves to promoting 'access to suitable English language tuition', focusing on basic, functional language skills required for, predominantly, lower-skilled, manual work. Later documents defined education as a 'major area of attainment' and a 'critical factor in the integration process' but were still focused on basic education.

Home Office research conducted in 2005 (Home Office, 2005) indicates that 56 per cent of adult refugees had qualifications and that 23 per cent were educated to degree-level, but the most recent policy documents mention only access to school places for refugee children and basic English classes. Successful indicators of 'achieving full potential' are limited to 'levels of English language attainment over time'.

The policy documents referred to above did not propose to count the number of refugees going to university, rather the percentage of *children* from refugee families going to university. Therefore the focus is on second-generation refugees. Second-generation migrants are generally more successful in all of the indicators of integration outlined in these policy documents than their parents. To us, this suggests some manipulation of data and an abandonment of first-generation refugees in policy terms. The highest level of educational attainment proposed to be monitored for first-generation refugees is vocational (NVQ, SVQ) with little account or recognition for the existing skills, qualifications and experience individuals bring with them.

It is argued here that the need of refugees wishing to access HE is a marginalised issue in UK widening participation policy too. Until the scope of the Aimhigher initiative broadened in 2004 (see HEFCE Circular, 2004), little evidence could be found of investment into the higher education needs and aspirations of refugees. However, working with refugees has disappeared from the latest Aimhigher guidance.

The HE sector has developed a broad range of experience and expertise on what works and doesn't work to engage underrepresented groups. Much of the energy within this work has been focused on working with young people, usually within the education system, and concentrating on issues of social class as the primary indicator for targeting activity. The difficulty of this model is that the particular circumstances of asylum seekers and refugees are not captured unless and until they become second-generation refugee learners as referred to earlier. Current widening participation policy does little to account for learners who are not accessing formal education or who may be engaging with learning in community settings.

The remainder of this chapter describes the development of a community/university partnership project called REMAS (Refugee Education Mentoring and Support into Higher Education). This project has been established in response to the policy shortcomings mentioned above and has been informed by community/university action research.

History and development of REMAS

History

In describing the REMAS project as it is delivered today and the partnership that oversees it, it is important to give brief attention to the history and impetus from different stakeholders within the two local universities (Brighton and Sussex) and the role of community partners in shaping and influencing the development of the service. This section briefly describes how two pilot projects undertaken by the universities led to the creation of REMAS as a joint service.

Working with refugee communities was flagged as a priority area of work in the original Cupp business plan. Consequently, a pilot project called 'Refugees Into HE' was one of the earliest commissioned projects by Cupp in 2003. The Health and Social Policy Research Centre (HSPRC) at the University of Brighton carried out a small piece of action research to investigate the needs of local refugees who wished to access HE.

The research team consisted of researchers and community members who jointly owned, managed and delivered the research. Community partners were paid for their involvement throughout the research. The main findings highlighted that targeted information, advice and guidance in community settings was essential in enabling refugees and asylum seekers to take first steps towards engaging in HE. A number of other findings echoed those outlined in numerous other widening participation research on barriers to accessing HE, but acknowledged that these barriers were compounded by other life experiences of being a refugee or asylum seeker (see Banks and MacDonald, 2003).

At the same time as this piece of research, the University of Sussex Centre for Continuing Education (CCE) had received European Social Fund money to carry out research into barriers into employment and training for refugees. CCE had been working with refugees and asylum seekers locally for a number of years, often in partnership with other local adult education agencies. Through this work CCE became aware that many such people were either unemployed or working in low-paid, low-skilled employment, despite having high level qualifications from their own countries of origin. The successful bid to the European Social Fund enabled CCE to interview local refugees and asylum seekers to explore their perceptions of the barriers to employment and training they faced and to develop and pilot a short orientation course to attempt to address some of their needs.

CCE worked in partnership with local agencies working with refugees and asylum seekers to identify people who would be willing to be interviewed and who might be interested in attending a course. Exceptionally skilled tutors worked alongside the researchers and the pilot group of learners to shape the course to the needs of the group. The resulting course, Ways into Learning and Work (WILAW), is a short course accredited at HE Level 1. Generic learning outcomes enabled the researchers to review and improve the course content in response to the pilot and supported ongoing curriculum development. WILAW now forms an integral part of the REMAS project.

Development

Building on the pilot work carried out by Cupp and linking with the ongoing work in CCE, both universities began discussions in 2004 to develop a joint service. Importantly, the feedback from the local communities to both universities was that development of a joint service was seen as paramount, with acknowledgement that refugees and asylum seekers did not identify or 'care' which university delivered it.

Aimhigher, a national initiative in the UK to increase the number of learners from non-traditional backgrounds accessing HE, expanded its brief in 2004 to include refugees as a priority area, resulting in funding being secured in September 2004 to develop a joint service between the two universities. In response to the pilot projects and ongoing discussions with community partners, REMAS was developed. Cupp continued to be involved with REMAS through its governance structures as well as providing administrative support in the start-up phase.

An important development for the joint project was the decision to create community-based advocates, called refugee outreach workers (ROWs), who are employed by the University of Brighton but work with and through local services and community groups. It is through these workers that the operational interface with all partners takes place. The University of Sussex continues to deliver the WILAW accredited programme as well as peer-support activities for service-users and ex-service users. The University of Brighton coordinates a revised mentoring programme, academic adviser network involving staff from the two universities and employs the ROWs for the project. More recently, it has led the development of an English for academic purposes module, delivered by the universities and community providers. The geographic scope also increased in 2004 to include Hastings and Crawley. RCOs and education providers continue to be involved in the governance of the project, with funding available to facilitate the involvement of the community and voluntary sector in the ongoing partnership working which steers the progress and development of the REMAS project.

A significant proportion of the activity of the project involves one-to-one advice and guidance, signposting and preparing individuals for the process of applying and entering university. Investing in relationships and building trust with individuals continues to be a crucial factor in the effectiveness of the project and the ROWs have been key in facilitating this by providing a brokerage service for enquiries and referrals. This is considered in more detail in the following section.

Case study examples of REMAS participants

K, 47, had a higher-education background in statistics in Iraq. She was referred to REMAS by a community education project. Having been out of education for many years and wanting to change field, she felt unconfident about her potential and met with the ROW to discuss her aspirations and needs. She then accessed a student mentor to work on what would be expected in her application. An information meeting was also arranged with an academic adviser from her chosen field of international relations. She was subsequently told that her application was of a very high quality and this resulted in her being offered unconditional places at the University of Sussex on four of her chosen courses.

M, 50, also from Iraq, had been a mathematics teacher. She had been given a flyer from a community venue about WILAW and subsequently took the course. She did not make an application at that time but continued to keep in touch via the participants' social group and met the ROW there. She made an application for mathematics with qualified teacher status to the University of Brighton and received an offer conditional on passing the Brighton GCSE English equivalence test. Coming from a different educational background, she was anxious about what she should study and the project arranged a meeting with an academic from the School of Education who talked her through the requirements, gave her titles of suitable textbooks and GCSE sample papers. If her test is successful she will be eligible for one of the postgraduate scholarships for refugees, recently instituted through REMAS by the University of Brighton.

Describing the partnership

REMAS as a project is supported by an overarching partnership involving stakeholders from both universities, other post-16 education providers, RCOs and services that work with refugees and asylum seekers. As outlined in the historical account of the project development, the scope of partners and the nature of their involvement has changed over time, ranging from designing and delivering action research to participating in the governance structures of the partnership which oversee the development of the REMAS project.

The REMAS partnership and the project it delivers functions at a strategic, development and operational level. At its core, the governance structure, chaired by a community partner, plays an important role in overseeing and steering the direction of the partnership and the project. This is not without tensions. As with any partnership, individuals have broader organisational objectives which they must ensure align to the aims of the partnership or, at least allow within those objectives, for partnerships such as REMAS to develop. Key to ensuring this has been the ability of the partnership to agree what Poxton describes as a mutual sense of purpose and joint agreement on future action (Poxton, 1996). This has been supported by the action research carried out prior to project development, effectively giving the mandate to partners, and particularly the universities, to develop the REMAS project.

There are difficulties in obtaining this mutual sense of purpose and engagement from community partners that emerge as consequences of the specific structural and ideological circumstances of the voluntary sector. The three main issues are resources, priorities and values.

The voluntary sector is characterised by an endemic lack of resources. Reliant on grant-based income, donations and, as we see it, unfairly negotiated statutory contracts, most organisations are chronically under-funded. With the exception of a few larger national charities, most organisations are unable to undertake substantial forward planning or long-range budgeting due to restrictive one-year funding allocations. Consequently they can lack a developed understanding of finance or market forces and are traditionally troubled by any mercantile endeavour. For the most part these organisations remain heavily cash-strapped. This is reflected in one key resource aspect: staffing.

Community partners cannot afford market-rate salaries; workers are either underqualified for their positions or, as is more usually the case, are overqualified and underemployed. Almost all organisations rely on some voluntary (unpaid) staff, and refugee community organisations are almost always entirely volunteer-run. In this resource-poor environment, personnel are not easily released for participation in steering committee meetings. The REMAS project has attempted to recognise this by paying community partners to attend meetings.

The institutional mindset of community participants is powerfully informed by these structural constraints in terms of identifying priority actions. Voluntary sector activity is often client-oriented and people-focused (e.g. advice surgeries, advocacy services). The main culturally-reinforced priority is to deal with 'frontline' clients, either on an appointment or a drop-in basis, with volume as a focus, and consequently overstretched capacity to deal with caseloads. The capacity-building and infrastructure-developing work that needs to be done to increase the service's ability to meet demand is frequently sidelined in favour of casework. Many organisations lack strategic planning personnel or any non-frontline managerial staff at all to undertake this kind of work. Other activities, such as external meetings with partnership agencies, are not regarded as of equal importance, meaning that workers can have difficulty justifying the time required by the partnership.

Justifying the diverted resources in terms of perceived value is the third main obstacle. Community partners may have difficulty identifying the direct benefit that particular partnerships may offer to their service or to their service users. When casework priorities are sifted in terms of need and the relative levels of suffering between clients, the proposed partnership activities need to offer something concrete and operational that is tailored to the immediate needs presented by the client group within the frontline environment.

Building on the strategic and developmental remit of the partnership, strong operational links have been made, via the work of the refugee outreach workers, with partners. Williamson (2001, p. 124) discusses the importance of such individuals to act as 'boundary spanners' within and across organisations. Sullivan and Skelcher (2002, p. 100) describe boundary spanners as people who are skilled communicators, talk 'the right language' in whatever forum they find themselves, have excellent networking skills giving them the ability to gain entry to a variety of settings and to seek out and 'connect up' others who may have common interests or goals. The ability to get the right individuals in post that can liaise and build trust between partners to work towards achieving the goals of the REMAS project has been integral to the success to date of the partnership and the project. The additional benefit here has been the exchange of expertise between university and community colleagues through these members of staff. Ambrose (2001, p. 30) discusses the importance of such staff retaining what he describes as 'frontline-ness: a sense of personal engagement ...being able to see something through to conclusion [and] working closely with other colleagues in another service to achieve a good outcome'. As the partnership and project grows, there are real tensions on the staff in these posts to maintain a 'frontline brief' but to share and input into the ongoing development and strategic capacity of the partnership. Box 8.1 gives some insight into these issues from the personal perspective of one of the refugee outreach workers.

Working through such 'horizontal' boundary-spanning requires management support through 'vertical' hierarchies in partner organisations if real strategic impact is to be achieved. The REMAS project and the partnership continues to work towards this with notable successes in influencing institutional outreach strategies; drawing down of additional funding for partners and inputting into developments of similar projects in other parts of the country.

Box 8.1

Barbara Bargione, Refugee Outreach Worker, University of Brighton

My role as refugee outreach worker requires me to liaise with individuals and groups from varying backgrounds and cultures and a number of local, national and international voluntary and statutory agencies, differing in size, structure and perspective – the 'horizontal' boundary-spanning referred to in the chapter.

Typically, as well as the diversity of the participants themselves, these might include local charities working with a small number of refugees, the Refugee Council in Britain and its international counterparts, the Local Education Authority, Student Loans Company, colleges of further education, a range of universities and academic organisations and personnel within them, DfES, community language providers, grant-making trusts, city council departments and referral services for a wide range of needs – health, housing, childcare, etc.

To make this complex interchange work, it is necessary to devote a large portion of time to establishing and maintaining relationships with individuals within the web of the work. Creating continuing trust between individuals and organisations with differing cultural and political agenda is not easy and the possibility for misunderstanding is great. For example, community representatives do not always understand the directness of British exchange and the potential for misunderstanding and even offence is present.

The 'language' the various groups use differs widely. As well as the aspect of communicating with speakers of other languages whose experience of education is diverse and whose confidence levels have almost without exception been affected by their experiences, the ability to transmit messages of complex information to a range of audiences, both orally and in writing, is key. A plethora of acronyms and jargon is used in the field of education and needs to be 'translated'. As outreach worker I may find myself giving a presentation on the project to a Vice-Chancellor or explaining it to the human rights section of a foreign embassy or a newly-arrived young asylum seeker. Additionally, we offer training and teaching skills. Training sessions for the community partner mentors have been developed and delivered and both outreach workers have taught on the WILAW course.

Agencies and participants are not always readily available. My role is a part-time one so contacting others who may also be in that position can pose problems. Participants often do not have access to email or telephone landlines and their mobile phones get lost, stolen and are often out of credit, due to the nature of their situation. Addresses change often as participants move around according to the vagaries of the rented housing sector, both statutory and private. For all these reasons, retaining lines of communication open is also integral to the work.

The main body of the work remains, however, to enable participants to access appropriate educational progression routes, to provide support in the formulation of personal goals and to develop strategies to overcome structural and personal barriers to achieving those. This requires the establishment of trust over a relatively long period of time, which may be months or in some cases has been up to two years. This is demanding, labour-intensive individual casework, often seeming to be a process of 'one step forward, two steps backward' as the aforementioned barriers can be numerous for refugees.

To sum up, the two aspects necessary to make the role work are to stay very much on the 'frontline' and to inhabit the space between the community and university, to be a good networker and keep relationships alive but primarily to be there one-to-one, to see each case through to potential being fulfilled in individual ways and to provide support for people's personal growth. To be a successful boundary spanner, that tension needs to be balanced and this is not always easy.

Assessment of the impact of 'partnership' and key learning points

This model of community–university engagement has provided numerous opportunities for reviewing existing practices within both universities and has enhanced the portfolio of outreach activity. It has provided an excellent opportunity for meaningful partnership work between the two universities, partner agencies and refugee community organisations.

Working closely together has enabled the project to 'track' service users and to respond flexibly to challenges as they have arisen. Collaborative effort and a flexible funding stream have enabled the team to respond creatively to participants' needs; for example the establishment of the 'participants' forum' offering peer-support and a means for current and former service users to contribute to the project. This joint approach illuminated the importance of continuing support during higher-level study at one or other of the institutions and has greatly enhanced the ability to identify and respond to issues which may have relevance beyond the experience of individuals.

Some of the barriers are institutionally-based and common to HEIs in general – being able to compare the approaches of two very different institutions has raised awareness that problems are not confined to a particular institution, giving partners the confidence to address issues through information sharing and lobbying.

The outreach workers and tutors have brought a wealth of skill and experience into the project and this has been the key to its success. The project has capitalised on the links it already had with community partners to great effect. Sometimes people have had to take a step back and acknowledge that this is not necessarily the best agency to provide a particular service. For example it was realised that academic advisers from within the university are very valuable but a mentoring scheme run by a voluntary agency was better placed to offer the broad-based mentoring this group requires than the project's own mentoring scheme.

Particular challenges arise for project staff in managing the expectations of the individuals involved. Participants in the project have a vast range of experience, aspirations and needs. However, even where prior experience and qualifications exist, appropriate academic language skills are often lacking and require further support. Ongoing support for the individual is also crucial to ensure they do not get lost in the system once they engage with it.

Considerable time has also been invested in awareness-raising of staff within each university. Developing strategic support for a partnership is important if maximum impact is to occur. This has in part been addressed by briefing sessions with academic advisers. Admissions tutors are also crucial to have on board and this remains a key area of work within the project. Staff from the language departments in both universities have been closely involved with the English language forum and will be vital in delivering the English for academic purposes module noted earlier. Sharing of information and drawing in expertise of staff in student services and admissions has also been an important aspect of the project. Working with Access and ESOL tutors in further education has become increasingly important and is a key aspect to the longer-term success of work in this area.

REMAS has benefited immensely from the participation of stakeholders in the project governance. Engaging the active participation of refugee community groups and their representatives helps to ensure that the project is meaningful to refugees. Apart from advertising the project to a key group it also helps to sell the project because participants feel that they have a vested interest in its success.

Inviting these representatives to become members of the steering committee and encouraging their participation in the decision-making process helps to bring their expert knowledge of the sector to bear upon the project design and implementation. Those who tackle the issues faced by refugees as part of their everyday work are able to bring an invaluable insight and wisdom based on their experiences and observations. Policy-level understanding of the situation is no match for grassroots vision when developing any scheme, let alone a user-led scheme addressed to social inclusion. The last point is that refugees need to be involved in a meaningful way even if only as a matter of principle. The ideal of partnership engagement is borne out by practice not by good intention.

With the REMAS project there are demonstrable and tangible benefits on offer to the refugee community but these have to overcome two issues. Firstly the community partners need to audit their users to ascertain the importance to them of HE as this is often not an initially-reported need and they may be unaware of its significance. Service users often tailor the presentation of their needs to their perceptions of the service's capabilities to deliver and so would not normally articulate HE desires to refugee community groups. REMAS, therefore, has a key role in raising awareness to community organisations that HE is a viable option for service users. Secondly, the steering committee needs to effectively demonstrate the direct utility of community engagement to the partners and to their individual client groups. Where this does not exist then partners on both sides will need to renegotiate the appropriate level of participation. If this renegotiation does not take place then participants may simply fall away.

The issue of resources is helped greatly by the provision of financial recompense to community groups attending committee meetings. This also assists participants to promote the project within their own organisations, providing that the guardians of their time are also the guardians of the purse. This feeds into the need for a dialogue between the university and the organisation itself, rather than just the participatory staff or the service users. Community buy-in can only be achieved once we have full organisation buy-in.

All partners share the view that involving refugees and their community organisations in a meaningful way in the governance process and training should not be underestimated but we have had to be realistic about the priorities of community partners – as noted earlier, attending a steering group meeting is often a luxury when time and resources are limited, even if funds are available to help.

Towards a model?

The authors have some reservations in describing the REMAS way of working as a 'model' since this might imply that it could be picked up and utilised elsewhere, whereas partners have found that what works for one group of people in a particular context, isn't easily transportable. Perhaps the most important attribute of our mode of working is its flexibility and adaptability and the 'model', in this sense, is continually evolving. With this proviso the following describes some of the ingredients for what the REMAS project believes has been a recipe for success.

Individual expertise

The skills and experience of individuals working for and with the project have been critical. All project staff are employed by one of the partner universities. They have been able to work closely with colleagues from the voluntary sector because there is substantial experience of working for this sector amongst project staff at every level. Similarly, the experience of working for two very different higher education institutions has brought insight and understanding to differences in operating contexts as well as strategic priorities relating to this kind of work. There is a need to understand and respect colleagues' professional cultures and ways of working and to ensure individuals can successfully span boundaries.

Where the project has not had the necessary knowledge or expertise it has worked with colleagues that have provided it. For example in struggling to meet the needs of participants to access affordable English language provision at an appropriate level, the project has brought together a large group of stakeholders representing a range of learning organisations across the further and higher education sectors, in both the statutory and voluntary sectors. This English language forum has been a valuable source of information as well as a vehicle for lobbying the decision-makers for progressive change and has been successful in securing funding to develop an English for academic purposes module.

Knowing our limits and sticking to them

The project's aim is to recognise its area expertise and to work ethically and responsibly within those boundaries. Crucial here is a shared 'ethos' as well as a common sense of the project's objectives. When people fall outside the project remit it is important to be able to refer them on to other organisations sensitively and supportively, which necessitates having a good working relationship with key organisations working with the same user group. Contacts with and through the overarching partnership, facilitated operationally and strategically through the governance structures, enable the project to ensure that participants are signposted in and out of the project accordingly.

Flexibility and responsiveness

This common sense of purpose is what enables the partnership to be flexible and responsive to the ever-changing circumstances of participants and the context within which partners are working. As outlined earlier, government policy can be short-term and short-sighted. Recent changes around immigration status for example have had huge implications for participants in terms of what courses they can access and the funding available.

Local policy initiatives are important too and the project aims to ensure that its modes of service-delivery are appropriate and complementary. For example, when one of the community partners received external funding to set up a mentoring service, REMAS worked alongside them and concluded that REMAS participants' needs would be best served by what was effectively a merger of the mentoring elements of the project with those developed by the community partner.

Conclusions

Whilst the authors acknowledge that the exact operations of the REMAS project might not be easy to replicate in other geographic environments, there are particular issues which relate to the nature of the partnership work that underpins the project that colleagues in other institutions and organisations might wish to consider if wishing to develop work in this area.

- Ensure strategic buy-in. Projects of this kind will only survive in the long term if they are able to demonstrate the strategic value of their work. This requires project workers and partners to work in tandem, delivering operational targets whilst ensuring there is capacity to develop strategic objectives.
- Be prepared to share power, through governance arrangements as well as deployment of resource. Remunerating community partners who bring their expertise to the table allows individuals to fully participate as well as recognising the constraints on them in financial terms.

- Encourage and develop the capacity of project staff and others involved in the partnership to span structural and sectoral boundaries. This requires real commitment of time and resource and is particularly important for 'frontline' staff.
- Allow time for trust to develop. Key to achieving this is effective communication in a way that promotes a 'shared' language and understanding. Regular reporting on project deliverables also enables trust to develop between partners.
- Be prepared to be flexible. Working across any sectoral boundaries requires this. Colleagues encounter different work cultures and constraints as well as differences in professional working. Process, procedure and clarity around roles and responsibilities are important to encourage the 'coordinated' partnership, as described by Mulroy (2004). However, application of this too early or too rigidly can stifle the entrepreneurial capacity and excitement that partners bring to the table in partnerships of this kind.

To achieve the 'co-evolutionary' partnership discussed by Pratt *et al.* (1998), it is fundamental that all of the above informs and sustains a shared vision and purpose so that, as in this particular case study, individuals who have huge amounts to offer society can contribute and realise their full potential.

With thanks to Barbara Bargione, Refugee Outreach Worker, University of Brighton

References

Ambrose, P. (2001) 'Holism and Urban Regenerations', in S. Balloch and M. Taylor (eds.), *Partnership Working: Policy and Practice*. Bristol: Policy Press.

Balloch, S. and Taylor, M. (2001) *Partnership Working: Policy and Practice*. Bristol: Policy Press.

Banks, L. and MacDonald, D. (2003) *Refugees in to Higher Education. A report from the Health and Social Policy Research Centre at the University of Brighton for the Community University Partnership programme*. Brighton: University of Brighton.

HEFCE (2004) *Aimhigher: guidance notes for integration*. HEFCE Circular, 2004/08.

Home Office (2005) *Integration matters*. London: Home Office.

Mulroy, E. (2004) *University civic engagement with community based organizations: Dispersed or co-ordinated models?* London: The Haworth Press.

Poxton, R. (1996) 'Joint approaches for a better old age: Developing services through joint commissioning', in M. Stuart (ed.), *Collaborating for change?* London: Kings Fund.

Pratt, J., Plamping, D. and Gordon, P. (1998) *Partnership: fit for purpose.* London: Kings Fund.

Stuart, M. (2002) *Collaborating for change? Managing widening participation in further and higher education.* Leicester: NIACE.

Sullivan, H. and Skelcher, C. (2002) *Working across boundaries.* Basingstoke: Palgrave.

Williamson, V. (2001) 'The potential of project status to support partnerships', in S. Balloch and M. Taylor (eds.), *Partnership Working: Policy and Practice.* Bristol: Policy Press.

Part 3

Doing research differently

Introduction

The next two chapters offer contrasting examples of 'doing research differently'.

Specifically, they explore participatory research – ways of doing research that involve the 'subjects' of the research in the research process: as the authors of Chapter 9 point out in respect of refugees, 'refugees themselves are almost invariably the passive recipients who have research "done to them" '. The projects described here turn that usual process on its head and describe the strengths and pitfalls of the experience of doing 'participatory' or 'insider' research.

Both chapters situate this experience in highly relevant and problematic policy terrain – the idea of extended schools, and the refugee experience. Both of these are ripe for new approaches to research, the one to assess whether and how, in the experience of those intimately involved, big policy ideas can really work on the ground amongst communities that face high levels of deprivation; the other to improve lives through the process of research as much as through the findings from that research. Both chapters emphasise rethinking the 'inside' and the 'outside' in the research and evaluation process; and on the nature and definition of expertise in research. This is challenging but very real for universities and for communities. These two chapters show the room for improvement in current practice, illustrating the impact of involvement in the research process on those taking part; and the considerable practical difficulties of doing this kind of work well.

Both show the reader 'the reality of working together [as] a process of constant experimentation, open exchange, iteration and evolution' (Morrice *et al.*). Both show the benefits to university staff and to the community members of working in different ways, although they also show that these benefits are not always easy to secure.

Chapter 9

Finding a voice: Refugees in research

Linda Morrice with Jonas Addise, Fayegh Shaafi and Elena Woolridge

Introduction

Refugees and asylum seekers have, particularly in recent years, been the subject of an increasing number of research projects. In this process the refugees themselves are almost invariably the passive recipients who have research 'done to them'. This chapter explores the process of recruiting, training and supporting a group of refugees to design and conduct their own research into refugee communities living in Brighton and Hove. It is written by one academic and three refugee members of the research team.

Background

Brighton and Hove has a relatively small, but diverse refugee and asylum seeker population.[1] It is estimated that there are between 150–200 asylum seekers and up to 5,000 refugees in the city (Chohda and Napier-Moore, 2005). However, there is a lack of reliable, comprehensive data on the numbers as some asylum seekers may be completely self-supporting and therefore not identified in any official figures, and once people gain refugee status, data is not collected. Under the Immigration and Asylum Act (Home Office, 2002) the Government has powers to disperse asylum seekers to various parts of the country, however, there is evidence to suggest that asylum seekers who have been dispersed out of London and the South East tend to return to these areas once they receive refugee status or leave to remain making it even more difficult to gain an accurate picture (Banks and MacDonald, 2003).

There are some long-standing and well established refugee communities in the city, for example the Sudanese, Somalian and Iranian (Hunt, 1998). Some of these no longer necessarily think of themselves as 'refugees' and are instead part of the larger black and minority ethnic community. More recently groups have arrived from areas of conflict including Iraq, Ivory Coast, Rwanda, Sierra Leone, Afghanistan and China (Chohda and Napier-Moore, 2005). Many of the more established communities have vibrant informal support and social networks. Others can arrive in

Brighton to find that there are very few other people from the same ethnic or linguistic background and the situation they find themselves in can be isolating and lonely.

A multiplicity of factors affect the refugee experience, including the circumstances of migration, the length of time and status in the UK, the size of the community, and the social networks and resources available to them. These factors, coupled with issues of ethnicity, race, gender, faith, age, class/caste, and educational background problematise the issue of refugee 'voice' and raise questions of who can speak on behalf of these diverse communities. In order to negotiate this diversity, we sought to draw on the first-hand experience of refugees from a range of communities across the city.

Our previous work with refugees and asylum seekers has involved research (Bellis and Morrice, 2003), and research combined with curriculum development and delivery (Morrice, 2005a; Morrice, 2005b). In all of this work the research design, tools, interviewing and editing of transcripts were done by white university academics who had no experience of migration or many of the other issues which might impact on the lives of refugees. We wanted to explore how the stories refugees told to other refugees might differ from the stories we'd been told in our research and what effect partnership working might have on the research. Funding from Brighton and Sussex Community Knowledge Exchange (BSCKE) enabled us to develop participatory research with refugees and to value their knowledge as partners rather than as objects of research.

Universities have traditionally been perceived as the primary site for the production and validation of knowledge in society, and as uniquely expert in research. Some would argue that this is their *raison d'être*. By engaging community partners to create and authorise knowledge, challenges these conventional conceptions. The term 'insider research' has been used to describe projects where the researcher has a direct involvement or connection with the research setting (Rooney, 2005). She cites arguments that insiders have a wealth of knowledge and understanding not available to outsiders, and that interviewees may feel more comfortable and freer to talk openly with someone with whom they are familiar.

The idea of partnership and collaboration with research subjects has a long history in anthropology and ethnography (Lassiter, 2005). Underpinned by Freirean notions of research for social purpose and transformation our aims were firstly to recruit, train and support a team of refugees in participatory research. Secondly, to establish a team of researchers to oversee the project and provide strategic direction. Thirdly, to explore what difference doing research this way might make to the research process and the knowledge generated.

Through previous work by the University, a significant number of refugees were identified who were unemployed or working in employment which didn't reflect their skills, knowledge, qualifications or levels of English language (Morrice, 2005a). Through providing the opportunity to work in partnership with university staff at the University we hoped to provide experience and support to individual refugees wishing to enter higher education.

The dialogue: nurturing and developing the partnerships

The first phase of the project involved working with a colleague with expertise in life history to develop and deliver a participatory research methods course. A flier on 'Researching Ourselves' was distributed through our networks and nine people came to the first session. Below Elena, one of the authors of this chapter, describes how the participants chose the research subject and the first challenge to be overcome.

> **Elena**: We designed a questionnaire on the course about refugees' experiences of education and work in the UK and in the country they came from. All of us on the course had high qualifications and had worked in good jobs before coming here and all of us were now wanting to study here or to find a job that was similar to the one we had before coming here. So education and work seemed a good subject. We then went out to do the interviews. At this stage we had some problems and challenges. The first was language difficulties. We all speak English as a second language and some-times it's difficult to understand what an interviewee is saying. When interviewing you can't keep interrupting and asking them to explain the meaning of a word which you don't understand or haven't heard clearly. It's alright if the person speaks the same language as you, but if they don't it's a problem. For the same reason transcribing tapes proved very difficult and time consuming when both interviewee and transcriber had English as a second language. So we decided to hand over the tapes and get someone else to transcribe them for us.

Next came finding the right refugee researchers with whom to partner. Although the publicity for the course clearly stated it was for refugees and asylum seekers, several people came who didn't fall into either of these categories, but who felt themselves to be 'refugees' in the UK. We had to confront the rather thorny issue of who to include in the definition of 'refugee' and to explore what was particular about the refugee experience. In the end we adopted an understanding of 'refugee' as those from outside the European Union and in the UK permanently. We also lost three initial researchers who moved during the project. We finally assembled a team of five key researchers, two women and three men, from five different refugee communities in the city: Eritrean, Ethiopian, Ukrainian, Iranian and Palestinian.

Nonetheless, the reality of working together was a process of constant experimentation, open exchange, iteration and evolution. The diversity of the partners required a particular focus on, and sensitivity towards, relationships, cultural differences and processes. Our dialogue was characterised by the tentative and exploratory nature of working together, in ways which were difficult to predict. Constantly checking back, confirming shared understanding, agreeing and making changes were an ongoing feature of the project.

The prior knowledge and understanding our researchers had of the refugee communities and cultures in the city was important in establishing mutual trust and respect between partners. The team was familiar with the university and the academics involved with this project through a *Ways Into Learning and Work* course (see Chapter 8). As Elena has suggested, they shared a common agenda of wishing to raise awareness of issues facing refugees. This shared commitment was a central unifying force (Suarez-Balcazar *et al.*, 2005), cutting across the agendas or interests of any single community.

Sustaining our partnership was complicated by the nature of the refugee experience which interrupted and intervened. Issues of homelessness, a deportation order and fear of travelling on buses following a racist incident inevitably took precedence. Like other socially and economically vulnerable groups, preoccupations with finding solutions to social situations were frequently just below the surface. All of these, coupled with everyday pressures, often made it difficult for the whole research group to meet up. Often only two or three partners could meet at any one time. This slowed the process of developing a sense of group identity and direction for the project. We tried to overcome this by adopting a range of styles of communicating and working together, including informal lunches and other opportunities to discuss the project and get to know each other better, and externally facilitated sessions to identify what we all wanted from the project and our ideas about its direction.

In this process, we confronted issues of power. Much of the partnership literature refers to power balances between partners (e.g. Matczynski and Penry, 1999). Universities are generally perceived as large, powerful institutions with access to significant resources. In this project, power and issues of inequality were embedded from the start. The University had initiated the project, written and submitted the proposal, with community partners joining once the funding to enable them to participate had been secured. However, it had been envisaged that once the research group was up and running, it would increasingly take a lead in determining priorities and direction: that power would be handed over, or at least shared on a more equal basis. In retrospect this underestimated the general power dynamics involved between the University and the refugee communities and the specific inequalities of working with individuals from marginalised and excluded groups.

It was only towards the end of the project that more equal partnership working emerged. The dialogue became more dynamic and self-assured, arising from the growing confidence of the researchers in their new role, the maturing of the partnership, and the opportunity for the community partners to demonstrate and share their knowledge, skills and capacities. Although a 'culture of learning' was established at the start of the project, in the initial stages much of the learning was about research skills and therefore predominantly the community partners were learning from the academic expertise. In the later stages, the refugee partners had greater opportunity to share their expertise and have their areas of strength recognised and more of a two-way learning environment was established. The point at which the refugee partners began to draw upon and recognise the value of their particular insights and understanding of the communities being researched marked a step-change in the flow of power in the project (see Suarez-Balcazar *et al.*, 2005, p. 90).

Doing it differently: the experience and impact of being a researcher

The extended interview that follows between the project coordinator and co-researchers explores how 'insider research' can make a difference to the process and direction of the research.

Researcher status

Linda: Do you think the fact that you were refugees made a difference to the research?

Jonas: Most people I've interviewed I know. They know me and they trust me, so they're not talking to a stranger. It's very easy for them to give correct and accurate information. They know they cannot lie or give false information, even if they want to. So I think it's going to be much more accurate and more honest. If they are interviewed by people with the same experience and people they know the result will be much better than talking to someone else for the University who they don't know. They know the information they give is not going to be transferred to the Home Office or some other place, so they say what they think and they are honest about their experiences.

Elena: I think people were more explicit and open with me because we're in the same situation. They might come from different countries but we're experiencing the same barriers and difficulties in this country. Then you can say anything because there's more trust and you can say more about your feelings and your experience. If you're interviewed by a British person and they ask you, for example, how you think refugees and asylum seekers are perceived by British people, they won't tell you the truth because they can't. If you've had a bad experience and you've been discriminated against and you have an opinion about this you won't say it to a British person interviewing you because you don't want to upset them. But if someone is in the same situation as you, you expect them to understand you properly. You can talk more openly about your negative experiences because you trust them more because they're in the same situation and you believe they will understand better.

Also, when you are interviewed by someone who is successful, for example, a lecturer at a university and you are someone who used to be successful in your own country and suddenly you're not successful at all anymore. You probably won't want to talk too much about that because you want to be perceived as still being on the same level as that person. If you were a lecturer and now you're just a usual person and you don't have the respect you used to have anymore. You still want to be perceived as being on the same level as that person; you still want to be seen as a professional and someone who knows things, and you want to feel respected. You don't want to talk about feeling lost and having a lot of problems; you don't want to show this negative side of your life. You're proud. Refugees are people who want or need to change something in their lives so they come to another country no matter what. They are often very desperate to change something and they are strong, proud people. To capture their experiences it is better that the researcher is someone in the same situation. It is just easier. You can share because you are both on the same level; you have the same status. People talked more openly about their negative experiences and this came through in our research findings.

Fayegh: Yes; sometimes if people have had a bad experience you can feel it with them and empathise. If people were upset I tried to calm them down or make them feel more comfortable by telling them some part of my story. In this way they feel better as there's someone who has the same experience. Trying to get into this country and trying to settle here are very difficult experiences; it's not easy. I still think asylum seekers are afraid. They are afraid of their status and that if they say something wrong that their status here will be in danger. For asylum seekers it is horrible; every day, every minute you worry what will happen to you, what the Home Office will decide, it's very frightening.

Linda: Has being partners in this project made any difference to you and your lives? Have you learnt anything or benefited from the experience?

Elena: It's helped me a lot because you see the other people with the same problem and you see how they experience and cope with this and what they do about it. You get ideas from them and you realise that you are not on your own. People around you have the

same problems so you can just share your experiences with someone. I think it's helpful for both of you – the researcher and the
interviewee.

It has had quite an effect on me doing this research; I'm very
involved in it. It's even changed my life a little. It's built my
confidence and my self-esteem. It's also affected my future plans.
I've been here for five years now and I still can't work in the field
that I would like to work, in the field that I used to work in my
country because of the exams I need to do. Five years have passed
already and I keep thinking I should just give up and do any job
here. But then doing this research I meet people who have
experienced more difficulty in their life and they want to achieve
something and they do achieve something no matter what. It gives
me the strength to do what I want, to try and achieve what I want
in my life and not to just give up. If they can do it, then so can I.
That's what I've gained from doing this research.

I have learnt how to communicate better with people from
different communities, different countries and cultures and different
educational backgrounds. Being a researcher on this project has
helped me develop my confidence. It's also a fast and easy way to
learn about life in another country. When you see real people doing
things it's easier to learn from them than from a book or the
internet. So you pick up ideas from the people you interview.

Fayegh: Before I started this research I wasn't that confident to
apply to university; I was going to delay for one year but then, doing
this research, I changed my mind; I applied to university and got a
place on the MSc. The interviews increased my confidence very
much. I was very quiet, always just listening. This has helped me so
much, now I'm not so afraid to talk and mix with people. I'm ready
for any interview and any research project; I'm not afraid! My life
has completely changed. My English has improved, but it's not only
the English language, but also interviewing people who had been
here for five or six years. They didn't know what to do, they were
just here doing nothing, waiting for someone to help them because
they didn't know how to get into university. I transferred my
information to them and that felt really good … So it's been a really
nice project: first you learn and then you help other people find
their way and that's enjoyable.

Jonas: This was the first time I've done research and since I also
want to go to university to study I thought this would give me a
chance to learn things that I might need in the future. I know I will
have to do research projects and I thought this project would give
me experience of working with people and doing research and
interviews. I have learnt how to conduct and do research and how
to do interviews. I haven't really learnt anything new about the

experience of refugees. The history might be different, but the process of seeking asylum is more or less the same.

Research content and direction

Linda: At some point, quite near to the end of the project, you decided we needed to change the focus of the research from education and employment to the social life of refugees and asylum seekers. Can you say something about that?

Jonas: We wanted to try and understand refugees as a whole without focusing on just a part of the refugee community or refugee experience. It was also sometimes difficult to find refugees with a high educational background. There are also refugees who don't have formal education and their voices should also be heard. What refugees experience in their day-to-day life is important. Social life is very wide and covers everything and includes everybody. Also, the first phase of the research project indicated how important social contacts and friends were in finding out information and getting advice.

In my experience refugees treat each other differently and are perceived differently depending upon how they came to the UK and what immigration status they have here – refugee, asylum seeker or failed asylum seeker. How people travelled to the UK indicates, for instance their social and economic status within their own community. People whose application for asylum has failed are more likely to find it difficult to make and maintain friends. We felt this was an interesting and important area …that's what we decided to do in the second phase of the project …It was not only our role in deciding on the area to research which made this research project different, but also the questionnaire we designed for interviews asked different questions from those which university researchers had asked in the past.

All people leave their country because they have problems; different problems. It is a normal question for refugees 'how did you come to this country; why did you come; who did you pay money to?' These are normal questions. People know each other so they tell; it's not a big deal. For a researcher who hadn't had these experiences themselves these might not be 'normal' questions and they might not feel comfortable asking about these very personal matters.

People might be embarrassed by how they came here. Some people might have walked or come in a small boat or in the cargo of a ship or they might have come by plane. In my community people are referred to as either 'camels', 'dolphins' or 'birds', depending on how they arrived. Some journeys are very traumatic. But everyone, no matter how they came here, has a story to tell.

Impact of university-refugee collaboration

Linda: Do you think this project, which has involved the University and refugees working in partnership, has made a difference to refugee communities in Brighton and Hove?

Elena: I think it has had an impact on the refugees that we interviewed. People appreciated being listened to, and although for some their fate is still in the hands of the Home Office, they know that the University was interested and concerned to try and improve the situation here. They perhaps see the University as a friendly place where they might perhaps one day be able to come to.

Fayegh: Yes; I think it's been really helpful to people. They knew that I was at university doing my MSc and they wanted to find out how to do it. You know their Bachelor degrees aren't accepted here. I know at least one of the people I interviewed who went on to approach the University about a course and others were really interested, so it does make a difference.

Jonas: I think refugees think it's better that their voices are heard and they know something will come out of this research, perhaps there will be changes. We've made two conference presentations. Maybe an article, maybe people's awareness will be increased. They know there won't be drastic changes tomorrow, but they want to participate; they want their voices to be heard, they don't want to keep quiet.

Conclusion: benefits and lessons learnt

The narrative accounts of other refugees' experiences served as 'tools for self-reflection' (Muchmore, 2002, p. 6). Much of the time this was an empowering and sometimes therapeutic process. Occasionally, listening to traumatic or painful experiences caused the researchers to reflect on their own experiences. It was particularly at these times, as Fayegh alludes to, that the boundaries between an 'outsider' (a university researcher), and an 'insider' (a refugee with similar experiences) become blurred, as stories were exchanged and experiences shared. As Naples (2004) suggests, insider and outsider positions are not fixed or static identities, but 'ever-shifting and permeable social locations' (p. 373).

The ethical implications for this kind of research came to the fore during this project and were explored and discussed. Relationships between researchers and subjects can be personal, and are likely to have existed before the project and continue after it has ended. The potential to undermine or damage relationships with friends and community members is clear. Decisions have to be taken on the spot during interviews and during writing-up about what material is appropriate and possible to include and what is not. Researchers are often confronted with these ethical decisions in life history and narrative approaches (Plummer, 2001; Muchmore, 2002). The issue becomes more complex where knowledge and information might have been given because of the insider status and personal relationship between the researcher and interviewee. Just as shared characteristics and experiences can give insider researchers particular insights and understanding, they can also raise painful or distressing memories. Muchmore (2002, p. 9) describes research involving personal and complex relationships as 'walking an ethical tightrope' in which there are no hard and fast rules for ensuring ethical behaviour, only guiding principles.

Through the process of collaborative working, university partners learnt the importance of being flexible and of letting go. Our focus shifted from research findings to the direction of the dialogue and the processes of working together. Willingness to throw out original plans, to completely rethink and to explore different ways of working was essential to the project's continuation. Without that flexibility we wouldn't have been able to train researchers as we went along or to have changed the focus in response to suggestions from the research partners. It was the refugee partners who felt that we were missing important aspects of the refugee experience and that we should widen the research remit. In many ways this was a key moment in the project; a moment at which a genuine two-way learning culture was established. The community researchers utilised and valued their experiential knowledge and understanding of their communities to suggest changing what and how we were researching.

Developing meaningful collaborative work where all partners feel confident and able to contribute on an equal basis takes time, patience and energy (Amuwo and Jenkins, 2001). For refugees, partnership building necessitates a slow and gentle approach with particular focus on relationships and sensitivity to cultural differences and language. This focus on process immediately sets up a tension, which has to be reconciled, with the outcomes-driven research climate in which university researchers' work.

A major project outcome includes mutual learning for all partners. The refugee researchers recognised individual benefits of enhanced capacity for higher-level study and research, improved English and communication skills. We also found that working on the project and being engaged with the University had a more general impact on self-esteem, confidence and sense of what we, as refugees, could achieve in the UK. Information and understanding was disseminated through the interview process, benefiting our community by contributing to the repertoire of communal resources. It has also built upon and strengthened the links between the University and the refugee communities in the city.

For the University, working with 'insider' researchers enriched our research and our understanding of the lives and experiences of refugees and asylum seekers. Interviewees were more comfortable talking with other refugees and the higher level of trust made them willing to reveal more about important aspects of their lives here, including prejudice and discrimination, and feelings of loss of professional identity and status. However, whether insider research produces more reliable data is a moot point: some argue that the insider's subjectivities and knowledge can lead them to make false assumptions and miss potentially important points (e.g. see Rooney, 2005). Their loyalties or hidden agendas can lead them to misrepresent or subconsciously distort data, and their relationship with their interviewees can have negative as well as positive effects. Rooney questions whether validity can ever be fully achieved and suggests there are no definitive answers to these questions, which arise in all research regardless of the researcher's position.

The research has certainly enhanced the university partner's experience and given a deeper and more complex understanding of diversity in all its forms. The research has consequentially reflected on how we might better respond to the needs of this group of potential learners: the curriculum and the sorts of support offered to refugees and other learners who speak English as an additional language or who are from diverse cultural backgrounds. The University has thus gained a body of research which can be used directly or indirectly to inform practice and curriculum development. We've also been able to realise our strong sense of social purpose and raised awareness of the barriers and difficulties facing refugees by dissemination events and conferences.

The research clearly highlighted the value and contribution which refugees have to make, and the need for universities to become more responsive and accessible to them. However, the complexity and political sensitivity of asylum issues in the UK mean that wider transformative outcomes for the University and the refugee communities will be harder to achieve.

Acknowledgements

The authors would like to thank their fellow researchers Mulugeta and Nada who contributed so much to the project in the early days, and all the participants who so generously gave their time and shared their experiences. Thanks also to Pam Coare, Sam Carroll and Nicky Conlan at the University of Sussex and Dana Cohen at the University of Brighton. Without their insight and wisdom the project would not have been possible.

Note

1. The term refugee refers to those who have been granted refugee status on grounds of the 1951 Convention on Human Rights and also those granted more temporary forms of protection such as Exceptional Leave to Remain or Humanitarian Protection. Asylum seeker refers to someone who has applied for asylum but is waiting for a Home Office decision. Here, unless stated otherwise, the term refugee is used to refer to both those who have refugee status and those who are still waiting for a Home Office decision.

References

Amuwo, S.A., and Jenkins, A. (2001) 'True partnership evolves over time' in M. Sullivan and J.G. Kelly (eds.), *Collaborative research: University and community partnership,* pp. 24–44. Washington, DC: American Public Health Association.

Banks, L. and MacDonald, D. (2003) *Refugees in to Higher Education. A report from the Health and Social Policy Research Centre at the University of Brighton for the Community University Partnership programme.* Brighton: University of Brighton.

Bellis, A. and Morrice, L. (2003) 'A sense of belonging: Asylum seekers, cultural difference and citizenship' in P. Coare and R. Johnston (eds.), *Adult learning, Citizenship and Community Voices,* pp. 69–73. Leicester: NIACE.

Chohda, N. and Napier-Moore, R., (2005) *'Refugee Week 2005. Understanding Lives and Sharing Journeys'. A report on the events and their contribution to community cohesion in Brighton and Hove.* Brighton: Brighton and Hove City Council.

Home Office (2002) *Nationality and Immigration Act.* London: The Stationery Office.

Hunt, D. (1998) *1991 Census; The Black and Minority Ethnic Population of Brighton and Hove.* Brighton: Brighton and Hove Race Equality Service.

Lassiter, L.E. (2005) 'Collaborative ethnography and public anthropology', *Current Anthropology,* Vol. 46, No. 1, pp. 83–107.

Matczynski, T.J. and Penry, R. (1999) 'Charging bulls: An arena for creating Charter Schools', *Education and Urban Society,* Vol. 31, No. 4, pp. 512–25.

Morrice, L. (2005a) 'Ways into work', *Adults Learning,* Vol. 16, No. 8, pp. 12–14. Leicester: NIACE.

Morrice, L. (2005b) 'Lifelong learning and the "outsider": The case of refugees and asylum seekers in the UK', in *Diversity and Difference in Lifelong Learning. The proceedings of the 35th Annual Conference of SCUTREA: Standing Conference on University Teaching and Research in the Education of Adults.* Falmer: University of Sussex.

Muchmore, J.A. (2002) 'Methods and ethics in a life history study of teacher thinking', *The Qualitative Report*, Vol. 7 No. 4. Available at: *http://www.nova.edu/ssss/QR/QR7–4/muchmore.html* [Accessed October 2006.]

Naples, N.A. (2004) 'The outsider phenomenon', in S.N. Hesse-Biber and M.L. Yaiser (eds.), *Feminist Perspectives on Social Research*, pp. 373–82. New York: Oxford University Press.

Plummer, K. (2001) *Documents of Life 2. An Invitation to Critical Humanism.* London: Sage.

Rooney, P. (2005) 'Researching from the inside – does it compromise validity? A discussion', *Level 3*, May: Issue 3. Available at: http://level3.dit.ie/html/issue3/rooney/rooney1.htm [Accessed November 2006.]

Suarez-Balcazar, Y., Harper G.W., Lewis R., (2005) An interactive and contextual model of community–university collaborations for research and action. *Health, Education and Behaviour*, Vol. 32, No. 1, pp. 84–100.

Chapter 10

Partnership processes in an evaluation of 'extended services' in a local secondary school

Peter Ambrose, Stuart McLaughlin, Tracy Whittle and Victoria Young

Introduction

The extended schools' programme was launched in 2003. The 240 schools funded under the £52 million programme are to provide services over and above delivery of the formal education curriculum. These services include childcare, health and social care, lifelong learning opportunities, family learning, parenting support, study support, sports and arts, and ICT access.

This chapter explores an evaluation of one such school, Falmer High School, funded by the Brighton and Sussex Community Knowledge Exchange. The school serves one of the most deprived communities in Britain with high levels of unemployment, low incomes, low educational aspirations and issues of substance and alcohol abuse.

Background

Falmer School faces considerable challenges, including over 50 per cent of students with special educational needs and over 35 per cent of students receiving free school meals. Educational attainment is low. Despite these difficulties, in recent years the school has made good progress in exam results and value-added scores.

Full Extended School status was seen as bringing the school the resources to work more closely with the local community and achieve its educational objectives by placing the school at the heart of the local community. To do this, the school focused on three key areas. First, to work in partnership with the Bridge Community Centre (on the school site) to provide learning opportunities for adults in the community; secondly, to provide access to health guidance, including sexual health guidance, for local young people via Mac's Place, a teenage drop-in centre based at the Bridge; thirdly, to develop a range of study support opportunities for students including a breakfast club, after school clubs and summer school.

The Evaluation

The Local Education Authority was one of 25 covered in a preliminary national evaluation of pathfinder projects carried out by Newcastle University in collaboration with the University of Brighton (DfES, 2004). The school wanted a more detailed account of its work as a full-service extended school and was keen to maximise the involvement of the school's stakeholders in the evaluation process. Cupp established an evaluation team using local people, supported by a university sponsor.

The evaluation set out to be an integral *aid to the development of the extended activities*, rather than as an imposition 'from outside'. It was therefore agreed that the indicators to be used, and the survey techniques utilised, should be developed collectively following discussions with key interest groups. The indicators would be quantitative and qualitative.

Perspectives

What follows shows the very real practical difficulties in achieving these objectives, from the perspective of those involved. These difficulties reflect some poor project management; the challenges of a large bureaucracy (the university) accommodating a small project in its personal and financial systems; the challenges of engaging local people; and the inherent weakness in evaluating a new initiative too soon after its launch. As such, there was considerable learning by all those involved during the course of the project and some adjustments were made to address the weaknesses. The knowledge gained during the project is also informing ongoing research at the University, the school's continuing efforts to relate to its community, and understanding of how to attempt evaluations in the future.

The team manager's reflections focus on the difficulties in assembling a team of researchers, on the initially inadequate project management, and need for more careful communication:

> We realised we had failed to put in place a memorandum of understanding setting out what we should expect from everyone. This would have let us act more quickly when things went wrong. It made us more vulnerable with so much turnover of personnel and collaborators. Assembling and supporting a team of local people to do the evaluation was highly problematic. There were conflicts of time with other work and personal commitments. The project required more flexibility than many team members had. The team was too small to manage staff absences and the irregular hours required to work were not readily accommodated by the University's employment processes. There were also financial difficulties for the team when team members had to wait over a month to be

remunerated. The sporadic working patterns and absence of a field office contributed to lost data when team members left, so we had to start the data collection again. Communication between stakeholders was inadequate, illustrated when evaluation forms from other stakeholders were distributed during the same week, generating much irritation from recipients.

The survey forms had been drafted in collaboration with all the managers of the services to be evaluated. In this sense they were participatory but they were being influenced not by local priorities but by future funding priorities, a more conventional research approach (Cornwall and Jewkes, 1995, p. 1,669). The wording of the questions did not always make sense to some of the students. Many young people, for example, did not know how to respond to the question asking their ethnicity, and could not see the point of some of the questions.

Some of these observations are echoed by one of the team members, who recalls initial euphoria about the project followed by very real difficulties of discontinuities in staffing and poorly specified project management:

Everyone was positive about the recruitment of local residents. The first few meetings I attended went smoothly and everyone seemed enthusiastic about the project and what it could achieve particularly as a joint working venture between the school, university and local community. Key members of staff were very keen to assist in the evaluation and gave their own input on the best ways for the evaluation proper to be carried out. It was exciting to be part of an innovative project.

By July 2005 two members of the team had left, and with it the data that was collated from the Bridge questionnaires was lost, this was a real blow to the remaining team members as a lot of effort and energy had gone into the work. New team members were recruited and a team manager was also appointed which gave us a boost. And although the team saw more members leave, several remained.

Collaboration certainly became easier as the unique strengths and resources of individuals were identified. Over the year we formed excellent working relations where everyone communicated well and our meetings were focused and productive. Everyone was taking on equal work. We recognised each other's strengths and weaknesses and were able to delegate the work accordingly, making for a smooth-running project, at least from our end!

The team members' experience shows the importance of continuity beyond the evaluation team itself:

Outside of the evaluation team there were also a high number of changes to the people working on the wider project. At the beginning of the project the steering group was made up mainly of the managers of the different branches of the Falmer Extended School, the University supervisor and research team members. This led to a very strong and focused steering group, with a high level of expertise being ploughed into the development of the evaluation. There seemed no questioning the stability of the project with such a team heading and guiding the work. However this sense of stability and dedication to the project began to feel very vulnerable when members of this team began to leave. When the Head of Community Services at the school resigned, I believe the absence of this particular member really hindered the project.

Their experience also highlighted some inadequate initial project management:

As a member of the team, it has been hard, at times, to feel positive about the project when there appeared to be so much confusion amongst school staff over what we were doing and what the school would gain from the evaluation. These problems were highlighted when the responsibility for the evaluation was handed over to the school, at the beginning of 2006. The handover process lacked cohesion and were it not for the stable and committed research team that were finally able to manage themselves I believe the evaluation could have collapsed altogether. On reflection, the handover needed to have more guidance from the University. As it was, forming the new steering group fell upon the hands of the research team. The academic side of the project had at that time not been adequately explained, and this left a void where complete knowledge and understanding were crucial.

High levels of staff turnover in the work being evaluated affected not only the services but the evaluation process. In evaluating Mac's Place, the team members note:

By the time the questionnaires were carried out the manager seemed to have a strong relationship with the young people who used it. Gathering the data was a real pleasure. The young people there were very welcoming and had a lot to give the evaluation, not only in their time but also their eagerness to complete the forms, which were done, I believe honestly, respectfully and thoroughly. However, the second survey was not the same experience. The young people involved had seen yet another manager leave. The premises were shut for a while. By the time of the subsequent survey there was a new manager but the positive attitudes towards Mac's Place were not so evident and the respect that had been shown to it, as somewhere safe to go for advice and support, seemed diminished. This got worse when the new manager announced that she too was leaving. I feel the results reflect this. It was harder to get questionnaires completed, and when they were they were not given nearly as much attention. I especially noticed a reduction in numbers using the facility. When Mac's Place closed we were unable to carry out the surveys for this last summer term. The results for Mac's Place remain incomplete. For the team this is a real blow. It is hard at times not to feel as if all the hard work and effort put in to evaluating Mac's Place has been a waste.

Nonetheless, this partner remains positive:

Even with all the changes to key members of the core project group the evaluation eventually found its rhythm. The data gathered so far has been a success. All of us on the team have found it interesting, and for some team members it has been a real change in the type of work they normally do. All of the team have learnt new skills, particularly with the computer training. Facing the challenges of working with all these partners and with young people has been rewarding. Learning of the positive effects that the Falmer Extended School is having on the young people and members of the community has made up for any disappointments that the organisational and management side of the project caused.

For the University supervisor, these very real on-the-ground difficulties are symptomatic of the nature of the intervention – the extended school initiative – and the way such interventions are conceived. Analysis over the last few years of the impact of small-scale local regeneration programmes on areas of multiple deprivation (including Stepney and Hackney in London, Hastings and East Brighton) shows the inherent weaknesses in the policy model given the local circumstances. One of the reports on these activities (Ambrose, 2000) reviews the critical literature on small-scale local regeneration programmes. In the case of both Stepney and East Brighton the array of problems faced by the local population can be related directly to globalisation processes and the near collapse of the local economies – in the case of Stepney by the London dock closures of the 1960s and 1970s and in East Brighton by the loss of something like 6,000 manufacturing jobs over much the same period. The calamitous impacts of these events include huge difficulties in accessing reasonably paid work, or sometimes any work, a consequent steep decline in household spending to support local commercial services of all kinds, decline in the quality of public services, increasing social stigmatisation and a deep collective sense of disengagement, verging on anger, as the rest of society is perceived to be enjoying rising standards of living. The local population are, in effect, the victims of world-scale processes of economic reorganisation of which they are not fully aware, and which were not of their making, but whose effects they feel sharply.

In the analytical framework offered by Habermas (1976) the government is likely to respond to these events not with structural changes (for example more direct investment in poorer areas funded by more steeply progressive direct taxation) but with a series of targeted, short-term and comparatively low-budget programmes. The political implication behind this strategy is that capitalistic organisation is delivering prosperity to the vast majority but that small isolated and residual pockets of poverty remain which can be addressed with area based initiative-type programmes. There is often the further implication that the programmes depend for their success on a more participative citizenry in the areas concerned – in effect that local residents should help by 'pulling themselves up by their own bootstraps' to use the terminology of the mid-1970s Community Development Projects programme.

In relation to the typically short-term nature of these area-based programmes, and the invariable desire of ministers to see 'quick fix' results, Pollitt has written usefully of the 'relentless restructuring' that has occurred in public management in the Blair era (Pollitt, 2006; Pollitt and Bouckaert, 2004). His basic point is that the speed of 'reform' (itself an interesting choice of word), accompanied by rhetoric about 'decentralisation', 'choice' and 'efficiency', is actually too fast to be coped with. Structures, processes and cultures of management cannot change at the speed required. The natural pace of recovery from the sorts of adverse consequences faced by east Brighton is at odds with the timescale of the plethora of 'quick fix', often ill-coordinated, interventions upon which ministers pin their reputations.

The relevance of this analysis can be seen in the 'extended schools' programme. The intervention is short term (two-years' money) and it was introduced in such a way that a 'year zero' period of thought, planning, team recruitment and the piloting of surveys was not built into the timescale. The effects of this are detailed in this chapter: the initiative is over almost before it has got up and running.

Yet potentially the introduction of a range of much-needed services for children and parents above and beyond delivering the educational syllabus, on a long-term and well-funded basis, would be an invaluable adjunct to more generally targeted economic regeneration initiatives in the area. But, as Habermas would have argued, it appears that the intervention has more to do with maintaining system legitimacy than with effecting structural change. The latter would require really serious public investment.

The difficulties arising for evaluating the initiative in this context are summarised here.

Rushed timescale

Overall, the project team agrees that the evaluation timescale was rushed. There was pressure from the DfES and the Local Education Authority

(LEA) to get evaluations of the extended schools programme underway quickly; and pressure to get the evaluation surveys and other mechanisms in place before there was time for adequate reflection and planning. It would have been more helpful to have had a 'year zero' in the programme during which issues of evaluation, and other issues, could have been thought out before the programme proper started. This wasn't helped when the original timescale slipped and funding was delayed.

Assembling and maintaining an evaluation team

Added to this, as noted earlier, the project underestimated the difficulties of recruiting a team of researchers. Initially it had been understood from the school and the LEA liaison officer that there was an active Parent Teacher Association (PTA) and that some members should quickly be recruited to form the team. In fact despite repeated efforts, and an advertisement in the school news-sheet, no one could be recruited from this source. Several members were recruited by word of mouth and by contact via the Bridge. Several of these had a number of complex family and health issues to deal with. When a team was assembled, the bureaucracy involved in appointing and paying team members via the University payroll system and the lack of a senior member to manage the team made the process more difficult.

The team formation problem was finally solved with the appointment of the team manager. From this point on the team quickly became fully operational although residual problems remained.

In retrospect it is not surprising that projects designed to have heavy dependence on involvement from local community members may find it difficult to recruit people in an area of multiple deprivation where almost everyone has some difficult family or financial issues to deal with in their lives. There is a considerable 'cultural gap' between the expectations within a university and those within a deprived community about carrying out specified actions to a specified timescale.

Inappropriate survey instrument

All the project team concluded with hindsight that the survey instrument was too complicated and inappropriate. The survey forms to be completed in the surveys of student responses were devised initially by the FSS coordinator and the University supervisor. They sought to cover all the outcomes set out in the Government's document *Every Child Matters* (Cm 5860, 2003) which specified a very broad range of expected outcomes and impacts of the extended schools programme.

After using the forms in the first full iteration of the surveys it was evident that even if the forms were completed under supervision, which was not always desirable in view of confidentiality, much of the language used was too complex for the age group being surveyed. Both the breadth of questioning, and the language, needed to be modified for later rounds of surveying, reducing the direct comparability of results from successive rounds of surveying. This could have been avoided with time to pilot the surveys, and/or if someone from the mid-teen age group had been part of the evaluation team from the beginning, and/or there had been a less precise adherence to the full range of Government impact dimensions.

Working with a large organisation

A number of issues arose from the need to work through the University's payroll and personnel systems. These, on the whole, proved to be poorly adapted to the needs of university/community projects of this kind. Difficulties included petty cash to pay small expenses; complications about placing team members on suitable pay scales to reflect the nature of the work being undertaken and the irregular time pattern; and issues about involving two 16-year-old members in the work.

Lessons learned

All those involved in the evaluation project and in preparing this chapter are clear that they have learned a lot from what went wrong. But they remain overwhelmingly positive about the potential for future collaboration, about improvements in ways of working and about broader learning. The team manager acknowledges that some of the difficulties reported could have been avoided if they had been more aware of the experience elsewhere: 'All those involved in university-community partnerships could benefit from reading the community development literature for insights on how community level variables might affect the collaborative process', for example, Flora and Flora, 1993, and Putnam, 1993 (see Todd *et al.*, 1998, p. 241).

The project manager continues:

> In spite of the shortcomings, the process of conducting the evaluation has enhanced the capacity for the community partners to implement and sustain evaluation systems for their services. The need to have a reliable system for collating and analysing evaluation data has been recognised by the school. An administrator for this task is to be recruited. Visiting other extended schools has provided insights in to other participatory methods that the school could employ to balance qualitative with the quantitative data. The Bridge now has an administrator with Excel skills that she uses to conduct the organisation's quarterly monitoring.
>
> In terms of developing wider capacity within the community, two former Falmer students have gained experience and training in data collection, analysis and report writing. Another team member has become more confident about her computer literacy skills.

Much of the learning concerns the expectations that projects should have about what is possible and how quickly progress can be expected. The team member reflects:

At the start of this project my perception of the problems of living in a deprived area were that children came from homes where parents did not work, families were living mainly on benefits, and children often did not receive the emotional support that is needed as they move through their teenage years, or encouragement for their educational success. What I have learnt since I began this job is that for most families this is untrue. I found that in reality most homes the children come from are made up of parents who do work, and often more than one job meaning many parents work unsociable hours for family life. Yet even with their parents' hard work, many children still seemed to be impoverished, and most probably live below the poverty line.

At the start of the evaluation project I was discouraged that we had been unable to recruit any local residents or parents to form our team of researchers. I believed this to be a sign of disinterest from parents in their children's educational welfare and experience, and for local residents a detachment of support for their local community. However I now believe that many people would not have been able to take this job even if they had wished as they are either working so many hours already or are part of a family where if in receipt of benefits like Working Family Tax Credit are forced to remain in a situation where only one parent can work.

Throughout this whole project I have felt increasing levels of frustration for families that face these sorts of hurdles. The unfairness of it all, in particular for the young people who are left having to care for themselves while their parents work, as I also discovered from this project the high numbers of children who were caring for siblings or disabled parents too. Seeing the children having to carry these burdens my eyes began to open to the inappropriate-ness of what is on offer to these children. I was there researching yet another government initiative aimed at giving children like these better chances in life, when it quickly became clear that these were not able to be delivered, and the children were not getting what they deserve. I was again frustrated in that I believe the Extended Schools Initiative has the potential to provide high-quality services for children, their families and the local community, but due to difficulties at times this was not happening. It was no wonder that when I came to survey the young people using Mac's Place many felt let down, as in two terms they had seen three managers come and go.

Working as a researcher on this project has only encouraged me to learn more about the lives of those living in deprived areas and in particular the effects of ever-changing government policies aimed at improving their lives.

Realistic expectations is a theme echoed by the University supervisor:

Involvement in the evaluation has been a learning experience. Contact with some of the children and parents in the area, and with members of the evaluation team, has helped to give a more direct insight into the range of problems faced by local residents in their daily lives. This serves to demonstrate how unrealistic, and in a sense unfair, it is to rely on 'resident participation' to achieve economic regeneration. Residents do not normally have the spare energy and time to 'participate' in managing improvement processes which, in more prosperous areas, residents assume will happen anyway.

The headteacher has reflected particularly on the role of the school and its capacity to include its pupils and other stakeholders:

The school has benefited from working with the University. We have a great deal to learn from each other and can achieve a great deal of mutual benefit from such work. The school did not have the expertise to set up an evaluation team and the advice and guidance of the University was invaluable and much appreciated.

The team found it difficult to gain the commitment of the school's community for the purposes of evaluating the full-service extended school activity. Not only was it a problem recruiting people to conduct the surveys, getting people to complete surveys was also an issue. This was the case for staff and students alike.

The process used to ascertain the views of stakeholders has also been difficult. Some of the questionnaires used were too complex and wordy for students especially. Perhaps using young people to design the questionnaires using student-friendly language would help.

We have also learned that surveying and gaining the views of students, staff and parents can be achieved more effectively if brought in-house by using a wider variety of evaluation processes. For example, using the school council, parents' groups, parents' evenings, etc. may be a better way of securing the views of stakeholders. However, the experience of working with the University and attempting to work with the community has taught us a great deal and informed the way forward for the future.

Conclusions

The project proved one of the most challenging supported to date by Cupp. Some of this was inherent in the context, some problems could have been avoided with better planning. Nonetheless much has been learned. Despite the difficulties and setbacks discussed, the project did meet its essential aim of carrying out an evaluation of an important programme of activities in Falmer High School, jointly managed by the University and community representatives.

References

Ambrose, P. (2000) *A drop in the ocean: The health gain from the central Stepney SRB in the context of national health inequalities.* Brighton: Health and Social Policy Research Centre, University of Brighton.

Cornwall, A. and Jewkes, R. (1995) 'What is participatory research?' *Social Science and Medicine,* Vol. 1, No. 12, pp. 1,667–76.

DfES (2004) *Evaluation of the Extended Schools Pathfinder Project (Research Report 530).* London: DfES.

Cm 5860, Every Child Matters Green Paper (2003). London: TSO. Available at www.everychildmatters.gov.uk.

Habermas, J. (1976) *Legitimation crisis,* translated by Thomas McCarthy. London: Heinemann.

Pollitt, C. (2006) 'Running out of or running into time? The pace of public service modernisation', Seminar on contemporary issues in public management, 13 June, 2006. Brighton: University of Brighton.

Pollitt, C. and Bouckaert, G. (2004) *Public management reform: A comparative analysis (2nd edition).* Oxford: Oxford University Press.

Todd, C.M., Ebata, A.T. and Hughes, R. Jr. (1998) 'Making university and community collaborations work', in R.M. Lerner and L.A.K. Simon (eds.) *University-community collaborations for the twenty-first century,* pp. 231–54. New York: Garland.

Part 4

Students and communities learning together

Introduction

The next three chapters concentrate on examples of students and communities learning together. They offer some conclusions about the key elements from such examples that can support both student learning in the community and community learning alongside university students as well as delivering individual projects of real impact.

The chapters illustrate how roles can shift in such learning partnerships, how far community and university partners can learn from each other, and how far each learns things not learnable in other processes. For the university students, the three projects described here provided the opportunity to test different skills and to develop ways of working not available in the classroom or studio. In particular, they provided the students with the chance to work with 'clients' and therefore to extend their repertoire for post-graduation life as practising artists or architects. The common view of the students involved in these projects is that they have learned at least as much as the community members. For the community members, the projects have given access to educational resources not conventionally available and have enabled a significant development in skills and confidence.

In addition, the three chapters illustrate not only the creative outcomes for the university and community students but wider educational benefits and insights into the problems and potential of such projects. In so doing they add detail to the question of higher education participation touched on in Chapter 1.

Chapter 11 describes one of the three pilot projects launched by Cupp at the outset. It illustrates powerfully the way in which roles and identities in community–university projects can evolve. It also illustrates the way the work itself needs to be reconceptualised and its organisation adapted to reflect the vibrancy of the activity and to make tangible the learning that has been gained.

Chapter 12 describes two examples of architecture 'live projects', 'working with real clients on real sites' and with the target of producing real outcomes.

Chapter 13 describes collaboration and mutual learning between a group of university students and local women residents. The chapter richly describes the powerful experience of participating in such a project and the challenge it offers to assumptions, understanding and the academy.

As Viljeon et al. comment in concluding their chapter, here we see 'successes, failures, warts and all' (p. 159).

All three chapters concern projects rooted in the creative disciplines at the university – art and architecture. They raise important questions for the nature of university arts education and for the power of art to challenge, communicate and inspire across difference, whether of material reality, personal circumstance, value or culture. As such, they are a particular and perhaps especially powerful expression of knowledge exchange and mutual benefit, through collaboration and creative dialogue.

Chapter 11

Access to art: from day centre to Tate Modern

Pauline Ridley and Alice Fox

Introduction

Access to Art (a2a) was one of the first Cupp projects and has been very influential in steering Cupp's direction. However, like other projects described in this book, its starting point was not an abstract desire to build collaboration partnerships but a real problem in the world – the absence of educational opportunities for artists with learning difficulties – which could only be addressed collaboratively.

The chapter is authored by two University members and includes the words of as many participants as possible, drawing on interviews, written reflections and video diaries. Some names have been omitted to preserve anonymity; where real names are used, this reflects an informed choice to have their contributions and achievements recognised publicly.

With or without learning difficulties, many of us prefer working with pictures rather than words. To help us remember and order our story, we begin with some images – snapshot memories from a journey that has now lasted several years – see Box 11.1.

Box 11.1a

May 2005. A bright morning. A group of people come over the brow of the new Millennium Bridge in London, still known as the 'Wobbly Bridge' after shaky beginnings. Our group is rather wobbly too, and rather late. We've already stopped several times to let people catch their breath or rest their legs; a silent decision is taken to blow the budget on taxis at the end of the day.

But now we pause to take in a wide view of our destination. With a little shock of recognition we realise that from our standpoint on the bridge we can see some familiar paintings through the upper windows of the gallery. Our work is on show at Tate Modern!

Box 11.1b

Another image, from Andrew's speech later that day. He has painted a self-portrait with a sad face. Scanned into his PowerPoint presentation, it helps him remember what he wants to say to the audience of artists, administrators and policy makers. He tells them that this is what he felt when his only chance to paint was in the art room at his day centre.

The whole group has come here to see their work exhibited but also to make sure that all these people get the point. They just want what other art students take for granted – teaching to help develop their own visual language as artists, a space to work together and the chance to sell their work professionally.

Box 11.1c

Flashback to 2004. A room in the college art building. Hot wax simmers gently on a side table; some students are making batik pictures on cloth. Others are working on different projects. Shirley and Rhian are making felt. Julie and Kelly are engaged on an elaborate narrative painting series. Keith and Paul are working on an enormous double canvas – Keith always prefers a large scale.

B is making prints; she smiles and hums to herself as she and her partner roll the ink on to the block. B won't be at Tate Modern, and she's not in our final picture – but her story needs to be told too.

Box 11.1d

April 2006 Another bright morning. Tutors are setting up two large adjoining rooms in the Phoenix Artists' Studios in Brighton. One is for the new students who've been coming here since October. Today they'll be painting a still life with brightly-coloured tulips to learn more about mixing colours.

Next door there are separate areas for work on individual projects. This is the first meeting of the original students since they won Arts Council funding to establish their artists' group. People start to arrive, greeting each other with delight. One tells us how excited he and his friend had been the day before. 'All day we were just bursting to get here.'

Now they are here, and the work can begin.

Background

The project grew out of work already underway between Carousel, a creative arts charity working with people with learning disabilities, and the University of Brighton, responding to research for the Arts Council (Fox, 2001). This had shown that learning-disabled people with artistic talent had very limited chances to improve their skills, confined to day-centre classes without professional help or equipment, or to non-accredited segregated courses.

The response was Access to Art, an inclusive part-time art course delivered at Sussex Downs College for students with learning disabilities working alongside undergraduate partners.

Thinking about the course was strongly influenced by Carousel's commitment to integrated arts practice and to testing how that could be translated into a formal educational context, to provide the first stage of an inclusive route to mainstream further and higher arts education.

The involvement of University of Brighton students was initially a pragmatic solution to the need for one-to-one support to enable the students with learning difficulties to be included in mainstream classes. The University students were recruited through an optional second year module, offering training in arts facilitation and a carefully structured programme of support. Their intended role was to provide general support to their partner and help them with practical tasks and communication with other students and staff. However, their role has evolved in response to changing circumstances, prompting questions about different models of inclusive learning, some of which have worked much more effectively than others.

Integrating the a2a students into the college's sixth form classes demanded more than was possible in such a limited time. Staff found it hard to manage some of the responses of the younger non-disabled students. Projects and teaching strategies tended to be designed to meet the requirements of the majority and it was difficult to adapt these for individual a2a students. Even with the assistance of their undergraduate partners, they needed more time to undertake set tasks, and more flexibility and choice in prioritising different elements. Experiences of failure damaged self-esteem and emphasised students' differences by highlighting what they could not do rather than what they could.

Difficulties encountered in that first year echoed longstanding debates about the advantages and disadvantages of 'inclusive' education. Ten years ago, the Tomlinson Committee cautioned that:

> Inclusive learning is not synonymous with integration. The best environment to match students' requirements will often be an integrated environment [...] but it will sometimes be a mixture of integrated and discrete provision or totally discrete provision as in specialist colleges. (FEFC, 1996)

More recently the Select Committee on Education and Skills looked again at policy relating to children with disabilities or special educational needs (SEN) and has endorsed the call by the Little Report (Learning and Skills Council, 2005) for a radical change in the planning and funding of post-16 education for people with learning difficulties. The Adult Learning Inspectorate also found a failure to meet the needs of young people with learning difficulties:

> Despite much rhetoric in the sector about inclusiveness and matching the needs of the learner, it is common practice to assess learners against the requirements of some form of accreditation ...not in relation to their individual needs. Rarely are strengths identified and built upon in a programme of learning. The assessment process too often results in establishing only a baseline of deficits [...] there is a wealth of energy and talent which is still denied its fulfilment.

(Adult Learning Inspectorate, 2006, pp. 5–6)

Art through integration

Though discrete programmes may make it easier to match teaching to individual needs, they carry important social and political consequences. In common with many disability groups, those involved in the project felt that educational segregation, however well-intentioned, perpetuates discrimination, misunderstanding and prejudices.

Learning from the difficulties encountered in the first year, but also the positive interactions between a2a and Brighton students, the course was restructured to centre on collaborative working across the two groups.

The first joint session of the term involved screen-printing individual T-shirts for each student. Focusing on a practical process helped the new partners to get to know each other quickly and avoided any shyness at meeting for the first time. The relationship was developed by a subsequent visit to the University where all the students put on a slide show. Brighton students were able to show their partners where they made their own work, and one pair attended a degree-level drawing class together.

Strictly speaking, this was not an integrated programme since the two groups of students, though working together, were enrolled at separate institutions on separate courses with different learning outcomes. But it supported the underlying aim of social inclusion, and because all activities and assessments were intended to be undertaken collaboratively, they could now be designed from the point of view of the students with learning difficulties. This has involved no loss of challenge for the University students. As we shall see, they have all been extremely positive about what and how they have learned.

The success of the reorganised programme has enabled it to be replicated in Hastings. In 2005, with help from the Cupp Knowledge

Exchange, Access to Art developed a productive new partnership with Project Art Works (PAW), a Hastings-based visual arts organisation which works with young people and adults with more complex needs.

Cupp funding enabled PAW, the University and Hastings College of Arts and Technology (HCAT), to create a new ten-week art course for students with learning difficulties and undergraduate art students from HCAT. Recruitment was mainly through local day centres. Over one hundred suitable participants were identified for the eight places.

PAW's expertise and dedicated studio space enabled the course to be expanded to include people with more complex needs. There were therefore three groups of participants: mainstream art students, people with mild learning disabilities and people with profound and multiple learning disabilities. The impact was immediate:

> I knew it was going to work after week one. I was so thrilled. I'd been thinking about this model of inclusion for five years and setting it up and finding ways to develop it ... I know that there have been details in the course that we can develop, but after week one I had a really basic feeling of 'this works. It's transferable. It can happen everywhere'. (*Alice Fox, University of Brighton*)

> There was no sense that there were different groups – just that everyone was working together and enjoying themselves and that everyone was equally valued. (*Anthony McIntosh, Hastings College of Art*)

> Before a2a we had not considered in detail how to deliver truly inclusive projects. However, we have been working on a vision and plans for a new arts centre ...'inverting the paradigm' of inclusion so that instead of adapting mainstream arts opportunities to the needs of people with disabilities ...we would be led by the needs of people with the most complex needs and then include mainstream audiences and participants ...a2a has been the first programme of work that PAW has delivered in partnership with others that has been really inclusive. That is a gift for which we are very grateful. (*Kate Adams, PAW Director*)

Curriculum development, teaching and assessment

Both the courses raise important issues about the nature of the arts curriculum and how to teach and assess art. These issues arise in a context where universities have considerable autonomy in setting their own course requirements, but FE colleges work with external accrediting bodies; where all education providers in the UK are required to make 'reasonable adjustments' to accommodate people with disabilities and to plan systematically to make their courses more inclusive (SENDA); and where academic standards must not be compromised.

Access to Art has always focused on what students can do rather than what they cannot. Nevertheless, it is common for people with learning difficulties to have problems with cognition and memory, and they may be less verbally fluent than their peers. Visual arts programmes assess students not only on their practical work but also their ability to offer a critical commentary on their creative intentions and decisions, and to locate their work within a historical and theoretical context. Our first challenge was therefore to explore how students' critical decision-making could be demonstrated in practice rather than relying on fluent written and oral communication.

Photographic records of work in progress were produced to help students recall the choices they had made and to provide assessment evidence along with video diaries. At the end of each class, the pairs of students filmed their work and recorded a brief discussion about the techniques and materials used, identifying particular highlights or things they would do differently another time. These video diaries helped to build confidence and the habit of critical reflection, and enabled the Brighton students to review their own development as advocates.

Meeting the demand for written theoretical assignments in existing units – even with the adjustments sanctioned by disability legislation – was more of a challenge. Eventually we opted for alternative funding arrangements through the Learning and Skills Council, to enable the course to be developed around the students, rather than trying to make it (and them) fit into pre-existing structures.

This freedom allowed more innovative approaches to teaching and assessment, many of which are transferable to university teaching. For instance, we have recently been exploring the systematic use of students' protective white overalls as a vehicle for reflection. Time is set aside for students to record the day's achievements and ideas and future plans by drawing, writing, printing or stitching on their overalls. This literal embodiment of experience provides a visible and tactile prompt which is particularly helpful for people with learning difficulties, and has been enthusiastically and creatively adopted by the University students. The possibilities of this approach have also attracted interest from staff in other subjects, seeking alternatives to the current dominance within higher education of purely verbal models of reflective practice.

Visual and experiential prompts are important throughout the course. Sessions begin with a review of the ground-rules agreed by the group to ensure a safe working environment. Each ground-rule has a specific hand gesture as a reminder and for use during quiet times or across a crowded room. One a2a student commented: 'We would be upside down without them'.

There is also a gallery of photos of each of the group members, their advocates, and all staff and support workers. a2a students check the gallery when they arrive each morning to see who is away or who to welcome back. The group then talks through the format of the day, noting how many sessions are left until the end of term. A customised wall calendar and day chart helps to reinforce this and avoid students being faced with sudden change. Such structure is important because many people with learning difficulties have experienced life in day centres and care homes with a high turnover of staff, where people who they see as friends may disappear without warning.

Terms end with a special 'goodbye' activity for the final week. In one such session all the students made prints about an enjoyable memory of working together and then swapped them with their partners. This allowed the advocates and a2a students to exchange a gift, a souvenir of their time together, providing a ceremonial 'full stop' to their shared experience.

Because many adults with learning difficulties have had limited opportunities to make informed choices about their own lives, the course has also been designed to help develop decision-making alongside artistic skills and self-expression.

After early 'taster' classes in print-making, painting, sculpture and textiles, for instance, students chose an area to specialise in for the rest of the term. This was an important decision that needed to be made on the basis of clearly remembered information and experience. Once they were ready to make a choice, they literally voted with their feet by standing next to the area representing the subject they wished to specialise in.

Students also need to gain the confidence to interact effectively with tutors and other students, to talk freely about their work and ideas, and above all to make their own decisions about what they are doing.

> It was fun and concentrating, thinking quite a lot, making decisions of whether we were finished or not and about eyebrows and all of that. (*Hastings Access to Art II student*)

An emotionally and physically safe environment is vital, and to achieve this involves establishing clear ground rules, mutual respect and (crucially) enough time for each student to have their voice heard.

> C is very proud of her work. She describes in detail how she makes or paints each piece; which she completes herself. (Someone else used to do her work for her, which defeated the object)... Finally someone can see beyond C's disability and encourage her to be herself. (*Parents of C, a Hastings Access to Art II student*)

However, learner autonomy should not prevent educational challenge. It is common for students with learning disabilities to be under-stretched, where carers and teachers have tried to protect them from mistakes or difficulties. Raising expectations means encouraging ambitious ideas and helping students to take risks and learn from, rather than avoid, mistakes.

This is one way in which the course differs from more informal arts activities for people with learning difficulties. Most art students have acquired basic visual knowledge and drawing skills at school. Without these, a2a students' ability to put their ideas into practice, and their opportunities for creative self-expression, would remain limited. Tutors must judge the right time to persuade someone to try a new approach rather than let them stick to familiar processes.

Observational drawing, especially life drawing, has been particularly challenging. People with learning disabilities are used to being stared at and scrutinised by professionals and the public, rather than themselves possessing the power of the gaze (Foucault, 1977; Reeve, 2002). They may find eye contact difficult and need support and training in looking skills. All kinds of visual exercises with viewfinders, photographs and digital video are used to improve confidence.

> We talked about the differences between our portraits, and [how] to mix flesh colours ...so I suggested using a photo of a friend. I could point at the photo and encourage her to look closely, and to then say whether the colour we were mixing was close, or needed to be darker or lighter ...I also put some paint on my hand to try to illustrate the differences between our colours and actual skin tone. (*Advocate diary*)

One student was reluctant to experiment with colour, so we brought in paint charts from DIY stores and encouraged her to pick the shade she liked best and then find out how to mix it. 'Mixing my own colours' was referred to with pride some months later when reviewing her achievements for the year.

Whenever students learn something new we also encourage them to make a note (written, drawn, collaged or photocopied) in their sketch books or on their overalls so they can refer to it later. This helps recall previous experience and reinforce the learning.

Some techniques are new to the University students, allowing the a2a students to share the knowledge they have gained previously.

> I learnt how to make a screen for printing and how to get the image onto the screen by exposing it [to light] then washing the emulsion off with a jet washer. [My partner] was really confident in this as he had done this many times before. (*Advocate diary*)

It is a novel and valuable experience for students with learning disabilities to teach someone else, so we have created additional opportunities for them to demonstrate techniques to other people. This is reflected in the 'milestones' for every process and learning outcome which we have now drawn up to help students recognise their learning and develop at their own pace. Each of these has four levels: 'I can do it with help/ by myself/ remember how/ show someone else how'.

Where are we now?

Access to Art has now begun to receive some national recognition, initially through a 2003 film *Degrees of Separation* in which the students showed their work and spoke about their ambitions. This attracted widespread interest and helped to publicise the project. By the time they completed the third and final year of the pilot course, the students had been invited by Mencap to contribute to an exhibition and conference on disability arts at Tate Modern.

It is tempting (and good for further fundraising) to present this as a simple triumphalist narrative: 'From day centre to Tate Modern in just three years'. But not every member of the original group completed that journey.

B was a talented and committed student, working quietly most of the time with her partner at the table in the art room, absorbed in her drawing and printmaking. But she required more support than the other students and needed a predictable and regular timetable. Occasional bouts of anxiety were expressed by shouting and swearing which could be heard in other classrooms along the corridor. This disruptive behaviour led to a number of requests for her to be excluded from the college, although disability legislation enabled this to be challenged. However, when funding difficulties led to an experienced tutor being replaced by a trainee, it became impossible to accommodate B safely at the college and she was unable to return to the course for the final year. This outcome is a source of continuing frustration to everyone concerned, and a reminder of how many barriers to integration remain.

However, the other members of the original group decided to stay together. As an independent artists' group calling themselves the Rockets, they successfully applied for funding from the Arts Council, which has allowed them to carry on working together once a week, with support from a tutor and some undergraduate helpers, in a rented professional space at the Phoenix Studios in Brighton. They benefit from being part of a wider artistic community, although some miss the social aspects of going to college, and recently held a successful exhibition at the Phoenix.

Access to Art has a new group of students and advocates and has also relocated to the Phoenix, partly because of space constraints on the main Sussex Downs campus and partly so that the two groups can work alongside each other. Andrew Apicella, one of the original eight, talked about how he could now advise other people:

> Whoever wants to can come to the Rockets group and then I would give them a bit of how to do it. They need the practice on the drawing first, and then if they want to go on the lino cutting they would know what to do because I've got some bits on my overall [a reference to his record of the process]. And [I would tell them] not to go too deep and keep your fingers away, never put your fingers where the blade is going ...

Everyone has gained from their engagement with the course and with each other. The regular reviews have brought big increases in confidence:

> Enjoy seeing myself speaking about my work, created drawings and stuck in pictures, lots of different ideas.

> I like seeing my work together – I have too much work but I didn't leave anything out.

> Made lots of paintings, made lots of cloth (batik) mixing own colour, video diary very nice liked it. Group nice, nice to look at famous artists' work. Enjoyed sketch book, learning to talk about work. Pleased with portfolio.

> (*All quotes from a2a student reviews*)

Two of the group, Andrew Apicella and Louella Forrest, have also given public presentations about their work and the project, while a print by Peter Cutts was chosen for the University of Brighton's Christmas card in 2005. Most of the other artists have also sold work, providing a small degree of financial independence, and had it reproduced in various publications about the project.

This kind of external recognition carries more than professional rewards. One student disclosed in a recent interview that the course had given her a new identity as a daughter – now that her work was publicly admired, she felt for the first time that her mother was genuinely proud of her.

Though their participation lasts only a term, the rewards for the University students have been equally tangible. They gain an intensive training in arts facilitation, and much else besides. One wrote:

> My traditional communication forms were challenged and I had to devise communication routes specific to the artist I was working with. I have increased my communication skills – I had to be creative to become an effective communicator … Not answering on behalf of others, letting the artists have the time to decide and speak for themselves. It challenged and increased my understanding of art and my own art skills. (*Brighton advocate*)

This student received a Higher Education Funding Council for England (HEFCE) Student Volunteering Opportunities Award for her work with a2a while the course itself was commended as 'an innovative model which should be adopted far and wide'.

The challenge of creative communication has inspired many of the students at Brighton and Hastings:

> Overall my experience at PAW has been totally positive. Not that its been all smiles and holding hands in unity … It was a lengthy and tiring procedure, coming to terms and peace with the fact that one must work with what they are shown [by people with learning difficulties], in terms of communication. I started to remember that

that is how you start to make friends, build relationships; it is a two way thing. Then I started to relax ... (*Hastings advocates*)

I found it was possible to communicate through non-verbal signs and through marks made in the art itself. This was incredibly exciting for me, as I have often found it difficult in the past to communicate in words with people who are articulate, let alone those with little or no speech, so this was an exceptionally liberating experience. (Brighton advocate)

'Liberation' is a constant theme, with students experiencing the course as a chance to rediscover the pleasures of art making for its own sake.

... I have gotten so much from the experience. It's given me a renewed appreciation for all the components of art; colour, space, texture, and the physical part of making ...

I learnt a huge amount from the [learning disabled] students themselves about how to draw without being too premeditated about the end result. This project gave us all the freedom to be uninhibited with a wider range of materials on a vast range of scales, from A6 portraits to enormous canvases we could throw things at or walk over.

... The more the project progressed, the more I felt able to be experimental with the art that was being produced, to get lost in the process without worrying about the end product ... (*Hastings advocate*)

Where next?

Despite the successes, a2a continues to search for sustainable funding and enough trained tutors to spread the scheme more widely. The project partners are currently developing a new training course for arts educators to help with this. As Alice says:

What do you need for it to happen everywhere?... It's about trying to make a change in education and provision that impacts on as many people as it can. I feel now there is a model that works. The serious ingredients are people that know what they're doing – people who are skilled and professional in the community/voluntary sector; and people who have a really particular range of skills (artistic, administrative, teachers, organised, in fifth gear a lot of the time).

Perhaps the last word should go to one of the former students. Interviewed about the past few years, Andrew was more interested in talking about the work he was planning next:

I would like to do a plane taking off, and then ...have two big squares added together. One big one here the other rocket would be on the stand waiting to take off to the moon and then turning into space then on the second one I will put a runway, a long runway, going from the one that I started on and then get the plane to take off – and I always do a curve at the end of the runway … you'll see the front wheel going up and you always see a curve to let you know the plane is going up and the wheels …[*his hand gestures in an upward curve*].

Later, he summed up the key point of a2a and the Rockets group:

I would say it's the learning that's important. If you can't do the lino cutting until you see somebody else doing it – that's what came into my head when I saw Leo …Learning is quite hard to start [but] once you get the hang of it, then you get …once you go, start guiding yourself, then you get the hang of it …[*and he gestures again, his hand swooping up from an imaginary runway*].

Authors' note

Early drafts of some sections of this chapter were included in the following conference publications, 'Access to Art: testing the limits of diversity and inclusion' *Diversity and difference in lifelong learning,* Proceedings of the 35th Annual Conference of SCUTREA (Standing Conference on University Teaching and Research in the Education of Adults) 2005, and 'Access to Art and the Overalls Project' Higher Education Academy *Curriculum Innovation for Diversity* September 2006.

The chapter is dedicated to Andrew Apicella, a key contributor, who died just as the book was going to press; one of the original members of the a2a Rockets group, his creativity and humour inspired everyone who knew him.

References

Adult Learning Inspectorate (2006) *Greater Expectations, provision for learners with disabilities.* Coventry: Adult Learning Inspectorate. Available online at http://www.ali.gov.uk/Publications/Publications/Feb-Jun_2006/greater_expections.htm

Foucault, M. (1977) *Discipline and Punish: The birth of the prison.* London: Penguin.

Fox, A. (2001) *Research into the training needs of artists with learning difficulties in East Sussex,* Unpublished report carried out by Carousel on behalf of the Arts Council. Carousel is available online at http://www.carousel.org.uk

Further Education Funding Council (FEFC) (1996) *Summary of the Report of the Further Education Funding Council Learning Difficulties and/or Disabilities Committee chaired by Professor John Tomlinson.* London: HMSO.

Learning and Skills Council (2005) *Through inclusion to excellence: The report of the steering group for the strategic review of the LSC's planning and funding of provision for learners with learning difficulties and/or disabilities across the post-16 learning and skills sector.* Coventry: Learning and Skills Council. Available online at http://readingroom.lsc.gov.uk/Lsc/2005/research/consultation/through-inclusion-to-excellence-summary.pdf

Mencap (2002) *Doing, showing and going: Mencap's arts strategy.* Available online at http://www.mencap.org.uk/download/arts_plan.pdf

Reeve, D. (2002) 'Negotiating psycho-emotional dimensions of disability and their influence on identity constructions', *Disability and Society*, Vol. 17, No. 5, pp. 493–508.

UK Parliament Select Committee on Education and Skills (2006) *3rd Report.* Available at http://www.publications.parliament.uk/pa/cm200506/cmselect/cmeduski/478/47804.htm

Chapter 12

Open architecture
Process and product

Andre Viljoen and Lynne Ward with Michael Aling, Dana Cohen, Margaret Maiden and Philip Miller

Introduction

The University of Brighton's Open Architecture project started in 2002 and since this time has worked on 13 different projects. This chapter focuses on two of these projects funded by Cupp, as case studies to delve deeper into the partnership elements involved in both 'process' and 'outcome'.

Background

Open Architecture is the name given to the organisational framework which facilitates community partnership projects within the University of Brighton's School of Architecture and Design. The programme gives students the opportunity to participate in 'live projects' – working with real clients on real sites with the aim of producing a real product, or built structure. Many of the projects have been located in deprived areas to tackle the complex social, economic and environmental issues that exist. Such issues of themselves require the involvement of a range of partners, providing immense opportunity and necessity for collaborative working, and require different roles to be taken on at different stages of the project. For much of the time, as proposals evolve through a process of design workshops and reviews with students, academics and community partners, the whole team works simultaneously as partners and learners.

Each partnership presents its own set of particular opportunities, requirements and challenges relating to desired outcomes, timescale, skills set available and budget. For a School of Architecture, these projects offer many opportunities for learning by 'doing', and this is a major driving force which encourages staff to want to overcome the practical challenges which may be evident from the outset of a project (Suarez-Balcazar *et al.*, 2005). A seminal and contemporary model for live architectural projects is provided by 'Rural Studio' in rural west Alabama (Oppenheimer Dean and Hursley, 2002).

Live projects therefore involve an assignment set for students, which requires them to work to a brief set by a community or commercial partner. Feedback from students shows they value the learning experience involved. Students who had actively participated in the two projects described here appreciated that the opportunities to acquire organisational and networking skills gave them the experience to gain professional skills, and helped them develop social skills such as working in large groups.

The two projects

The two projects are the 'Shade' project at Kingston Buci First School and the Youth Shelter project at Parklands Park, both in a deprived area of West Sussex. The Shade project had a brief to design and construct a shaded play and seating area in the grounds of a primary school. The Youth Shelter project aimed to construct an innovative structure in which older children and young people could play and hang out. The projects were supported with £20,000 from the Brighton and Sussex Community Knowledge Exchange (BSCKE) to develop design proposals and seek additional funding bids. Construction costs were excluded. The money bought out teaching time for a subject leader and funded a full-time associate post over a year. Three students who had worked on a previous Open Architecture project took on the associate post on a job-share basis. The School of Architecture's research room and workshops were made available for the duration of the project. University staff and departments not directly involved with the project provided some technical support and our professional partners gave their support, advice and involvement free of charge. Enthusiasm, commitment and active involvement were also provided by members of the community. Essential insurance cover in the form of professional liability and personal cover were made available through the University and the BSCKE team oversaw the monitoring of the projects.

In the summer of 2004 four architect graduates had successfully built a play structure at Kingston Buci School working in partnership with the pupils. Due to its success the headteacher asked if the students would be prepared to work on an additional project to design and construct a shaded play and seating area in the school grounds.

The project began in April 2005 and prototypes of the design were built in May 2005, with the intention that construction could be supervised by the associates in the summer of 2005.

The project was designed with 30 pupils from a particular class. The associates held a daylong workshop where children were asked to build large shading areas using provided materials. The associates acted as technicians and helped the children erect their desired shaded area from large cardboard posts, card sheeting, tarpaulins and string, and also documented the workshop. Later the associates returned to the class with a range of scale models translating elements of the children's ideas into designs for more permanent solutions. The children found the choice of proposals exciting and held a vote for their favourite.

Structural Engineering advice about the structural requirements of the design and its safety led to design changes to reduce the overall cost. Meanwhile, however, the school had been unsuccessful in its initial application for capital funds of £5,000, and was now under review due to demographic changes resulting in the need for fewer school places. As a consequence, further development of the Shade proposal did not proceed.

The Youth Shelter project was initiated when the community development officer from Adur District Council approached the School of Architecture about the need to build a youth shelter for a community suffering from low income, poor health status and, of particular concern, extremely low academic achievements. Consultation suggested a real lack of facilities and services for young people, who wanted somewhere to 'hang out' and meet with friends. They envisaged a youth shelter which would be more innovative, exciting, involving and welcoming than the traditional metal constructions in other areas. A project to design and construct a shelter with the active involvement of local people was devised, that would create the shelter and also, by working with the community, increase community involvement, social capacity and cohesion.

Working with young people was inspiring; but like the Shade project, resulted in an initial design that was ambitious and costly. A second stage of design development was required to create a safe construction within budget, with the continued consultation of the young residents.

Like the Shade project, the initial funding bid was unsuccessful. However, this had an unexpected positive effect in that it really tested the strength, resolve and robustness of the partnership. All partners supported those who had submitted the bid and the sense of involvement and commitment increased.

Learning in partnership

The first learning outcome was perhaps not surprisingly, the need to identify the partnership. At Kingston Buci School the pupils and staff were easily identified, a single administrative infrastructure existed for the whole community, and young children were easy to engage in the 'designing through play' strategy which the associates and teachers adopted. The partners here were relatively stable.

For the youth shelter, the same community was less easy to define. Working with youth clubs was successful as there was a captive audience of young people and an extremely innovative design emerged. Yet it could be argued that this failed to engage with 'hard to reach young people', including those who had been excluded from school (and so could not attend the youth club due to its location on school grounds); or who chose simply not to attend the club.

Our commitment to partnership was based in our desire to implement a 'whole system working' approach, as devised by Pratt *et al.*: 'Whole system working helps people make organisational connections that enable them to find sustainable solutions to local concerns' (Pratt *et al.*, 1999, p. 3). In a whole system, all parts are interconnected, adapting to change and evolving, with each element playing an important part in the system as a whole, and addressing issues such as trust, power, passion and sustainability.

We found that successful learning in partnership, in which our projects were part of a whole system, required us to trust local resourcefulness (Pratt *et al.*, 1999). In both case studies local people were consulted about their needs and then took a lead role in the design and location of the structures. The involvement of the community development officer and headteacher helped to bridge any potential gap that existed between the University partners and local partners. Both were trusted by the young people involved and both trusted and had confidence in the abilities of local people. Nevertheless, the University members had to adapt to working with young children and other community members who had little experience of architecture and architects, and to work hard themselves to gain trust.

Passion is also key to partnership working: 'people choose to participate when they feel passionate about something' (Pratt *et al.*, 1999, p. 18). We found that all partners were passionate about the projects, many giving up their spare time, unpaid, to participate. The community members, young people and children were particularly passionate about the impact of the projects for them. Where intense passion exists, there is also the possibility of 'burnout' of individuals, particularly those in the community sector that are doing this work in their 'free time'.

Learning in partnership required us all to address issues of power. In the case of the youth shelter, we found an informal web of communication and relationships, a diverse range of partners and different cultural and organisational structures. This complicated power structure may have been a stumbling block for the project, leading to logistical and time problems, but it reflected the project's ethos of local people being key drivers. Participants told us:

I feel important in this project. (*Sophie, age 15*)

There hasn't been one leader, this is a partnership project. (*Chair of community group*)

The project has been led by different people at different times, according to the point we've been at in the project and who has had the relevant expertise. (*BSCKE Development Manager*)

Maintaining the capacity for students and community partners to work together successfully placed an onus on good communication. Inadequate communication is often cited as a cause of failure in collaborative projects (Hornby, 1993). Traditional methods of staying in touch through daytime telephone calls and email proved inappropriate for the youth shelter project. The young people would have preferred text messaging as adults from the community were unavailable during office hours because they held down full-time jobs unrelated to the project. The sheer volume of work of many partners also made staying in touch difficult at times, with innovative projects of this type losing priority to statutory duties of the post holder. Involving community members in deprived areas also posed a challenge: whether through despondency, despair or membership of transient populations, some of the most disenfranchised local residents chose not to become involved.

More positively, we chose to celebrate success and believe it is significant in cementing partnerships (Australian Government: Department of Transport and Regional Services, 2003). We found local newspapers willing and keen to publish news items, often as features, relating to Open Architecture events. The effectiveness of these with respect to building esteem within the partnership came as quite a surprise.

Both projects learnt hard lessons about funding, for community and university participants. We learnt from these projects that the conventional chronology to realise a built project –

• design development and final specification
• construction
• running and maintenance

– cannot apply in a community partnership project. These projects need to be able to guarantee funds from the outset, starting with the running costs. Putting these funds in place requires time, knowledge and its own funding. This capacity is rarely possessed by a loose network of partners.

The whole issue of how and who raises funds provokes an important question about how partnership projects are viewed. Both projects were working in areas with high indices of social deprivation; both addressed issues of social inclusion and aspiration; both could be seen as being exploitative, of the communities of Kingston Buci School and Parklands, and the 'professional' partners, all of whom contributed significant time and effort, and built upon the expectations of the community, only to fall foul of the main reason for the high indices of deprivation, a lack of money.

Our experience is that, working within a competitive funding environment requires a clear funding strategy at the start of a project. Successful projects require community partners who are willing and able, often with external support, to take on the responsibility for leading fund raising.

The emphasis on learning through partnership should not obscure specific learning outcomes for the students. Design is at the centre of interest for

Open Architecture. There must be the opportunity for students to engage in a challenging design process, in which preconceptions are distinct from constraints, such as budget or timescale.

All the projects undertaken by Open Architecture so far have taken much longer to complete than anticipated, due to the number of parties involved, the time required to build and sustain relationships with a range of stakeholders, and unforeseen circumstances. Some design work had to be undertaken voluntarily by the associates as funding became depleted.

The two case studies show that the students have learnt a great deal about the nature of developing a sophisticated design idea with input from direct and articulate clients, and about dealing with external constraints. Students who have participated in these projects are in a far stronger position to set up as independent practitioners, and also to make clear choices about how they might wish to practice in the future. The close relationships with clients/future users, which proved so beneficial in developing appropriate design solutions and sustainable design solutions, is not always evident in commercial practice, where standard, and not necessarily appropriate solutions may be demanded by clients.

Reflections

Our involvement in the two projects described here prompts reflection. Firstly, there is the issue of flexibility. In comparing different models for university and community engagement, Mulroy, and Strand et al., note the need for flexible curriculums within universities (Mulroy, 2004; Strand et al., 2003). Finding ways of accommodating this flexibility within academic programmes such as Architecture, where the requirements of professional validating bodies tend towards a rigid curriculum is a real challenge that requires further discussion, development and consensus at a national level.

Secondly, there is a difference, inherent in live practice work and partnership working, between consuming and participation. In the case studies much of the partnership value was gained by giving voice to community members as participants not merely consumers. The point was to identify valid needs for which appropriate, particular and sustainable solutions owned by the communities could be developed. Superficial needs could have been met more cheaply and without the ownership by selecting an off-the-shelf item from a catalogue of playground equipment. The projects tested the notion that bespoke constructions better met the needs of their users.

Thirdly, the projects showed the cost of collaboration. Much literature suggests (Lerner et al., 1998) that university partnership projects are about building esteem within communities whilst working to tackle poverty. The added value given to improvements, which result from intensive partnership working will therefore come with a cost. The practical consequence is that projects can become bogged down in futile debates which aim to compare the cost of a mass-produced standard product, with a one-off-design for a particular situation. Value needs to be given to the process of arriving at a particular design and to the wider benefits which will arise from communal ownership of that process.

Fourthly, the relationship between process and outcome is complicated. Both case study projects have met the strict requirements of the BSCKE award, which was to develop design proposals and funding bids, but neither has received funding to cover the cost of construction. In the case of Kingston Buci School this was largely unavoidable: the County Council's school review resulted in a proposal for the school to change its function to a 'children's centre'. For the youth shelter project an unsuccessful bid was submitted. At the time of writing, a new funding bid has been submitted by the local authority, demonstrating an ongoing commitment to the project.

Although nearly all partners viewed the construction of the Shade Project and the Youth Shelter as the desired outcomes, other significant positive outcomes can be identified. The educational and aspirational benefits of both projects for school pupils and young residents have been noted by many including the headteacher, the chair of the residents group and Ofsted.

> The experience of working with other groups was very positive. Whilst needing to be flexible, the school gained a tremendous amount from the project. Pupils were able to see how their ideas were turned into reality, whilst the staff were amazed at how diligently the students undertook the task and saw it through to conclusion. (*Headteacher, Kingston Buci First School*)

> Visits out of school and visitors to the school also help to enrich the curriculum, for instance when architects and artists help pupils to improve the outside environment. (*Official OFSTED School Inspection Report (Sept 04) for Kingston Buci First School*).

> It is fantastic and reassuring that there is the help and expertise to bring about the changes we need in our community. (*Chair of Community Group*)

The university has been demystified. The projects have helped communities to visualise and be actively involved in positive change in their environments. University students were afforded valuable opportunities to engage in live projects, amounting to more than simply 'work experience'. The organic nature of development in these projects led to a real world experience: successes, failures, warts and all. Community 'professionals' have rethought how they work.

> All partners have been committed and prepared to put in the effort and support required. There have been no sleeping partners. This project has completely changed the way that I now work, with

partnership working being key to the initiatives I am involved with. (*District Council (Parks) Group Manager*)

The main benefit of the project has been the extremely successful and rewarding partnership working. (*District Council, Community Development Officer*)

We hope all these are durable legacies from the partnerships described in this chapter.

References

Australian Government: Department of Transport and Regional Services. (2003) *Community and Campus – the benefits of engagement. Research findings.* Web site accessed 25 May 2006, http://www.dotars.gov.au/rural/rdp/compendium/research_findings.aspx

Hornby, S. (1993) *Collaborative care. Professional, interagency and interpersonal.* Oxford: Blackwell Scientific Publications.

Lerner, R.M. and Simon, L.A.K. (1998) 'The new America outreach university', in R.M. Lerner and L.A.K. Simon (eds.), *University-community collaborations for the twenty-first century*, pp. 3–23. London: Garland.

Mulroy, E.A. (2004) 'University civic engagement with community-based organizations: dispersed or coordinated models?' *Journal of Community Practice*, Vol. 12, No. 3–4, pp. 35–51.

Oppenheimer Dean, A. and Hursley, T. (2002) *Rural Studio.* New York: Princeton Architectural Press.

Pratt, J., Gordon, P. and Plamping, D. (1999). *Working whole systems.* London: Kings Fund.

Strand, K., Marullo, S., Cutforth, N., Stoecker, R. and Donohue, P. (2003) 'Community partnership practices', in K. Strand, S. Marullo, N. Cutforth, R. Stoecker and P. Donohue (eds.), *Community-based research and Higher Education: principals and practices* (pp. 43–70). San Francisco: Jossey Bass.

Suarez-Balcazar, J., Harper, G.W., and Lewis, R., (2005) 'An interactive and contextual model of community–university collaborations for research and action', *Health Education and Behaviour*, Vol. 32, No. 1, pp. 84–100.

Chapter 13

'Art in the Woods': An exploration of a community/university environmental arts project

Juliet Millican with Sue Nunn and Alice Fox

Introduction

'Art in the Woods' is a project involving students from the Faculty of Arts and Architecture and women from an arts group based on a local council estate. This chapter offers some conclusions about the crucial elements in partnership projects that create learning opportunities for students in community settings. It draws from models of service learning in the US and Australia, and looks at how we have adapted these to fit our particular context in the South of England. The chapter explores the collaboration and mutual understanding that grew up in the project and the significance of art as a cross-cultural language in building relationships between people with very different personal histories. It draws on video diaries made during the project. While the project itself lasted for only a few weeks, the chapter suggests a longer impact on the people involved and the potential for developing in all participants a broader understanding of other ways of living.

Background

Art in the Woods involved nine art students from the University of Brighton and six women from a local council estate across four days in National Trust woodland on the edge of the South Downs. The project participants foraged in the trees and wrestled with plants and logs to create huge, organic woodland sculptures. The sculptures, a giant, a spider, a web, some rabbits, emerged from their joint experience and the forms suggested by the landscape and the materials on hand. These sculptures still nestle snugly among the trees, sprouting bluebells and celandines and offering shelter to local wildlife. Their size and capacity for growth indicate the achievement of their makers in placing their own mark on the landscape. They represent the start of an ongoing partnership between two very different groups of people and what can be achieved through collaborative working.

The idea for a partnership project was initiated by the National Trust warden who attended a presentation on a2a (see Chapter 11) and saw the potential for groups to work on National Trust land. The coming together of three partners, the University, a community arts group and the National Trust, provided the opportunity for the students to work together in a space that was both neutral and equally challenging to both student groups, each of whom generally inhabit very different areas of the city, and on a different scale. Getting to know and overcoming the geographical challenges of working there contributed to confidence raising and provided them with a sense of belonging in a place they had not previously visited.

Service Learning

Service learning, an American term, links university students with community groups as part of their degree studies. It combines credit-bearing and service activity with reflection in order to expand a student's knowledge of course content and discipline as well as their sense of civic responsibility (Bringle and Hatcher, 1996). Service learning outcomes for students typically focus on four domains: personal competence; interpersonal relationships; an understanding of community service as a charitable responsibility; and an understanding of service learning as social justice (Wang et al., 2005). This model of 'service' has since been challenged somewhat in the UK (Holland, 2005; Tett, 2005), and the US (Lewis, 2004), and perhaps fits more into a now outdated 'welfare' rather than a 'rights based' approach to community development. Cupp's key philosophy of mutual benefit, of knowledge exchange rather than knowledge transfer, does not sit well with the notion of 'service'. The Student Learning in the Community model that we have evolved at Cupp is based on attitudes to learning that have more in common with Dewey, Piaget, Kolb (1984) and Freire (1996). Kolb's model of the learning cycle stresses the importance of reflection, of practical experience and active experimentation alongside theoretical learning. Freire highlights the value of experience and reflection on experience of action. While the US model combines what it sees as a 'service experience' with academic content, in Cupp we are more concerned with developing interpersonal skills among all participants and looking at the relevance of academic learning to understanding community issues. The aim of this project was more to involve both groups making art collaboratively in an inclusive environment.

The artists

The women artists came from a local family centre meeting weekly as a group at the primary school on the estate where they lived. The arts group fulfilled a dual role, as 'time out' and support for people whose lives were under pressure, and an opportunity to explore creativity and learning. For many, the group was something of a lifeline. When asked to get involved in this project the women felt they were providing the students with the opportunity to learn more about community arts groups and what life was like for them. They felt they would be sharing their experience with the University and felt they might learn something about art as a result. The women from the art group rarely got the opportunity for a more prolonged experience of making, away from the demands of home, family and children. Four days spent in a completely new environment seemed a good way to provide them with space to focus on themselves and their abilities. Meeting and working with university students offered the potential for breaking down barriers with the University on their doorstep.

Similarly the art students rarely got the opportunity to socialise with people other than students and their immediate peers. Most were living in shared student houses, working in part-time jobs and spending their days painting alone in their university studio and their evenings going out with friends. Many had come straight from school or from gap years spent travelling. They had limited experience of what life might be like for a mother in public housing.

There is a widespread sense of low self-esteem on this estate, in common with any council estate on the outskirts of any major city. Low income, poor employment prospects, poor literacy skills, large families and a lack of local facilities result in an atmosphere of economic and emotional deprivation in which it is difficult for the individual to thrive. The women from the art group, like many residents, were acutely aware of their position in the wider society of the city. Often self-conscious, they felt they were looked down upon by other residents. They would frequently say things like 'When I go down to the town I feel everyone is looking at me as if I've got where I live tattooed on my forehead', and 'people outside here think we are all druggies and thieves just because we live here'. There are whole areas of the city where they will not shop and try not to go, as they feel they do not belong. There was a hope that this project might address some of these issues and help them feel more comfortable among different people in other areas.

There is a very different culture among young students at the University. While their student income is low, they study in the city centre, close to the museum, historic buildings and a range of music and arts venues. While many students come from other parts of England they are brought together as a discrete group, associating almost entirely with other arts students, where they have a small amount of allocated studio space and a lot of allocated studio time. Unlike the women from the art group, for whom their two-hour session a week might be their sole opportunity to think about themselves away from the pressures of home and family, most of an art students' time is devoted to 'developing their art'. This project was one of the few modules not focused on either art history or personal practice, and all the students who opted for it did so because they wanted the experience it offered.

Each group thus brought a different range of skills. By forming relationships and working together, they stood to gain more than they would from working alone. The coordinators saw it as an opportunity for participants to develop greater empathy, and to develop confidence in each individual's talents and worth, through the medium of art.

The learning partnership

Other chapters have explored the power dynamics and the roles of different partners in the Cupp projects. Todd *et al.* (1998, p. 243) suggest that in partnerships between the university and the community: 'Collaborations work best when the partners involved share a similar vision of how to work together'. They suggest three potential models for such collaborations: faculty as consultants, faculty as equal partners and faculty as learners. They suggest that, whilst it is essential to adopt the role that works best in each instance, in a true partnership model, the university 'must be willing to view collaborators as equals in the creative process and willing to invest the time and energy needed to integrate the knowledge of the various partners' (Todd *et al.*, p. 243). True partnerships can only come from a situation in which one partner is not always in charge – 'it is the synergy between the groups rather than the contribution of any one group that is responsible for the outcomes' (Todd *et al.*, p. 245). This invariably requires care where the university, as in this case, is responsible for funding and administering the project. It is facilitated by the willingness of the coordinators to share the different knowledge and skills they bring. Strand *et al.*, put 'sharing worldviews' and 'agreement about goals and strategies' as fundamental characteristics of potential collaborators (2003, p. 43). In this project the long-term friendship between the university lecturer and community group leader went a long way to ensuring the project's success. As in the Open Architecture projects, building trust is essential. From a strong base in the knowledge each of the coordinators had of their different groups, with clear roles and expectations at the beginning, grew the necessary trust and confidence for mutual learning and knowledge exchange (Garlick and Pryor, 2002).

Suarez-Balcazar (2005) emphasises the importance of respecting the culture of the setting and the community in partnership programmes and warns against partners imposing their own culture or values on the partnership. In this project, both groups were anxious about meeting and working with the other. The University students were interested to know about life on the estate, but were quite terrified about handling face-to-face relationships with the people who lived there. The women's group was sure that students would be posh, standoffish and difficult to relate to. They concealed their fears behind a bravado based on greater age and experience. They had practical concerns – about toilets and facilities and being away from their children in an emergency, and about getting to the site. Artistically they worried about not having any ideas, and that the students would think they were stupid. The university students who were used to making and creating things from different materials, to being given projects to design and develop, and to being in new and unexpected situations, anticipated feeling intimidated by working with women whose life experiences were on a much greater scale than their own.

However, in this project, it was clear both groups had much to offer. Students brought with them greater experience of making and a greater confidence in their own creativity but they lacked the practical and quick thinking skills that many of the women possessed. They soon developed a great respect for the women's problem-solving abilities and they enjoyed their sense of humour and willingness to pitch in. They liked the feeling of being able to share the skills they had developed while at university. Overall they were aware of how privileged they were at having time to study and the range of experience and opportunities this gave to them.

Outcomes

The groups worked together for four days using only those materials that were available within the wood or in the surrounding area, binding them together with biodegradable materials, twine, natural paste, the odd nail. They constructed large-scale pieces of art that would not be possible in their studios or school environment. Their inspired response to the woodland and its materials resulted in a highly refined level of visual interpretation. Both groups learnt from the realities of their interaction. The women's art group enjoyed meeting new people, noting how 'everyone has their own group, a normal day would not bring this, we wouldn't normally socialise with people from the university'. They commented on how, before they met the students they 'didn't think they would be in the same league'. The university students talked about how much they learned from the women's problem-solving skills, discussed the experience of overcoming their lack of confidence and learning to work collaboratively.

Those hoping for a future in professional art commissions clearly benefited from the experience of community involvement and community art – fine artists seeking public art commissions need to demonstrate how the process of making art will enrich the life of the local community and to work with and relate to people of different ages and backgrounds. But in addition to this there was a huge amount of incidental or additional learning. The expansive woodland gave the students the opportunity to make work on a large scale.

Box 13.1

'I had the best time.'

'When I sat down for a cup of tea on my own, I'd look round and one of the students was sitting down next to me and talking with me like we were friends, it was great.'

'It really increased my confidence.'

'Since we got back, I've made some flowers out of sticks for my Mum's front garden; my son's been collecting sticks to make things too.'

'There was an old branch down in our garden, and I let my boys (aged six and eight) take the bark off with butter knives. They loved it. I told them they'd done it so carefully, next time I get my money I'm going to get us some chisels.'

'I went out there last weekend with the kids, it still all looks great.'

The women felt they developed self-esteem and confidence in their sculpture and themselves. See Box 13.1 for some of their Comments. They learnt from the university students' knowledge and artistic skills and experienced a different environment where they had greater freedom to express themselves artistically.

Reflections

The longer-term benefits to the women's art group and to individual partnerships are difficult to measure. Material conditions remain a real restriction to more in-depth study. A certificate presentation organised at the University was a genuine celebration and brought them into what had previously been seen as inaccessible territory. But for some, even the logistics of attending the presentation were not easy. Similarly, despite their enthusiasm for the project, for what they achieved in the woodland, and their pride in it, many cannot easily revisit the site due to lack of transport. While the project in some small way contributed to their sense of belonging, in the countryside, on the university campus and among groups by whom they had previously felt intimidated, their opportunities to access these remain limited. In spite of their claims that 'students are just like us really' one of them mentioned seeing a student from the project in town a week later, and not feeling able to say hello. They tackled new challenges, met new people and accessed places they had avoided in the past, and in a small way challenged their sense of self.

But the initiative needs to be built on if it is to have a longer-lasting impact. Art, like music, has always acted as a cross-cultural language – enabling dialogue between people from different places and experiences. One of the key values of projects such as this is the ability to enable dialogue and the development of relationships between people with different life experiences, in the process of making art. Art can reach people, move them, inspire and challenge them, and achieve this 'vital engagement' in ways that no other discipline or approach can (Phillips, 1997; Rogers, 2005). Hawkes (2001) observes that it is through the amorphous dimension of art and culture that social cohesion, community vitality and genuine engagement can be achieved.

At the beginning of the twenty-first century, when social divisions appear increasingly impermeable, the ability to build relationships with people different to ourselves is arguably more important than ever. In this context, universities have committed themselves to widening participation, opening their doors and to seeking mutual benefit through collaborative endeavour. This project suggests such commitments can be realised.

Todd *et al.* suggest:

> Within academia there is no longer one reality of the world. We need a multiplicity of approaches to address the complexity of problems before us and the multiplicity of contexts in which people now reside. To achieve this goal we must re-evaluate how we teach students. More than ever we need students who are broadly educated, who are exposed to many different populations, contexts and methods of enquiry during their training and who can integrate research and practice to address critical social issues. (Todd *et al.*, 1998, p. 251)

The community–university partnership described here through the medium of an inclusive arts project, has hinted at the potential for curriculum innovation for increasing institutional accessibility, and for transforming people's view of the world and their place in it.

References

Bringle, R.G. and Hatcher, J.A. (1996) 'Implementing service learning in higher education', *Journal of Higher Education*, Vol. 67, No. 2, pp. 221–40.

Dewey, J. (1897) 'My pedagogic creed', *The School Journal*, Volume LIV, No 3 (16 January, 1897), pp. 77–80.

Freire, P. (1996) *Pedagogy of the oppressed.* London: Penguin Books.

Garlick, S. and Pryor, G. (2002) *Universities and their communities – creative regional development through knowledge based engagement.* Report for Department of Transport and Regional Services, Canberra.

Hawkes, J. (2001) *The fourth pillar of sustainability: Culture's essential role in public planning*. Melbourne: Common Ground Publishing.

Holland, B. (2005) 'The growing role of community engagement in US higher education', *B-HERT News* 21, pp. 2–4.

Kolb, D.A. (1984) *Experiential learning: Experience as the source of learning and development*. Englewood Cliffs, NJ: Prentice Hall.

Lewis, T.L. (2004) 'Service learning for social change? Lessons from a liberal arts college', *Teaching Sociology*, Vol. 32, No. 1, pp. 94–108.

Phillips, L. (1997) *In the public interest: Making art that makes a difference in the United States*. Crosswell, Pembrokeshire: Comedia.

Piaget, J. (1971) *Biology and knowledge*. Chicago: University of Chicago Press.

Rogers, M. (2005) 'Social sustainability and the art of engagement – the small towns: big picture experience,' *Local Environment*, Vol. 10, No. 2, pp. 109–124.

Strand, K.J., Cutforth, N., Stoecker, R., Murullo, S., Donohue, P. (2003) *Community-Based Research and Higher Education: Principles and Practices*. San Francisco: Jossey Bass Wiley.

Suarez-Balcazar, Y., Harper, G. W., and Lewis, R. (2005) 'An interactive and contextual model of community–university collaborations for research and action', *Health Education and Behaviour*, Vol. 32, No. 1, pp. 84–101.

Tett, L. (2005) 'Partnerships, community groups and social inclusion', *Studies in Continuing Education*, Vol. 27, No. 1, pp. 1–15.

Todd, C.M., Ebata, A.T., and Hughes, R., Jr. (1998) 'Making university and community collaborations work', in R.M. Lerner and L.A.K. Simon (eds.) *University-community connections for the twenty-first century*, pp. 231–54. New York: Garland.

Wang, Y., Ye, F., Jackson, G., Rodgers, R. and Jones, S. (2005) 'Development of Student Service Learning Course Survey (SSLCS) to measure service-learning course outcomes', *IR Applications*, Vol. 3, pp. 1–15.

PART 5
What works

Introduction

The three chapters in the last part of the book provide differing perspectives on how to reflect on and evaluate community–university partnerships. Chapter 14 provides a detailed model for reflecting on whether or not the conditions are right for setting up such a partnership in the first place. It is a model developed through the experiences gained during one particular partnership project that involved therapeutic services for disadvantaged children. In Chapter 15 it is Cupp itself which is under the spotlight, and the chapter reports on an external evaluation undertaken to examine 'what makes community–university partnerships "work"'. It extrapolates factors drawn from interviews by the independent evaluator authoring this chapter, and puts these in the context of the literature on critical success factors. The last chapter in the book is a look to the future to explore what has been learned to date and the issues that arise in moving onto the next phase of work at Brighton.

Although the evaluations offered here – and hopefully the preceding chapters on individual projects – show a positive account, they do not gloss over the difficulties. Cupp did not come as a pre-designed package. It has, as we have made clear throughout this volume, been refined and redefined 'in the doing'. These chapters attempt to sum up what has been learned to date and how that is informing our thinking as we continue to evolve the work represented here.

Chapter 14

An ACE way to engage in community–university partnerships: Making links through Resilient Therapy

Angie Hart and Kim Aumann

Introduction

This chapter explores aspects of the learning and practice development that have been made possible through partnership. We give an account of the dynamic individual and agency partnerships that have emerged in relation to Resilient Therapy (RT), and document some of the challenges such a partnership faces as we move towards sustaining it.

We set out our discussion in relation to a model that one of us has developed through working with Cupp. This framework draws on current organisational and network theory as well as empirical examples from community–university knowledge relations. The model is built around seven dimensions: attractions, conservation, crevices, contingencies, expectations, enlightenment and emergence, ACE for short, and it can be used as an evaluation tool in assessing such partnerships.

In order to illustrate these dimensions we start by asking you to picture the authors of this chapter: Kim the director of Amaze, a parenting charity, and a university student; Angie an academic at Brighton University and the academic co-director of Cupp. Angie is also a child and family therapist on a service level agreement between the university and the NHS. Both are mothers. Kim's children are typically developing, Angie's have special needs. It is Kim's job that Angie's mothering role connects with, as Amaze supports parents of children with special needs. So no surprise then that Angie has been a member of Amaze for ten years. That's longer than Kim has been director of it. The Resilient Therapy approach is set out in Box 14.1.

In this article we look back on our work together to consider what the successes have been, and what challenges still need to be tackled. As we do so, we generalise from our own work to consider what others might take from it. Hence, we use the model we shall call ACE for documenting the drivers, processes and outcomes of partnership working between university and community collaborators (Hart, Blincow with Thomas, 2007).

BOX 14.1

Resilient Therapy (RT): A box of ordinary magic tricks

Masten termed resilience 'ordinary magic' (Masten, 2001). Her idea inspired our use of the magic metaphor to produce materials with parents/carers and young people. RT makes explicit the kind of 'ordinary magic' that needs to happen to foster resilience in disadvantaged children. The approach strategically focuses on 'scaffolding' resilience for these children through the imaginative and creative therapeutic work of resilient promoters such as mental health practitioners, social workers, teachers and parents. The box of tricks provides a strategic framework, together with more specific help and advice. Hence applying RT involves a relentless search for resilient actions that improve outcomes in situations of high disadvantage. This project captures the critical success factors at play in RT and disseminates them.

www.cupp.org.uk/projects/magic.htm

The birth of an idea

Kim and Angie were not the only partners involved in the fairly organic development work of RT. Others joined our community of practice which includes social services, a local charity supporting disadvantaged children, schools, the local education authority and a number of departments in the National Health Service (NHS). Two organisations stand out as key partners: Amaze and the local Child and Adolescent Mental Health Service (CAMHS) where Angie works as a research practitioner.

Throughout the first year, the university partner led the work and the other two main organisations worked with her, but not so much with each other. Fast forward to today: this is still the case. Until now the pace of movement seems justified. We needed to focus on developing RT as a discrete entity in its own right, with its own conceptual framework and internal coherence as a working practice. Too many organisations formally involved in the project might have detracted from that task. However, reflecting on this tight organisational partnership makes us think that if we want our work embedded across a range of organisations, and to increase the pace of dissemination, from now on we need to encourage horizontal links to develop between Amaze and CAMHS and indeed between other organisations.

Whilst organisationally we have evolved RT using this fairly measured approach, we have included many individual people along the way; so plenty of other people might have joined us. Following Wenger *et al.* (2002), we call this loose group of people and the work that we do an emergent community of practice (CoP). This is 'a kind of community created over time by the sustained pursuit of a shared enterprise' (Wenger, 1998, p. 45; see also Smith, 2003). Wenger and Snyder depict it like this: communities of practice are 'groups of people informally bounded together by shared expertise and passion for a joint enterprise' (Wenger and Snyder, 2000, pp. 139–40). The emphasis here is on the voluntary origins of such practice. People in such communities want to do things together. Such self-direction will enable them to 'share their experiences and knowledge in free-flowing, creative ways that foster new approaches to problems' (Wenger *et al.*, 2002, p. 5). However, communities of practice are not without leaders and champions.

The impetus for, and subsequent development of our RT work grew as a synergy of different policies, structures and day-to-day practices. National public policy emphasising user involvement, partnerships between statutory and voluntary sector providers in service to disadvantaged children and their families were key ingredients that set the scene for our work. Sustained commitment at a national level to tackle inequalities in health and the consequences of these for disadvantaged children and their families was also in the picture as was. An emphasis on the concept of resilience in academic literature and in practice accounts were further contributing factors. A national focus on local parent support training brought Amaze as an organisation more fully into the picture.

In the university context, the local development of our Cupp programme promised support to community–university partnerships that tackled inequalities and disadvantage. Nationally, Centre for Knowledge Exchange (CKE) funds were being made available to further this work (see Chapter 2). These synergies enabled modest funds to be secured to support the work. This also provided a structure within the university in which the project could gain momentum.

Dimensions of the framework

Helping practitioners, community members and university workers discover how they can best achieve effective partnership needs unpacking. Yet we do not think that it is possible to provide an absolute blueprint for partnership working. A fairly loose structure and project plan encourages organic development in unexpected, yet uniquely creative ways. Much of the work of community–university partnerships is experimental and experiential; innovation depends on these. Go too far the other way however, and nobody knows what they are doing. As Brown and Duguid (1998) argue, in knowledge exchange work, structure and organic flexibility do need to work in creative tension to curb the worst excesses of each other. There is then merit in providing a framework that provides both a sounding board against which prospective project partners can try out their ideas and a method of benchmarking the status of the partnership along different dimensions at its inception. ACE (see Figure 14.1) is our attempt to do just that. This section summarises the seven dimensions of ACE and illustrates its relationship to our partnership working.

Figure 14.1 The ACE Way

Attractions – What draws the partners to each other?

In the current climate of multi-agency working and the ease with which we can work with others via email, there are a plethora of potential partners for many of us in our working lives. What is it that draws particular partners to each other and helps us stick together in the absence of a contract? One answer is that we are brought together through passion for a common purpose. Social scientists have drawn attention to effective partnerships where professional or work-related passions that colleagues share are often enhanced by personal bonds of friendship and broader shared interests (Fineman, 2000; Jones *et al.*, 2006).

The ACE framework conceives of attractions as different forms of 'capital' that prospective partners bring to the table. In our resilient therapy work we can retrospectively identify the following: purpose, financial, leadership, personal capital, organisational capital, status capital and what we call Aristotelian capital as attractions for different partners. Let us now explain each of these elements in turn.

Regarding *purpose*, we certainly shared a passion for the key issues in RT. For example, as an organisation Amaze was committed to working with disadvantaged families, but they were struggling to do enough with parents managing behaviour issues. For Amaze the RT project was a chance to shine a torch on what they were doing with this particular group of families. And Angie had built up research and practice expertise in working with disadvantaged children and their families over many years.

Financial attractions worked one way since collaborators were drawn to the university because it has (at least modest) finances to support partnership working. However, it is also the case that the other main partners have put in a great deal of resources in kind. The energy that the project has generated has resulted in many people working out of hours.

Regarding *leadership*, as partners we never had an explicit discussion about who was best suited to lead the project, although up until now it has been the university partner who has taken most of the initiative. She led on writing a book on RT (Hart, Blincow with Thomas, 2007), set up workshops, seminars and conference presentations and led on funding proposals. As RT grows, this role looks set to change in some ways with Kim now leading on writing an RT handbook for parents, and Amaze holding the purse strings for that project. Other partners are beginning to take the lead elsewhere. Kim clearly recognised the benefits of being led at the outset: 'If you don't take the lead you've got the chance to be a bit more playful and experimental.'

Personal capital was another driver for Kim. 'I felt quite isolated. There aren't many people in the city who are interested in my field of work or our perspective, so here was a potential colleague. We were both able to work flexibly, out of hours and coped with last minute frenzied planning. And I like ideas and Angie is full of them, so that's a real attraction. You don't get much chance to ponder when you're managing a service.'

An attraction here for Angie was that she perceived Amaze to have particular creative flair. They were unencumbered by conventional ways of presenting information, and put effort into making their meetings accessible to parents. This helped Angie experiment further with her own style.

Organisational capital refers to the attractions that particular organisations bring to the table. Looking back, it was the other lead partner CAMHS, that Amaze wanted to develop a working link with, not the university. Amaze knew parents needed better support around behaviour management. Angie's research-practitioner role and her membership of Amaze were the bridges that led to Amaze linking up with CAMHS. This further alerts us to the need to think about the relationships between multiple partners, not simply assuming, and concentrating on dyadic connections between the university and its partners. Over time though, motivations shifted. As the RT project grew, Amaze became more attracted to the university's organisational capital. They saw the university as a high-status partner for funding applications.

Some partnerships with university academics are driven by the *status* afforded by the university. However, in our context this was not initially the case. The lesson here for others is that the power of academic status should never be assumed. There is work to be done communicating the benefits. Kim reflects: 'We were a bit sceptical about working with the university at first. Our committee is very adamant that our work should be practical and not theoretical. We are avowedly political about not doing research for research's sake. But fortunately the trustees were willing to make an exception.'

Working the other way, Angie had simpler motivations to work with Amaze. She explains, ' "Street-credibility" in the ACE framework is shorthand for academics drawing on "natural laboratories" for our empirical research work. There's a growing need for us to demonstrate real understanding of, and involvement in, the lives of research participants. As a parent-led organisation, Amaze is intimately connected to parents struggling with disadvantaged children.'

However, retrospective analysis of our project suggests that organisational capital as a motivation should sound warning bells. As a rule of thumb, it is acceptable to community groups, but only when accompanied by other forms of capital. Indeed, academics have developed a bad press with community groups because they focus on this above all else for the short while they are involved with the research. Academics stand accused of not really understanding the people with whom they are trying to work, and not really caring that much about developing a thorough understanding. The emphasis is on analysis of findings and then dissemination in learned journals. In our case the hybrid identity of one of us helped get beyond these perceptions.

Aristotelian capital sounds a bit pompous, and you can blame the university partner for thinking of it. But we've stuck with the idea because Aristotle was deeply concerned about leaders acting in a way that promoted the common good, and his ideas remain influential. For example, Richard Layard, a London School of Economics scholar and government advisor promotes Aristotle's notion of the good life in explaining keys to happiness (Layard, 2004, 2005). It is not about charity and self-sacrifice. It enhances our work.

Conservation. What are the unique differences that need to be conserved? What difference does one partner have that another would like? Where are the similarities?

When initial passions have died down and become assimilated into daily partnership practice, where do we go next? We need to focus on conserving. Following Østerlund and Carlile (2005) we have elevated conserving differences over and above points that so often get made in partnership literature on the need for boundary spanners, culture brokers and interpreters between partners (Østerlund, 2006; Wenger, 1998; Wenger *et al.*, 2002). There is much empirical evidence to suggest that effective partnerships include people with hybrid roles and identities. The most obvious example here is that Angie is a university academic, a CAMHS practitioner and an Amaze parent. As time goes on, the other principle project partners have developed hybrid roles through formal affiliations with the university.

However, with so much blurring of roles and identities, and the possibility for the various attractions of the partnership to pull us in many different directions, it seems even more incumbent on us to maintain a focus on where differences and complementarities lie. Hence we need to be very clear about what should be conserved in a separate state. The very notion of partnership depends on it, and without this perspective the concept of exchange seems meaningless. For Amaze, unique links is what they have singled out for conservation above all else. Indeed, those links are key to making Amaze attractive to the university partner.

Amaze has a deep commitment to the community of parents of children with special needs. This gets expressed through efforts to protect their confidentiality, convey their experience accurately, and represent their interests fully to service planners. They have experience of working with parents in groups and facilitating their involvement in new initiatives. Alongside this, Amaze's unique knowledge of the local arena, network of services and government agendas provides them with a perspective that nobody else has. Any work in our community of practice that does not draw on Amaze's unique difference in this regard, or that threatens to undermine it, is unlikely to be taken forward.

For the university, a unique difference is their relentless emphasis on teaching, scholarship and the dissemination of findings. University partners have been educated to focus on evidence underlying practice and their appraisal and reward systems require dissemination of research and scholarship nationally and internationally. This difference can be put to work for the community partner – it can help them work more effectively from an evidence-based starting point, and provide authoritative arguments for practice development.

Once our differences are articulated, we can focus on developing a 'shared repertoire' (Wenger, 1998, p. 83) of routine activity through which people connect, and helpful symbols such as 'boundary objects' and brokers. Boundary objects are joint 'products', for example shared language, project plans, policies and other documentary outputs. A sense of common allegiance can be enhanced by these. In RT we have developed many such boundary objects. This chapter is certainly one of them.

Contingency

Contingency theory in the philosophy of science informs this dimension. This explains that any two conditions will always be moderated by a third, and therefore are always contingent on other factors (Donaldson, 2001; Galtung, 1967). This idea has been taken up in the management literature in the form of contingency management. The claims are that there is no intrinsically best way to manage; rather, the best management approach is contingent on the interplay between the situation and the characteristics of an organisation.

So what contingencies might be apparent in our particular community-university knowledge relation? For the purposes of illustration in this paper, we will outline just two. The strong culture of autonomy both amongst academics and amongst voluntary sector workers is important to grasp. This has certainly helped drive our work forward. It is worth noting that none of our main partnerships have emerged in a context of tight managerial control. In community–university knowledge exchange, it may well be that where a high degree of autonomy is not present, true knowledge exchange may be seriously limited. This assertion warrants further empirical investigation.

Crevices – what holes might we fall down?

Because we feel that there is often too much emphasis on what can go wrong, rather than what can go right, crevices hold a somewhat grudging place in the ACE framework. Retrospectively we can identify certain elements that could have led us to fall down a hole. Perhaps we were particularly lucky that they didn't. Some of the ones that we faced are certainly generalisable to other community–university partnerships. Here are just two examples.

Angie is very attracted to reading and talking about academic scholarship, and derives much work satisfaction from talking about academic knowledge with peers. She couldn't rely on this particular community partner to fulfil that need. Kim reflects, 'I can see that my limited capacity to offer academic cut and thrust might irritate my academic partner ... it takes me a long time to get through this [academic] stuff, and also I have to brace myself for the anxieties it provokes. Perhaps it's only really now, when I feel that the relationship will be sustained, that I think it is actually worth the bother.'

Another example of a crevice is that where universities are concerned, lengthy and bureaucratic processes that are difficult to circumvent can dampen passion and enthusiasm. Angie reflects, 'For project planning, you really do have to consider which elements are particularly threatened by the inflexible wheels of university bureaucracy and plan accordingly. Personnel recruitment and the payment of service users are both key areas that have raised challenges for us.'

Expectations – What kind of a relationship do you expect to have? What model of knowledge exchange is implied in this particular relationship?

This aspect of the framework asks us to look closely at the expectations we have of our prospective partners, to understand what they are and to consider whether or not they are realistic given what we know by now about our mutual attractions, conservation, contingencies and crevices. In particular, it focuses on our expectations of the knowledge relationship.

A distinction can be made between knowledge transfer and knowledge exchange. For our purposes in this paper, the dimensions of knowledge transfer and knowledge exchange can be understood as each occupying opposite ends on a knowledge relations continuum. There is elitism and status inequality implicit in the notion of university knowledge transfer and we recognise the unique merit in a more egalitarian exchange. Employing the notion of a knowledge relations continuum enables us to appreciate that our knowledge relations do not need to be set in stone. As we have seen in our own partnership, whilst we have always termed our work knowledge exchange, in reality we did start off further down the university knowledge transfer end. However, this is not now where we find ourselves.

Enlightenment – How do we change as a result of joint enterprise? How have things changed around here? What have we learnt to do differently?

In our partnership, some demonstrable changes have certainly occurred. The way in which trust relations have developed between us stands out. We can, to some extent, take each other for granted in a way that we could not before. Advice and support in both directions is on tap. But what are the consequences of this mutual trust and support for future work? One is that the development of this relationship enables us to move more quickly. We can seize opportunities that might previously have taken months to bring to fruition, or which we may have missed out on.

A further example of these mature relations of trust is that to some degree they allow us to swiftly move into different structures and relationships that assume each other's participation. Maturity brings the opportunity to develop exchange relationships that more closely resemble what anthropologists have described as 'gift exchange'. These are exchange relations based on cultural, rather than economic capital (Mauss, 2000). In such relationships neither university nor community partners will require immediate recompense for their gift rendered. Delayed reciprocity begins to feature, and to become embedded in the culture of each organisation. An example from our work is that whilst Amaze gets some benefits from writing this book, it is clearly a university led and university-motivated project, closely aligned to our core business of research, scholarship and their dissemination. And yet the organisation has partici-pated fully.

Let us now turn our attention to our shared passion. What can we say that we now do differently as a result of partnership working to improve the odds for disadvantaged children? For Angie, 'I'd be really surprised now if I set up an innovative research project without community partners thoroughly involved in it ... My former ways of working, where the practice outcomes of research and scholarship were, if I'm honest, somewhat vague and elusive, seem almost unthinkable now. And I'm now more attuned than ever to using the status of the university wherever we can to promote the interests of disadvantaged children and their families.'

From Kim's perspective, she has the following to say: 'Our organisation has changed a lot as a result of our joint work ... It has given us a better language to talk about our work. We know how to articulate clearly to others much of what we were doing already. Another example is that we now automatically do a literature search to check the evidence-base before we even think about setting off on a new piece of work. And we've got a much better understanding of monitoring and evaluation which has enabled us to improve our processes.'

Emergence – What new space might open/has opened up? What does it look like? Can we go so far as to describe them as spheres of innovation?

This dimension of the framework helps us structure our thinking about whether indeed something has, or will emerge from knowledge exchange that is more than the sum of our parts.

We have all started to spend more time on each other's territory, Kim has particularly appreciated the library, computing facilities and opportu-nities for academic debate that the university affords. However, we would not want to go so far as to occupy a completely new space, for example setting up another organisation external to all of our current affiliations. Our partnership to date has benefited from the Cupp approach (Hart and Wolff, 2006), where there is strong partnering of academics and practi-tioners and even research practitioners in a combined project that links many separate organisations together, with the university as a lynchpin. Lots of different people have been involved in the development of RT and there has been some cross-fertilisation so we have been able to get a rounded final product and new knowledge/understanding. However, its development needs a lead person, a champion, to link the range of players and hold the strands together.

From the perspective of the main community partners it seems very clear that the tripartite coming together of health and welfare organisations on the one hand with parent groups on the other within the umbrella of an academic institution would have been hard to assemble without the hosting arrangements and resources a university provides. Adherence to evidence-based and research-literate processes here is key and highly valued. It can act as a powerful counterbalance to organisations operating as evidence-free zones. A key point here too is that the university has a key role and that the other organisations would not have worked together in this way without it. The status afforded by the university, precisely because of its reputation for knowledge transfer is another point to be made here (Blincow, 2006). Hence we will probably continue to evolve our work with the university as the lead player.

A strong claim in the higher education policy documents is that knowledge exchange such as that of the RT project will lead to innovation and then on to major social and economic transformation beyond the separate participating organisations (Secretary of State for Education and Skills, 2003). There are some signs that knowledge exchange activities push us in this direction, and certainly towards what Wenger defines as a new 'landscape of practice' (Wenger, 1998, p. 118). So we should ask ourselves, what has our partnership done for disadvantaged children and their families? What has emerged that was not there before for them?

At this point in time the absence of rigorous and systematic evaluation we risk over-claiming for our partnership. In our work so far we have managed to provide a comprehensive and clearly articulated account of how practitioners and parents can bridge the gap between what resilience research tells us is helpful to children and what they are in a position to do in reality. We have also evaluated our workshop programme and can say with confidence that parents and practitioners exposed to our methods tell us it has made a difference to their thinking and to their practice (Freeman, 2006). From practice discussions, meetings and supervision we witness how RT has become embedded in our own working practices, and that of colleagues. Teaching the method to students on professional courses at both of our local universities (Brighton and Sussex) produces documented evidence from students that RT makes a difference to their outlook and practice. It may then, with so many perspectives covered, not be too much of an over claim to say that we are changing the culture of practice locally. We have incorporated RT into a parent support course, the evaluation of which shows that parents feel that their confidence and skills in parenting have increased. And finally, our scholarship and dissemination programme ensures that we drip feed our work into a wider orbit.

However, we have not as yet systematically captured the impact of RT on our practice with individuals in CAMHS, nor with our work with individual parents in Amaze. A very complex (and consequently expensive) long-term evaluation of the impact of RT remains to be undertaken in order to show whether our method really does promote sustained change for disadvantaged children. One thing that we have learnt from our work so far is that more sophisticated evaluation methods are needed to capture the outcomes of what we do. These are certainly ambitious aims and are unlikely to be realisable through the modest funding underpinning RT so far.

So the answer to our question about whether a new space has emerged in terms of hard outcomes for children remains elusive at this point. Despite all the complexity, along with enlightenment, the dimension of emergence is essential to hold in mind.

Conclusion

This chapter has provided an account of one partnership in our RT work, and attempted to understand how it has developed and been sustained. To do this, we used ACE, a framework for evaluating community–university partnerships. We did not self-consciously set our work up in this way, so we have analysed the attractions of our partnership retrospectively.

It is surely the case that partnership cannot be artificially fabricated. However, operational managers and prospective partners might use the ACE framework to help maximise opportunities for action. Thinking through attractions, conservation, contingencies, crevices, expectations, enlightenment, and emergence can steer partnerships in helpful directions and orientate novices to the landscape of community–university partnerships. Furthermore, if prospective partners thought-shower the different dimensions of the framework and find little of substance, it may alert them to the fact that this partnership is unlikely to succeed. For operational managers, the ACE framework may be useful for thinking through the allocation of scarce funding. We are not suggesting that operational managers in community–university partnerships cease taking risks on partnerships. The complexity of discovering what actually works in these relations points to the worth of not playing things too safe. However, where resources are tight and the fit is vague, *perhaps* less money should be gambled on partnerships that predict very weak associations with the dimensions of ACE.

We are careful to say 'perhaps'. This is because there is a great deal in this area that we do not know for sure. Sophisticated research on the precise nature and form of community–university partnerships would be needed to progress this agenda. And at this stage of our development it is sufficient to keep the claims and the hope of their eventual fulfilment in our consciousness.

References

Blincow, D. (2006) Personal communication (Derek Blincow, Consultant Child and Adolescent Psychiatry, Sussex NHS Partnership Trust).

Brown, J. S., and Duguid, P. (1998) 'Organising knowledge', *California Management Review*, Vol. 40, pp. 90–111.

Donaldson, L. (2001) *The contingency theory of organisations.* Thousand Oaks: Sage.

Fineman, S. (2000) *Emotion in organisations.* London: Sage.

Freeman, M. (2006) *Evaluation of "Box of Tricks"*, unpublished report.

Galtung, J. (1967) 'On the effects of international economic sanctions with examples from the case of Rhodesia', *World Politics*, Vol. 19 No. 3, pp. 378–416.

Hart, A., Blincow, D., with Thomas, H. (2007) *Resilient Therapy with children and families.* London: Brunner Routledge.

Hart, A. and Wolff, D. (2006) 'Developing local communities of practice through local community–university partnerships', *Planning, Practice and Research*, Vol. 21 No. 1, pp. 121–38.

Jones, C., Ferreday, D., and Hodgson, V. (2006) 'Networked learning a relational approach – weak and strong ties', *Lancaster University: Proceedings of the Networked Learning Conference.*

Layard, R. (2004) Happiness and public policy, *LSE Health and Social Care Discussion Paper Number 14*, pp. 1–16. London: London School of Economics.

Layard, R. (2005) *Happiness: Lessons from a new science.* London: Allen Lane.

Masten, A. S. (2001) 'Ordinary magic: Resilience processes in development', *American Psychologist*, Vol. 56 No. 3, pp. 227–38.

Mauss, M. (2000) *The gift: The form and reason for exchange in archaic societies* New York: W. W. Norton.

Østerlund, C. and Carlile, P. (2005) 'Relations in practice: sorting through practice theories on knowledge sharing in complex organisations', *The Information Society*, Vol. 21, pp. 91–107.

Østerlund, C. S. (2006) 'Combining genres: How practice matters', *Proceedings of the 39th Annual Hawaii International Conference on Systems Sciences (HICSS'06).* Hawaii.

Secretary of State for Education and Skills (2003) *The future of Higher Education.* Cm 5735. London: HMSO.

Smith, M. K. (2003) 'Communities of practice', *The encyclopaedia of informal education*, available at www.infed.org/biblio/communities of practice-.htm. Accessed June 2007.

Wenger, E. (1998) *Communities of practice: Learning, meaning, and identity.* Cambridge: Cambridge University Press.

Wenger, E., McDermott, R., and Snyder, W. M. (2002) *Cultivating communities of practice.* Boston: Harvard Business School Press.

Wenger, E. and Snyder, W. M (2000) 'Communities of practice: the organisational frontier', *Harvard Business Review*, Jan–Feb, pp. 139–45.

Making community–university partnerships work: The key success factors

Debi Roker

Introduction

This chapter describes some of the key success factors involved in making community–university partnerships 'work'. The information presented is based on research undertaken by the author into the community–university partnership programme (Cupp). The chapter summarises the learning from the research to date, focusing on both the University of Brighton's and community participants' views and experiences.

In the early stages of the Cupp programme, an external evaluation of the programme was commissioned. Following a competitive tendering process, the author was appointed to undertake this evaluation. The evaluation was not on a large scale (accounting for one day per month of the author's time), but aimed to take an overview of Cupp projects and activities, focussing on the experiences of those involved.

The information in this chapter was collected in a variety of ways, including face-to-face and telephone interviews, focus groups, and self-completion questionnaires. Over 50 people were involved in total. A focus of the interviews was on what people thought were the key success criteria. First, however, some context is provided – what sorts of community–university partnerships have taken place elsewhere, and what key 'success' factors have been identified?

'What's worked' in community–university partnerships elsewhere?

There is a growing literature on community–university partnerships across the world, and much of this information (both published and unpublished) is referenced throughout this book. Much of this literature refers to factors that have contributed to the success of projects and activities.

The majority of the publications in relation to university-community partnerships come from the United States (see for example Lerner and Simons, 1998). It is useful to identify the main 'success' factors that have been identified by some of these writers.

A key text in this respect is Todd, Ebata and Hughes (1998). These authors state that progress in community–university partnerships has been slow, because of the complex interaction of organisations and people. This theme is reflected by a variety of writers on this topic (for example Suarez-Balcazar, Harper and Lewis, 2005). Interestingly, Todd *et al.* also stress that collaborations between universities and communities are usually thought of as collaborations between *individuals* in both these settings. Todd *et al.* offer an alternative perspective: 'Although we tend to think of collaborations as interactions between individuals, in fact, collaborations represent the interplay between systems' (Todd *et al.*, 1998, p. 231).

Connected to this point about the importance of systems, these authors suggest that those involved must discuss, and agree, the boundaries around their work. Thus, for example, is a particular collaboration aimed at influencing pupils at a local school, or is it more about parents, staff and the local community around the school? As the authors describe it:

> It is important that collaborations carefully define the level at which change is desired and include stakeholders in the collaboration who are able to effect change at that level. (Todd *et al.*, 1998, p. 238)

Having a shared (and agreed) vision of the objectives of a project or activity is therefore central to success. These early conversations must, Todd *et al.* believe, reflect the often very different interests and priorities of universities and communities. All those involved in a collaboration must learn about and understand the other group's perspectives, their different priorities and methods, and the different ways in which they might monitor and evaluate what they do.

In addition, Todd *et al.* describe two broad sets of factors affecting the success of collaborative projects between universities and communities. These include factors within the university, including senior staff commitment, availability of resources, and infrastructure support (such as administrative time, personnel input, finance support, etc.). At the community level they focus in particular on what they describe as 'entrepreneurial social infrastructure'. This refers to the existence of community resources and cohesion, at the human, financial, and technological level.

A detailed review of the literature in this area is outside the scope of this chapter. However, there are some consistent themes that emerge from the literature, in terms of those factors that are associated with success and 'what works'. These factors can be summarised as follows:

- a *shared vision* about the aims of university-community collaborations in general, and individual projects and activities in particular
- *mutual benefit* and learning
- *good personal relationships* and 'openness' to new ideas and ways of doing things
- individual and organisational *flexibility*
- senior staff leadership and commitment

- *commitment and enthusiasm* from universities and communities
- organisational infrastructure and support

Given the number of times that these aspects come up in the literature as 'success' factors (albeit with different language and concepts used), they provide a useful structure to the Cupp evaluation results described in this chapter. To what extent is Cupp able to demonstrate the seven factors above? Are there other factors that help us understand 'what works' in Cupp activities?

Key success factors in Cupp – similarities and differences

The factors associated with community–university success in the literature are reviewed below, focusing on the experiences of Cupp participants.

A shared vision

In the interviews, the author explored how people viewed the aim of Cupp in general, and their project or activity in particular.

The participants' views could be broadly categorised in two ways. First, there was one (relatively small) group of participants who felt distanced from the broader Cupp programme, as they were mainly involved in only one project or activity. This group of participants found it difficult to describe the aims of Cupp, because they didn't necessarily see themselves as part of this broader programme. It should be stressed that many participants did not see this as particularly problematic. They knew the aims of their project or activity, and felt very engaged in this. Whilst not always sure about the 'vision' of Cupp, they clearly felt they had a shared vision and ambition for the work they were engaged in.

The second group of participants, who formed the majority, were able to describe the aims of Cupp in some detail. However, few had a single 'line' to describe the aims of the programme, but rather listed a combination of the following three aims, as given below:

To help improve the lives of disadvantaged groups and communities

This aspect was mentioned repeatedly, in particular by the community participants. For example:

> It is about making a difference, definitely. It's focussing on the people at the bottom of the pile. Refugees, asylum seekers, gay and lesbian youth, older people. All these groups, those who are most vulnerable. That's why I'm involved anyway. (Community participant)

To help share university expertise with the local community

In talking about the aims of Cupp, many of those interviewed talked about traditional views of universities as 'ivory towers'. A key aim of Cupp, participants felt, was to challenge this image, and to share university expertise with its local community. For example:

> There is that view, you know, that we're here ... we're here in our ivory tower ... doing nothing (laughs). The Cupp stuff aims to challenge this, to show that we have something to offer. (University participant)

To help community organisations to benefit from the resources and expertise held at the university

Many of the respondents commented on the wide range of community and voluntary groups in the local area, and how these could benefit from greater involvement with the university. For example:

> ... it's about making partnerships, working together to make a difference. (University participant)
>
> ... there's a lot of money there, a lot of resources. This project is all about opening it up, making resources available to the community. (Community participant)

Whilst there is clearly overlap between these latter two aims, it was particularly the community participants who focused on using university resources to *benefit* local people.

Interestingly, few participants used the phrase used by most senior staff in Cupp – 'mutual engagement for mutual benefit'. This is an interesting finding. Does this mean that, according to Todd *et al.* (1998) that Cupp participants do not have a 'shared vision', one of the key success factors in this kind of work? It is difficult to offer a clear conclusion to this. However, despite the broad-ranging descriptions of Cupp aims described above, there was a core of 'exchange' and 'sharing' of expertise at the heart of most people's definitions. There was also a link to social justice and tackling disadvantage in many people's descriptions. Using this assessment, Cupp can be seen to have a shared vision, albeit one expressed at a number of different levels. As projects and activities grow and develop over the long term, it will be interesting to see if there is greater clarity about aims and objectives of the programme as a whole.

Mutual benefit

Most participants highlighted some form of mutual benefit from Cupp, where both universities and communities gained something from collaborations. Although there were many similarities between the ways in which mutual benefits were identified by the community and university partners, there were differences. First, the main themes in terms of benefits and outcomes identified by *university staff* were as follows:

University students gaining a range of skills

This was a very commonly-mentioned outcome from the Cupp programme. For example:

> ... for the students, it was a real eye-opener for them, it really was. Seeing how [group of people] lived, the realities of their lives, for a lot of them the struggles that they have just surviving day to day. It was a really important developmental opportunity for our students.
>
> ... they [department's students] have got a huge amount from it. Interpersonal skills, wider experience, research skills.

These responses were particularly common amongst those university staff whose students were *actively* engaged in the local community, such as by visits, themed days, or collaborative activities. An example of this was university pharmacy students working with elderly residents locally to help them to understand their medication.

University teaching has improved

Most university staff felt that their teaching had improved as a result of their Cupp work. For example:

> I do think about my teaching differently now, what I'm doing, how I'm doing it, and in many ways who it's for. Yes it's had a huge impact on my teaching, and research, for me and many of my colleagues.
>
> Doing [the project] has made me re-think my teaching, a lot I'd say. It's, I suppose, it's grounded it, if that makes sense. It's made it more real.

One university lecturer described, for example, how they had built 'real-life' case studies into their teaching about social issues. This 'brought teaching to life' and led to much greater levels of discussion and debate. In addition, where students had been involved in active engagement in the community, they brought these experiences to teaching.

Making research 'real'

A number of the university staff members who were interviewed talked about how Cupp had made their research more 'real'. By this they meant, for example, that they were able to 'test out' ideas:

I understand this group [of disadvantaged people] much better, in a more, well, honest way than I did before.

What I do feels a lot more real now, I suppose that I'm talking about real people and real issues. Being part of it [a project with a community group] yes, it's made it real for me.

Personal and professional development

Many of the university staff talked about 'unexpected' benefits from their involvement in Cupp projects and activities. These were wide ranging, but can best be classified as personal and professional development resulting from Cupp involvement. For example:

... in a strange way, well, I suppose, it's that I'm more confident. All those meetings, developing the partnerships, all that. It's made me feel 'yeah, I can do this, I do have something to offer.'

Second, the views of *community participants* are described below in terms of how they saw the mutual benefits and outcomes from Cupp.

Contact with 'experts' – people who have skills that the voluntary and community sector does not always have

This theme came up repeatedly in the interviews with community participants. For example:

... a huge boost for us, really. We just don't have the money to buy in the people we're working with on this project.

... there's a huge amount of specialist knowledge there [the university] and it's great to be able to tap in, to tap into it to help our work.

It should be stressed that many community participants were initially sceptical about whether the university really had anything to offer. Whilst not all events or activities necessarily proved 'successful' from the community's point of view, most were convinced that the university was worth pursuing.

Learning about research and evaluation

This positive outcome was mentioned by the majority of the community partners. The research skills most commonly mentioned included doing needs analysis, monitoring and evaluation, secondary analysis, and undertaking original research. Many of the respondents had considered many aspects of research as 'beyond them' before becoming involved in Cupp. For example:

We're really into it now, we've become research bores (laughs). Yeah, you know it's all 'we could do this, we could do that'. It's made us realise that a lot of research is just common sense, and we can do it ourselves.

Many participants also then reported using research and evaluative methods in their work, to identify the needs of clients for example, or to support a funding bid.

Improved networking for staff and the organisation

Cupp was seen by many participants to have helped them to develop a range of new networks. These networks were seen as invaluable for both informing and disseminating current work, and developing future work.

Getting funding to undertake joint projects and initiatives

Securing funding, or gaining an improved knowledge of funding sources, was a frequently-named outcome of Cupp involvement by many respondents. For example:

It's really opened up things for me, for us. We've found all these great sources of funding that we never knew were there.

Helping organisations to think more strategically

Many of the community participants stressed how valuable it was to have university staff available who could 'play devil's advocate' in a helpful and practical way. This, many said, had helped their organisation to think through the evidence-base for their work. For example:

... sometimes it's painful, but it has helped to have someone ask us difficult questions. Our work is better as a result.

One community worker, for example, explained how a session with a university researcher made them realise that their definition of an 'evidence-base' for their work was very different to that which was being used by most funders. As a result they changed the way in which they collected monitoring and evaluation information.

Giving the work of community organisation 'authority' and 'credibility'

Having the 'university tag' as one person described it, suggested that a project or activity has been properly thought through and planned, and that it was evidence-based. For example:

> ... it does give us an edge, shows that we've done it properly. Yes it looks good for us, that we've had this involvement with the university.

As can be seen from this section, both university and community staff could identify a list of ways in which mutual benefit had occurred through collaboration between the university and the community. This is not to say that it was always 'plain sailing' – many relationships and collaborations faltered and struggled, and most had times when they were considered as in trouble. However, what most people believed 'got them through', and that contributed to success in projects, was the factor described below.

Good personal relationships and 'openness' to new ways of doing things

Todd *et al.* (1998) and other writers, have identified how successful community–university partnerships are characterised by good personal relationships and 'openness'. This was repeatedly highlighted by both the university and community participants who were interviewed. For example:

> It's essential, you have to like people, get on with them, have some sort of rapport. It's not about being best buddies, you know (laughs) but feeling you can do business. (University participant)

A common theme from the research was that successful community–university partnerships involved people being willing to listen and learn from each other. This was not just a matter of approach – it was a really practical issue. One of the themes that came up regularly was about the different language and systems used by universities and communities. These were often impediments to joint working, and had to be 'got through'. For example:

> ... it is different. People in the university world and the community have different ways of thinking, use different jargon. It has been difficult to get through that ... (University participant)

For a small number of those involved, this had become an impediment to join working. This was either because of the slowness of administrative systems in the university, or a feeling that the university did not respect and value the expertise of community workers. Most people, however, believed that you have to persevere to get through these sorts of issues and difficulties:

> They talk a different language sometimes, the university. But you have to stick with it. Keep asking questions. 'What's this?' and 'what does that stand for?' Don't be afraid to ask, or it'll just go over your head. (Community participant)

Many of the participants commented on how it was difficult for new partnerships to get through the barriers of different language and procedures. They often talked about the importance of having a 'broker' (in this case Cupp staff) to negotiate the relationships. The Cupp team were seen to 'interpret' different agendas and priorities, explain different language and procedures, and encourage collaboration. This theme is returned to later in the chapter.

Individual and organisational flexibility

A key element that emerged was the importance of compromise and negotiation in making collaborations between universities and community groups 'work'. Most commonly, participants talked about the importance of a flexible approach. In addition, some participants described the importance of not being 'precious' about things, such as particular approaches or methods. There were some tangible examples of the importance of compromise and negotiation. Several community partners, for example, expressed irritation with some of the priorities of university staff. For example:

> They want to write all these articles in journals that no ones reads. It's so irritating, you know, 'does that matter?' I ask them. (Community partner)

> The RAE I think it's called, you know, academics talking to other academics and all the ivory tower stuff. (Community participant)

Despite these irritations, however, the two individuals above also acknowledged that they had to 'live' with this:

> … but, you know, I have to live with it. That's how they [academics] are judged. It's important, you know, to them for their careers. It's not for me, but, yeah, I have to accept it's something they want out of our project. (Community participant)

In addition to accepting the different agendas and work priorities of community groups and universities, participants talked about the need not to be 'precious' about things. As this university staff member described it:

> … as an example. I'd say the university is very informal in many ways, you know this contract goes to this person, and then another one is slipped their way (laughs). But [community group] weren't like that. They were really strict with equal ops and stuff. So everything had to be open and advertised. Early on that really irritated me, but I could see that was what they did. I had to give way, you know, bite my tongue. (University participant)

A worker from a community group described a similar issue:

You can't be precious, you know? Like this is our ethics, or how we do things, and you need to fit round us. We've all had to compromise a bit. It wouldn't, like, wouldn't work otherwise. (Community participant)

Senior staff leadership and commitment

The literature in relation to community–university partnerships states that senior staff leadership and commitment is a key characteristic of successful collaborations. It is interesting that, as a theme, this was rarely mentioned by those interviewed in the research. However, this should not be read as implying that participants did not view senior staff as not supporting the project or activity that they were involved in. Rather, it is likely to be a reflection of the fact that many of those who were interviewed were researchers and community members working 'on the ground' of Cupp projects and activities. Thus the issue of senior staff support for community–university partnerships was not asked about directly, and rarely came up spontaneously.

Commitment and enthusiasm from universities and communities

Many of the participants in the research talked about the importance of some 'fairly simple things' in getting partnerships going, and keeping them going. One of the most common 'what works' factors mentioned in the research, concerned all those involved being fully committed to the work. This was most often described as being 'genuine', 'being committed', and 'really wanting to make a difference'. Where this commitment was lacking, or was half-hearted, relationships and partnerships often floundered. For many of the participants, a commitment to social justice had to be there for a community–university partnership to survive, and to thrive. For example:

Yes, I work at the university but I'm not doing this, working in this area for nothing. I believe in it. And I want to work with groups that share that view. That's why it's worked with [community group]. They're there, on the ground, but I'm here too, if you see what I mean. We're just coming at it from different angles, but we have the same aim. (University participant)

The final section of this part of the chapter explores a key aspect that is said to contribute to the success of partnership projects – organisational infrastructure and support.

Organisational infrastructure and support

Most of those who were interviewed in the research did not believe that community–university partnerships came about naturally, or organically.

Thus they considered that occasional links between universities and communities were developed, but often in a very individualised or ad hoc way. Most participants talked about the importance of a specific programme such as Cupp, in forging, developing, and negotiating links. The majority of those interviewed believed that their collaboration would not have happened without the Cupp programme. This begged the question of what infrastructure and processes are needed to support the development and maintenance of effective community–university partnerships. Drawing on the experiences of those interviewed, the following aspects are considered to be particularly important:

- *Organisational structure and 'push'* – by this respondents talked about such things as a central body (such as the steering group) to organise and facilitate collaborations, and to assist with disagreements and problems. Such a body was seen as essential in keeping a 'forward momentum' and pushing the university and the community to explore different options and different ways of working together on issues.
- *Providing a 'first port of call'* – here respondents talked about the importance of having one or two named individuals that both community and university people could go to for advice, or with enquiries. This prevented, as one respondent put it, having 'a great big wall of faces and bureaucracy' to work through. Thus having a Helpdesk manager, and a Project Manager, was seen as important to facilitate signposting.
- *Financial support* – here participants talked most commonly about the importance of having project funding for joint activities, including covering staff time. However, what people also found important was having small amounts of money (or provision in kind) for such things as meetings, refreshments, transport, etc.
- *Administrative and technical support* – in this context participants were mainly referring to two distinct but connected elements of Cupp. This included 'traditional' administrative support, in the sense of the co-ordination of meetings, management of room bookings, chasing up payments, etc. In addition people referred to technical support for particular issues, such as making a video, or using a particular type of software. One participant described these as 'bedrock issues', which provide the foundation for effective joint working.
- *Networking and learning opportunities* – having the infrastructure of a programme like Cupp enabled people both to network and to develop learning opportunities. Many people considered this a particularly important element of joint working. Thus people referred, for example, to finding out about individuals, organisations and networks that could help support their work. They also heard about events and activities where they could learn more about the area they were interested in. One participant described this as 'glue, the sort of glue that can hold it all together, keep people engaged with each other'.

These various elements of Cupp infrastructure were, of course, seen as closely interconnected.

Conclusion

In conclusion, this chapter has aimed to synthesise the main factors that make community and university partnerships 'work', drawing on data from the external evaluation of the programme. As has been demonstrated throughout this chapter, there were many very positive comments made by evaluation participants about Cupp projects, processes, activities and outcomes. Both community and university partners considered that Cupp promoted shared benefit, and shared learning, and addressed key issues of disadvantage and social justice. As the evaluation (and the other chapters in this book) make clear however, it was not all plain sailing. Setting up and maintaining community–university partnerships is never a simple process, and there are inevitably difficulties, controversies, and tensions. Many of the respondents in the evaluation described Cupp as a complex process, akin to a 'journey'. What came through most strongly, however, was the positive learning that has come out of Cupp. This included the key factors that contribute to the success of university-community partnerships that have been described in this chapter. It is appropriate to finish with the following quote from a community participant, who was initially sceptical of what could come out of university-community collaboration:

> ... it's been amazing for me, I have to say. Because I was sceptical, I wasn't sure it could work. But it does, it's really working AND it's making a real difference to people's lives. (Community participant, Cupp)

References

Lerner, R. M. and Simons L. A. K. (1998) *University-community collaborations for the twenty-first century*. New York: Garland.

Suarez-Balcazar, Y., Harper, G., and Lewis, R. (2005) 'An interactive and contextual model of community–university collaborations for research and action,' *Health Education and Behaviour*, Vol. 32 No. 1, pp. 84–100.

Todd, C., Ebata, A., and Hughes, R. (1998) 'Making university and community collaborations work', in R. M. Lerner and L. A. K. Simons, *University-community collaborations for the twenty-first century*. New York: Garland.

Chapter 16

View to the future: What have we learnt and where might we go next?

Angie Hart and David Wolff

Introduction

This chapter, written by and from the perspective of two of the editors of this book, reflects on what we have learnt from our Cupp initiatives to date, drawing out common issues illustrated in the individual chapters. It also tentatively sets out some possible points of departure for future engagement activity and offers a view on how we may approach some of the challenges we face.

We believe Cupp has been a proven mechanism for developing sustainable partnerships between the university's schools and local communities, through community and voluntary sector organisations, for mutual benefit. There is great confidence in Cupp acting as a 'point of entry' to the university for project work, brokerage, joint bids, research and practice development. As we saw earlier in this book, Cupp has strong support from the university's governors, senior management, academics, staff and students across the institution. It links with other social engagement activities; has been independently evaluated; and enjoys local, national and international respect. The volume and range of activity has been considerable.

These are some of the successes. What of the challenges that yet remain?

Six main challenges inform this chapter. First, we aspire to involve others more deeply. Although, as the preceding chapters illustrate, we have made progress in working with community organisations, Cupp has capacity to further the systematic involvement of community members themselves, particularly the most disadvantaged. And even involving community organisations every step of the way, meeting their needs and ours, defeats us at times. The issue of involvement also holds relevance for students. Much has been achieved here, but with the right resources in place we could achieve greater reach and greater student involvement in the governance of Cupp and its projects.

Secondly, we want the next stage of Cupp to see a shift from a series of projects to a sustainable programme. Some of this is implicit in the change of funding to be part of the university's main budget for its core costs (which we address below). But achieving this shift requires us to determine what organisational shape Cupp should take, and how it should link with other engagement activities.

The third and related challenge is to think hard about 'scaleability': how big should Cupp grow and what is the best balance between breadth and depth. We have to ask whether one of Cupp's critical success factors has been its relatively small-scale and highly focused nature. For the future, other questions include whether Cupp concentrates on deepening what it is doing and sustaining existing individual pieces of work to their next stage or whether it should assume existing pieces of work can now fend for themselves and concentrate instead on starting new pieces of work.

The fourth and ongoing challenge is to find innovative solutions to the complexities of evaluating and demonstrating the impact of this kind of work. Although the evaluations included in Part 5 of this volume, of both individual projects and the Cupp programme as a whole, are largely positive, they are rarely if ever couched in the sort of quantifiable ways required of much public policy, particularly if specific public funding is to be secured. Like much of that realm, they have yet to tackle the issue of underlying economic benefit. The university's 2007–12 Corporate Plan commits the institution to increasing its community engagement activity during the next five years, and to demonstrating this through an initial and subsequent audit. Similarly, commitment to the Talloires Declaration, described in Chapter 1, requires that the University will carry out an audit of engagement.

This leads to the fifth challenge, which concerns the policy context. Nationally, the funding council's own strategic plan makes much of the broader role of universities in public life, and of changing expectations upon them. It is seeking to complement its well-established emphasis on knowledge transfer and business interaction with more recent notions of public engagement and knowledge exchange (see Chapter 1).

Finally, against that national policy context, the completion of this book coincides with a time of major change in the institutional operating context for Cupp. As explained in Chapter 1, we received a 'golden hello' to the world of community–university partnerships from Atlantic Philanthropies, and developed an excellent working relationship with them as the initial funder for Cupp. Since then their funding priorities have changed and they are unable to support us further. The new University Corporate Plan has taken economic and social engagement to heart and the university has decided to fund Cupp's core costs as part of its mainstream budget. In this context, Cupp has ceased to be a separately-funded initiative and has become part of the institutional infrastructure, one of a range of initiatives seeking to achieve a broad set of institutional objectives. This is more than merely a change in funder. It implies a change in the scope of funding and raises for us the challenge of generating project funding; of keeping partners fully involved in decision making; and of how to address the other issues raised here in a new context.

In this complex terrain we need to develop work in collaboration with community partners and with other colleagues and students in the University, and to do so in ways that fit with the opportunities available and the emerging policy context. The shift to funding Cupp as a core function of the university changes the way in which answers to these challenges need to be agreed – and also what these answers are likely to be.

The remainder of this chapter therefore offers some thoughts to stimulate debate about how we might prioritise our efforts. It also considers ways in which we might conceptualise and operationalise Cupp for the next phase. We have three major issues to consider; what are the *areas* of work on which we might concentrate, and we cover this in a section below entitled 'addressing inequalities'. The second section, 'communities of practice', considers Cupp's *organisational* form. Finally, 'pursuing mutual benefit' addresses issues of *outcome*.

Addressing inequalities

Running alongside the initiation and development of Cupp is the debate about what universities are for and how they should relate to those who are outside them. The university's new Corporate Plan 2007–12 aims for the institution 'to become recognised, as a leading UK university for the quality and range of our work in economic and social engagement and productive partnerships'. The plan further commits the university to consolidate progress in widening participation in higher education where it interprets participation as not only about individual access to a higher education qualification and the related social mobility but also about the more general accessibility of the university's resources. The university is therefore committed to opening itself up in a number of ways and to redefining what is meant by higher education participation, as discussed in Chapter 1.

As Chapter 2 shows, Cupp refocused itself within its first phase of funding to concentrate more explicitly on two areas of work, namely tackling disadvantage and promoting sustainable development. Recently we have added a third: enabling social enterprise, and thus far we have promoted a fairly broad interpretation of each remit. Both sustainable development and social enterprise came on stream in Cupp a bit too late for inclusion in the project chapters of this volume.

But why have we placed each of these under the umbrella of addressing inequalities? To some readers it may seem that the latter two are quite different agendas, but our understanding sees them both falling broadly within the remit of addressing inequalities. We have three reasons for this.

First, our work in relation to disadvantaged communities can be broadly understood to be a quest to address inequities; for example access to art in Chapter 11 and access to higher education for refugees, as we saw in Chapter 8. Addressing inequities of access to the university can of course be understood as part of our response to the widening participation agenda discussed in Chapter 1.

Second, we see 'sustainable development' as situated in the inequity caused by environmental degradation. The argument that richer nations and richer individuals within nations do more damage to the environment but suffer fewer consequences is compelling (Harris, 2000, p.5).

Third, social enterprise, as the Nonprofit Good Practice Guide suggests, is 'A nonprofit venture that combines the passion of a social mission with the discipline, innovation and determination commonly associated with for-profit businesses ...' (see Nonprofit website).

It is yet to be decided if our future Cupp strategy will to go so far as to concentrate *all* our efforts on those social enterprises that promise the most in addressing inequalities. The same goes for our engagement with disadvantaged communities and with sustainable development.

However we choose to answer these questions, as we move into the next phase of Cupp's development, we will need to ask what our commitments will look like in practice. In particular, should we maintain the focus on working with and through community organisations or should we do more to work directly with individuals; and how should we understand community – as distinguished from social – engagement.

There are now a handful of Cupp projects in 2007 that increasingly involve marginalised individuals themselves in a direct, sustained and reciprocal relationship with the University. The projects represented in this book demonstrate that on the whole, we were not at a stage of development that could embrace and sustain such inclusive practice. This type of engagement – what we call Socially Inclusive Engagement – sits towards the furthest end of what might be described as an 'engagement continuum' for higher education. It tackles a major challenge facing universities: engaging members of the public who are least likely to have ever had a formal relationship with higher education through teaching, research or knowledge 'transfer', but for whom a relationship with us holds promise.

An important question for us, therefore, as we help to shape the next stage of Cupp's development, is whether this principle should inform all our practice. If achieved, it would indeed be a powerful model for making university knowledge and skills practical and accessible; informing people's life choices; and increasing well-being. However, the specific communication and access challenges of this socially inclusive engagement are considerable and require specialist skills and partnerships. This point is well made by Ridley and Fox in Chapter 11.

As we set forth on the next stage of Cupp we will have to think carefully about the limits of what is possible, about what is the best way for the university to add value, and about the gains and losses in impact that might be involved.

Communities of practice

The second idea that we think will help us address our six practical challenges concerns 'communities of practice' as an organisational form.

Through project work, the steering group and other brokerage mechanisms, we have developed some Cupp relationships of real depth. As this book illustrates, Cupp involves a complex mix of activity and a web of relationships that did not have neat university structures within which they could be fostered and accommodated. Questions have included: the organisational relationship between Cupp and other university functions including those aimed at widening participation and supporting business-university interaction; how best to ensure sustainable cross-faculty academic and student buy-in; and how to manage the complexities of working across different university sites. As Cupp has evolved, we have found the concept of 'communities of practice' (CoP) valuable in helping us to both describe our work and to cultivate activity.

The concept of CoPs is a practice theory. This means it starts from an emphasis on what people actually do in the world-practice or activity. According to practice theorists, we define, develop and learn how best to do what we do in doing it, rather than always behaving according to an abstract rule about how to act in a given context (see Østerlund and Carlile, 2003, p. 95). The literature on CoPs is diffuse but has a number of core components. In thinking about the future of Cupp, we are finding that a number of features of CoPs are particularly relevant.

First, there is an emphasis on sharing: CoPs are defined as 'groups of people informally bounded together by shared expertise and passion for a joint enterprise' (Wenger and Snyder, 2000, pp. 139–40).

Second, they do not define some members as experts and others as non-experts. The idea is that everyone can learn from each other once people are clear what the different skills are around the table. Whilst CoPs are not without leaders and champions, the concept emphasises the dynamic nature of group development. For example, Lave and Wenger (1991, p. 29) see the idea of legitimate peripheral participation as 'a way to speak about the relations between newcomers and old-timers … newcomers over time move from peripheral to full participation, building a sense of belonging and shared identity.'

Third, they are fluid, and do not have set start and end points:

> They come together, they develop, they evolve, they disperse, according to the timing, the logic, the rhythms, and the social energy of their learning. As a result, unlike more formal types of organizational structures, it is not so clear where they begin and end. In this sense, a community of practice is a different kind of entity than, say, a task force or a team. (Wenger, 1999, p. 96)

Fourth, although fluid, they do have a sense of purpose, 'a passion for a shared interest', and this is about change and improvement. People join a

CoP to learn how to approach a given task or issue in a better way, and to put that learning into practice (Wenger et al., 2002, p. 5).

Fifth, they are concerned with, and driven by a focus on what occurs on the boundaries between different stakeholders and their affiliations. One aspect of this debate concerns what are termed 'boundary spanners' – culture brokers and interpreters between partners (Wenger, 1999, p. 109). This dimension highlights the value of members working across organisational and disciplinary boundaries, and promotes the fostering of news ways of working for which current structures and processes are not adequate. It helps avoid getting bogged down with working strictly within teams and conventional organisational hierarchies. In Chapter 14, Hart and Aumann explore how 'brokering' by boundary spanners, who are members of multiple constituencies, introduce elements of one practice into another context. These individuals need to be able to manage their ambivalent position in order to translate and align differing perspectives. And they need sufficient legitimacy to carry influence as well as to address conflict effectively. In our work, partners arrive with many differences, the value of which are not always easily articulated and understood.

Spatial issues hold strong relevance for boundary working across community and university contexts. The entire Cupp enterprise is to an extent about 'reach' and accessibility. Several chapters in this collection make the point that university partners needed to confront disparities from the early stages of the partnerships. Are academics implicitly expecting community practitioners to always come to them? Might some meetings or seminars be best delivered on university territory and others in the community? We have found that providing library cards and access to desk space can help community practitioners feel more included as mutual partners on projects, and can certainly make project work more effective. Likewise, as we have demonstrated in this book, some academics are spending much more time on community ground. MacDonald et al. in Chapter 7, explained in relation to their neighbourhood renewal project that one of the researchers was employed by the university, but based within the Neighbourhood Renewal team in the Local Authority.

Sixth, the concept helps to think about the nature of knowledge and how it is defined, developed and disseminated – at the heart of the university endeavour. 'Communities of practice' is a way of thinking about ways of working and of handling knowledge that typifies the shift from what has come to be known as Mode 1 to Mode 2 knowledge (Gibbons et al., 1994; see also Part I Introduction).

The concept of CoPs can, in this context be helpful, because we have seen that it can help us shift university culture and practice towards types of knowledge that are more productive in addressing 'real world' issues and in delivering real engagement. If Mode 2 knowledge already typifies knowledge that helps us understand how best to approach difficult social problems that defy current organisational structures and processes, Modes 3 and 4 bring us dispositional, transdisciplinary, political and change-orientated knowledge. Using the notion of CoPs may lead us towards what we have described as Mode 5 knowledge, with an emphasis on the co-production of knowledge by universities and communities.

Finally, thinking in terms of CoPs helps us to think critically about aspects of power.

Power and CoPs

Whilst we recognise the CoP concept to be helpful in developing our work, the issue of organisational and personal power is one that has repeatedly been made in this volume. Eraut (2002) and Miller *et al.* (2001) found that issues of differing power and status and different allegiances can constrain multiprofessional co-operation and learning. Relations may also be shaped by gender, ethnicity, age, sexuality, and disability (Clark and Newman, 1997; Balloch *et al.*, 1999). These issues ring true for relations between universities and communities (for example, see Conlan *et al.* in Chapter 8).

Universities have considerable power and it would be naive to ignore this. Also, universities, their funders and stakeholders have their own processes, perceptions and priorities.

Using the notion of CoPs can help here by forcing the various partners to recognise their individual sources of authority, but also to see the potential in everyone for contributing, whatever their structural position and organisational affiliation. We need a degree of realism here.

Pursuing mutual benefit

The third idea shaping our thinking as Cupp moves ahead is to maintain an emphasis on achieving mutual benefit as an outcome. One of the key aims of Cupp, right from the start was to 'Enhance the community's and University's capacity for engagement for mutual benefit.'

Mutual benefit is an interesting notion, particularly in relation to ideas about knowledge and CoPs. The former debate, as we have seen, concerns not only what counts as knowledge but who is understood to create it: where does expertise lie? The latter requires us to recognise the differences between members of a CoP as much as their common interest. In higher education policy and practice, conventional discourse has referred to knowledge transfer, where knowledge moves from a more knowledgeable partner (the university) to another less knowledgeable one. Some consider there to be elitism and status inequality implicit in the notion of university knowledge transfer (Hart and Wolff, 2006). Knowledge exchange challenges some of this – where a genuine sharing relationship is in order, in which knowledge is shared and created between partners and expertise is more dispersed.

Some aspects of Cupp's work have adopted a knowledge transfer model, for example, the Helpdesk. And it may well be appropriate for us to continue to develop some of our functions in this vein. Indeed, one reading of a social justice agenda would always see merit in sharing the technical expertise of the university without expecting anything in return.

This caveat aside, a future model of Cupp is likely to see us increasing our commitment to knowledge exchange, in which the university's knowledge is changed through the project process as much as that of the partner organisation. In Chapter 13, Millican *et al.* argue (see p. 161), 'True partnerships can only come from a situation in which one partner is not always in charge ...' In our view, expecting and working towards mutual benefit is an important discipline. It does not overlook the fact that different kinds of expertise reside in different places. Rather, it assumes that these various sorts of expertise together create more than the sum of their parts and that all partners can learn from each other. We recognise the unique merit in a more egalitarian exchange, with the sustainability it encourages and enthusiasm of academics and students to participate particularly worth mentioning.

However, finding the right fit, and then proving this to be the case, are continuing challenges.

Below we extrapolate from our work to date to summarise what communities and universities can, in our experience, hope to give and receive from each other.

Universities offer:

- Disciplinary, policy and research knowledge
- Staff time
- Student time
- Money
- Status especially in perceived independence
- Brokerage
- Technical skills training (e.g. research)
- Learning and discussion forums
- Contribution to community governance
- Curriculum and teaching
- Contributions to grant applications

Communities and their organisations offer in return:

- Experiential knowledge
- Access to community members
- Staff time
- Real world testing grounds for academic knowledge (both research and teaching)
- Research skills
- Research team contributions
- Contributions to university curriculum
- Opportunities for students to engage with local people

- Contribution to university governance
- Contribution to funding applications

In some cases this is relatively straightforward. However, as Viljoen *et al.* in Chapter 12 note, in others it is harder: Hart and Aumann in Chapter 14 suggest that maturity in relations of trust brings the opportunity to develop exchange relationships that more closely resemble what anthropologists have described as 'gift exchange'. In such relationships delayed reciprocity begins to feature, and to become embedded in the culture of each organisation, without looking for short-term or individual tangible gains.

Pursuing mutual benefit then looks set to offer a welcome challenge for us as we move forward in Cupp. Even more of a challenge, as authors in earlier chapters (see Chapter 1, and Chapters 14–15) of this book suggest, is *demonstrating* the benefits. We have begun some of this work; our external evaluation of Cupp is captured in Chapter 15, and the university has committed to an institutional audit of its community–university partnership activity as a further step along this road. For this task we will look to the Talloires initiatives, the benchmarking work undertaken in the US, and to UK developments in Strathclyde, Bradford, Herefordshire and Cambridge (see University of Cambridge, 2004; PACEC, 2006; Pearce, Pearson and Cameron, 2007; Tufts University, 2007; Universities UK, 2006; CIC, 2005).

However, as others have pointed out before us, the complex social and economic processes involved make demonstrating impact at the level of citizen health, local population etc., labour intensive and methodologically challenging. Placing an economic value on these 'activities of a societal nature', is according to Pearce *et al.* who have attempted to do so, particularly problematic (see Pearce, Pearson and Cameron, 2007, p. 33).

With the resources available to us thus far in Cupp, it is little wonder then that we have not yet managed to capture the long-term effects. And it is ever more important that we find innovative ways of doing so.

Conclusion

This book has introduced various ways of planning, describing and evaluating activity developed and delivered through the Community-University Partnership Programme. The chapters seek to offer a useful guide to any university or community manager, planner, academic, student, community member and practitioner, who wish to develop ways of operating across the university-community boundary for mutual benefit. But alongside the tools introduced here, the volume also makes clear that much of the work of community–university partnership is experimental and experiential: innovation depends on these. Go too far the other way however, and nobody knows what they are doing. The dangers are that projects fizzle out, drift aimlessly towards at best a limp, and at worst a destructive, conclusion. As Brown and Duguid (1998) argue, in knowledge exchange work, structure and organic flexibility do need to work in creative tension to curb each other's worst excesses.

As we have seen in this volume, there is nothing in community-university partnerships that place them above the dilemmas and difficulties found in other areas of collaborative working. The risk of conflict is inherent, and often poorly disguised by the rhetoric of 'partnership working' (Aldgate and Stratham, 2001), or a 'common philosophy' (Miller, et al. 2001) in inter-agency and inter-professional practice. In other contexts professional turf wars (Eraut, 2002), agency politics (Roaf, 2002) and unconscious organisational processes (Granville and Langton, 2002; Obholzer and Roberts, 1994) familiarly derail the best of intentions for joint practice. Bureaucracies can dampen passion and enthusiasm.

Written as a community–university collaboration (acknowledging all the limitations and difficulties that this implies), this volume has sought to articulate *some* of the challenges that our work entails. And this final chapter in particular, contributes our thoughts on where Cupp's future priorities may lie. Articulating the challenges is always tempting, possibly because in the range of tasks that lie before us, it is one of the easiest. More difficult, and yet far more interesting is to acknowledge the positive possibilities and to turn them into action.

Hence we want to end on a note of enthusiasm. We have touched on the complexities of organisational form and processes, difficulties delivering individual projects, and some real policy dilemmas. Yet our concern in this book lies more with the spaces – metaphorical and physical – that we have found at both the policy level and in our own working arrangements to develop a more collaborative and a more entrepreneurial culture, and to dramatically increase the capacity for, and quality and impact of, community–university engagement.

References

Aldgate, J. and Stratham, J. (2001) *The Children Act now: Messages from research. (Studies in Evaluating the Children Act 1989)*. London: Department of Health.

Balloch, S., McLean, J., Fisher, M. (eds.) (1999) *Social services: Working under pressure*. Bristol: Policy Press.

Brown, J. S. and Duguid, P. (1998) 'Organizing knowledge', *California Management Review* Vol. 40, pp. 90–111.

Clark, J. and Newman, J. (1997) *The managerial state*. London: Sage

Committee on Institutional Cooperation (CIC) (2005) *CIC reports: Draft resource guide and recommendations for defining benchmarking engagement*. Available at: http://www.cic.uiuc.edu/groups/CommitteeOnEngagement/ archive/documents/EngagementReportREV2-22-05.pdf. Accessed 19 April 2007.

Eraut, M. (2002). 'Conceptual analysis and research questions: Do the concepts of "learning community" and "community of practice" provide added value?', Paper given to annual conference, American Educational Research Association, New Orleans: pp. 1–13.

Gibbons, M., Limoges, C., Nowotony, H., Schwarzman, S., Scott, P., Trow, M. (1994) *The new production of knowledge: the dynamics of science and research in contemporary societies.* London: Sage.

Granville, J. and Langton, P. (2002). 'Working across boundaries: Systemic and psychodynamic perspectives on multi-disciplinary and inter-agency practice', *Journal of Social Work Practice*, Vol. 16 No. 1, pp. 23–7.

Harris, J. M. (2000) 'Basic principles of sustainable development', Global Development and Environment Institute Working Paper 00–04. Available at: http://www3.ima.kth.se/nordenvt20/3c1397/Harris00.pdf. Accessed April 2007.

Hart, A. and Wolff, D. (2006). 'Developing communities of practice through community–university partnerships', *Planning, Practice and Research*, Vol. 21 No. 1, pp. 121–38.

Higher Education Funding Council for England (HEFCE) *HEFCE Beacons for Public Engagement , Invitation to apply for funds December 2006/49* at http://www.hefce.ac.uk/Pubs/HEFCE/2006/06_49/ (Accessed 20th January 2007).

Laing, S. (2006) Community-university partnership conference. Introduction by Pro-Vice Chancellor. Brighton: University of Brighton. Available at: http://www.brighton.ac.uk/cupp/pdf%20files/why_community.pdf.

Lave, J. and Wenger, E. (1991). *Situated learning: Legitimate peripheral participation.* Cambridge: Cambridge University Press.

Miller, C., Freeman, M. and Ross, N. (2001) *Interprofessional practice in health and social care: Challenging the shared learning agenda.* London: Arnold.

Nonprofit Good Practice Guide. See website at http://www.npgood practice.org (Accessed 17 April 2007).

Obholzer, A. and. Roberts, V. Z. (eds.) (1994). *The unconscious at work.* London: Routledge.

Østerlund, C. and Carlile, P. (2005). 'Relations in practice: sorting through practice theories on knowledge sharing in complex organizations', *The Information Society*, Vol. 21, pp. 91–107.

Pearce, J., Pearson, M. with Cameron, S. (2007) *The ivory tower and beyond: Bradford University at the heart of its communities.* Bradford: University of Bradford.

Public and Corporate Economic Consultants (PACEC) (2006) *Economic and social impact of the University of Hertfordshire on Welwyn Hatfield.* Cambridge and London: PACEC.

Roaf, C. (2002) *Coordinating services for included children: Joined up action.* Buckingham: Open University Press.

Tufts University (2007) *Strengthening the civic roles and social responsibilities of Higher Education – building a global network. The Talloires Conference 2005.* Available at http://www.tufts.edu/talloiresnetwork/conferences.html. Accessed 19 April 2007.

Universities UK (2006) *The economic impact of UK higher education institutions – a report for universities UK by Ursula Kelly, Donald McLelland and Iain McNeal.* University of Strathclyde. London: UK.

University of Cambridge (2004) *University of Cambridge Community Engagement 2003–04.* Available at: http://www.admin.cam.ac.uk/offices/community/community_report.pdf. Accessed 19 April 2007.

Wenger, E. C. (1999) *Communities of practice: Learning, meaning, and identity.* Cambridge: Cambridge University Press.

Wenger, E. C., McDermott, R., Snyder, W. M. (2002) *Cultivating communities of practice.* Boston: Harvard Business School Press.

Wenger, E. C. and Snyder, W. M. (2000) 'Communities of practice: the organisational frontier', *Harvard Business Review* Jan–Feb, pp.139–45.

Biographies

Jonas Addise

Jonas Addise was born in Eritrea and grew up in Ethiopia where he attended Addis Ababa Commercial College before coming to the UK. Jonas is now settled in the UK and studying at university. He also works as a community interpreter.

Michael Aling

Michael Aling received his BA (Hons) in Architecture at the University of Brighton in 2004, after which he was involved in the formation of the Open Architecture Studio as a research assistant until the end of 2005. Michael is now studying for a postgraduate diploma at the Bartlett School of architecture, UCL.

Peter Ambrose

Professor Peter Ambrose holds degrees from London, McGill and Sussex Universities and taught at the last of these for 35 years until his retirement in 1998 since when he has been a Visiting Professor at University of Brighton. His current research interests centre on the effect of poor housing on health. He has produced seven books and about 160 other publications.

Kim Aumann, Jenny Broome-Smith and Ros Cook

Kim Aumann, Jenny Broome-Smith and Ros Cook all work at Amaze, a Brighton-based charity providing information, advice and support for parents of children with special needs. Their work has been cited by the Joseph Rowntree Foundation, the Audit Commission and Ofsted Joint SSI Inspectors as an example of excellence. Kim led the development of

Amaze from the outset with a conviction that parents have the capacity to create positive futures for their families, despite the obstacles of prejudice and discrimination. She believes the voluntary sector is uniquely placed to improve the life chances of disadvantaged groups. Jenny has a background as a medical researcher. She brought her passion for action research to the creation of the Compass, the city's database of children with special needs. Ros is a parent of a child with special needs. Her commitment to social justice has been the common thread throughout 20 years working in the statutory and voluntary sectors. Collectively they aim to leverage change by breaking down the gaps between theory and practice.

Susan Balloch

Professor Sue Balloch is Professor of Health and Social Care at the University of Brighton. She is also Director of the Health and Social Policy Research Centre and joint Academic Director of Cupp. She is the co-editor of several recent publications from The Policy Press, including *Partnership Working: Policy and Practice* (2001), *The Politics of Evaluation: Participation and Policy Implementation* (2005) and *Care, Community and Citizenship* (2007).

Paul Bramwell

Paul Bramwell is from the Working Together Project, a charity providing training for the not-for-profit sector in Brighton, Hove and Sussex.

Daren Britt

Dr Daren Britt is a Senior Lecturer at the University of Brighton where he leads a professional diploma in 'Substance Misuse Intervention Strategies'. Daren is a person-centred counsellor and works with adult men who have experienced childhood sexual abuse. His interest is in seeking to identify how residential substance misuse practitioners experience and conceptualise childhood trauma amongst their client groups and how this informs practice.

Jenny Broome-Smith

(see under Kim Aumann)

Dana Cohen

Dana Cohen manages the Brighton and Sussex Community Knowledge Exchange (BSCKE) at the University of Brighton. Located within the Community University Partnership Programme at the University of Brighton, BSCKE supports the development of socially-transformative projects involving students, academics, volunteers, service users and staff from community organisations. Dana is also a psychotherapist in private practice.

Nicky Conlan

Nicky Conlan works at the University of Sussex in their Centre for Continuing Education. She jointly manages the REMAS Project for Refugees, alongside colleagues from the University of Brighton. She also works as a research fellow.

Ros Cook

(See under Kim Aumann)

Mark Cull

Having worked for Barclays Bank for 14 years, Mark changed careers in 2001 to work for Hove YMCA. Mark has worked in various roles within the organisation and was working with young homeless people when he developed the LGBT youth homelessness research project. Following the publication of the research report, Mark is now disseminating the report to local stakeholders, government departments and members of parliament.

Alice Fox

Alice Fox is a senior lecturer on the Access to Art Project in the Arts Faculty, University of Brighton. She is a visual arts practitioner/filmmaker and has been working with people with learning disabilities in the arts since 1992. Recently she has been researching and developing inclusive teaching and learning strategies.

Stuart Gill

Stuart Gill is currently the Training Manager with the West Sussex Drug and Alcohol Action Team. His responsibilities include co-ordinating a wide range of training opportunities across the diverse variety of agencies in the statutory and independent sectors delivering interventions into substance misuse. He has been closely involved in partnership working with further and higher education providers to expand the choices of education and training provision to ensure that all those working or wishing to work in the substance misuse field have access to high quality training.

Sarah Hardman

Sarah Hardman is Deputy Director of the Sussex Learning Network. Prior to taking up this role, Sarah managed the Neighbourhood Renewal programme for Brighton and Hove, part of the government's national agenda for regeneration and social inclusion. Sarah's background is in education and marketing, and she has worked in the public, private and voluntary sectors.

Angie Hart

Professor Angie Hart is Professor of Child, Family and Community Health at the University of Brighton, and Academic Co-Director of Cupp. She is also a child and family therapist in the local health services, and the parent of three children with special needs, adopted from the care system.

Philip Haynes

Philip Haynes is a Reader and Deputy Head of School in the School of Applied Social Science, University of Brighton. He previously worked as a probation officer and social worker, specialising in substance misuse. His current research interests include the organisation and management of public services and the application of online learning and information technology in higher education.

Stuart Laing

Professor Stuart Laing is Pro-Vice-Chancellor (Academic Affairs) and Professor of Cultural Studies at the University of Brighton. He was previously Dean of the School of Cultural and Community Studies at the University of Sussex. He was involved in the formation of Cupp and is Chair of the Cupp Steering Group.

Dee MacDonald

Dee MacDonald is a Research Fellow within the Health and Social Policy Research Centre. Research interests include the Community and Voluntary Sector, public service delivery and neighbourhood renewal. She is also Curriculum Lead for the community practice strand of the Sussex Learning Network, working towards ensuring coherence in educational provision for those working in and with communities.

Elizabeth Maddison

Elizabeth Maddison is Head of Strategic Planning at the University of Brighton. She is also chair of the Association of University Administrators Planning Forum. She was formerly a member of the secretariat of the National Committee of Inquiry into Higher Education. She is the co-author, with David Watson, of *Managing Institutional Self-Study* (Open University Press, 2005) and is the author of the funding bid that initiated Cupp.

Margaret Maiden

Margaret Maiden is Headteacher at Kingston Buci First and Nursery School in Shoreham, West Sussex. Margaret is an experienced headteacher and completed an MA in Education at Sussex University. She is committed to developing stronger links between her school and the wider community and chairs the Locality Extended Schools Group.

Elaine McDonnell

Elaine McDonnell was Project Administrator for Cupp from its inception in March 2003 to October 2006, coming to the role from the Brighton Business School where she worked as a School Administrative Assistant. Elaine is currently Office Manager for the West London Lifelong Learning Network.

Stuart McLaughlin

Stuart McLaughlin is Headteacher of Falmer High School in Brighton.

Philip Miller

Philip Miller received his BA (Hons) in Architecture at the University of Brighton in 2004, after which he was involved in the formation of the

Open Architecture Studio as a research assistant until the end of 2005. Philip is now completing his postgraduate diploma in Architecture at the University of Brighton.

Juliet Millican

Juliet Millican manages 'Student-Community Engagement' programmes within Cupp at the University of Brighton. She has also worked on widening participation and community education programmes in Africa, India and the UK and published on adult education and literacy. Current research interest concerns transformational learning and student/community engagement in post-conflict societies.

Linda Morrice

Linda Morrice has worked in adult and community education for almost 20 years. She has always had a particular interest in refugees and asylum seekers with whom she has learnt, taught and researched in a variety of contexts and projects. Linda is a Lecturer in Continuing Education at the University of Sussex.

Carol Mullineux

Carol Mullineux is a qualified and experienced youth and community worker who has worked locally in both the statutory and voluntary sectors. For several years she was involved with the Coalition4Youth which supported young people's participation in decision-making within Brighton and Hove. She has co-ordinated several participatory evaluations of projects.

Sue Nunn

Sue Nunn is a sculptor and community arts practitioner. She has worked on several large-scale publicly-sited sculptures. In parallel, she has run art courses with a wide variety of groups, in recent years focusing this work on a deprived outer city area of public housing.

Hazel Platzer

Dr Hazel Platzer is a Faculty Fellow with HSPRC and an independent research consultant. She conducts qualitative research in mental health and has completed a large number of evaluations and needs assessments working closely with the community and voluntary sector. She has particular expertise in conducting sensitive research with hard-to-reach and socially-excluded communities.

Pauline Ridley

Pauline Ridley is based in the Centre for Learning and Teaching at the University of Brighton. Her involvement in curriculum development and research for the Access to Art project combines her educational interests in inclusive teaching practices and the development of visual literacy in higher education.

Polly Rodriguez

Polly Rodriguez joined the Cupp team in October 2003. As Research Helpdesk Manager for Cupp, her job has involved designing and developing a research support service for local community and voluntary organisations. A substantial element of Polly's role has involved supporting the development of research partnership projects and research collaborations between University of Brighton and the local community. Prior to this Polly held a research post in the Health and Social Policy Research Centre at the University of Brighton.

Debi Roker

Dr Debi Roker is Co-Director of the Trust for the Study of Adolescence. Debi has spent most of her career as a researcher, and has long been interested in collaborations between researchers and practitioners, particularly in the charity sector. Debi was commissioned to undertake the external evaluation of the Cupp programme, and copies of her reports can be found on the Cupp website.

Fayegh Shaafi

Fayegh Shaafi is a Kurd from Mahabad in Iran. He has been in the UK for three years. Fayegh is currently studying for his Masters Degree in Civil Engineering after which he hopes to either find work as a civil engineer or study for a Ph.D.

Stephen Silverwood

Stephen Silverwood is a published author and freelance journalist. He has an MA in Anthropology. He currently manages several refugee and asylum-seeker projects in the voluntary sector.

Andre Viljoen

Andre Viljoen is an architect and Subject Leader for undergraduate architecture at the University of Brighton's School of Architecture and Design. He runs the final year of the undergraduate architecture programme and established 'Open Architecture' to facilitate the integration of live practice into architectural teaching. His research focuses on sustainable design.

Lynne Ward

Lynne graduated from Lancaster University in 1989 with a B.Sc. in Ecology. She spent a brief spell in the NHS before entering local government where she works today. She is the Community Development Co-ordinator at Adur District Council and is also completing an MA in Health Promotion at the University of Brighton.

Tracy Whittle

Tracy Whittle trained as a Registered Nurse and then went on to study Social Policy and Administration at Sussex University. After graduation she went on to work in the Voluntary Sector in Sussex in a variety of roles including providing casework, service co-ordination and community development. She is currently a Carers' Development Worker.

David Wolff

David Wolff is Director of Community University Partnerships Programme (www.cupp.org.uk), the subject of this book. Prior to this David worked in the community and voluntary sector in the fields of homelessness, advice and information services; project management and in the use of IT. He has occupied roles as a service delivery worker, manager, director and consultant.

Cherie Woolmer

At time of writing, Cherie Woolmer was Widening Participation Manager at the University of Brighton and project manager for the Refugee Education, Mentoring and Support (REMAS) project. She is now project manager of the South West London Academic Network (SWan). Cherie has ten years' experience of working with women's mental health charities and teaches at the University of Brighton.

Elena Woolridge

Elena Woolridge worked as a paediatrician in the Ukraine but has been unable to get her medical qualifications recognised in the UK. She has recently completed a Holistic Therapies course and now works as a self-employed holistic therapist. She is enjoying still helping people to be healthy.

Victoria Young

A law graduate, who has worked as a researcher for an MP in Parliament and the LB Greenwich Extended Schools Pathfinder Project. After volunteering for Falmer High School's Community Services she took the role of one of the researchers on the Falmer 'extended schools' project.

Glossary

a2a	Access to Art
ABI	Area-Based Initiative
ACE (way)	attractions, conservation, crevices, contingencies, expectations, enlightenment, emergence
AS	Asperger Syndrome
BHDVF	Brighton and Hove Domestic Violence Forum
BME	Black and Minority Ethnic
BMEC	Black, Minority Ethnic Communities
BSCKE	Brighton and Sussex Community Knowledge Exchange
CAB	Citizens Advice Bureau
CAMHS	Child and Adolescent Mental Health Service
CBR	Community-Based Research
CCE	Centre for Continuing Education (Sussex University)
CE	Community engagement
CKE	Community Knowledge Exchange
CPD	Continuing Professional Development
CRB	Criminal Records Bureau
CRF	Community Research Forum
Cupp	Community University Partnership Programme
CVOs	Community and Voluntary Organisations
DAATs	Drug and Alcohol Action Teams
DANOS	Drug and Alcohol National Occupational Standards
DATs	Drug Action Teams
DDN	Drink and Drug News
DfES	Department for Education and Skills
ES	Extended School (see FSS)
ESF	European Social Fund
ESOL	English for Speakers of Other Languages
FEFC	Further Education Funding Council
FSS	(Extended) Full Service School
GCSE	General Certificate of Secondary Education
HCAT	Hastings College of Arts and Technology
HE	Higher Education
HEFCE	Higher Education Funding Council for England

HEIs	Higher Education Institutions
HEIF	Higher Education Innovation Fund
HEROBAC	Higher Education Reach-Out to Business and the Community
HSPRC	Health and Social Policy Research Centre (University of Brighton)
ICT	Information and Computer Technology
IELTS	International English Language Testing System
IT	Information Technology
LEA	Local Education Authority
LGBT	Lesbian, Gay, Bisexual, Transgender
MOU	Memorandum of Understanding
NESTA	National Endowment for Science, Technology and the Arts
NHS	National Health Service
NR	Neighbourhood Renewal
NT	National Trust
NTA	National Treatment Agency (for Substance Misuse)
NTORS	National Treatment Outcome Research Study
NVQ	National Vocational Qualification
OCN	Open College Network
OFSTED	Inspectorate for children and learners in England
PAW	Project Art Works (Hastings)
PTA	Parent Teacher Association
RAE	Research Assessment Exercise
REAP	Bradford University metrics: reciprocity, externalities, access, partnerships
REMAS	Refugee Education Mentoring and Support
RIBA	Royal Institute for British Architects
RCOs	Refugee Community Organisations
RT	Resilient Therapy
SCIP	Sussex Community Internet Project
SEN	Special Educational Needs
SENDA	Special Educational Needs and Disability Act 2001
SMEs	Small and Medium-sized Enterprises
SMPQ	Substance Misuse Practitioners' Questionnaire
SRG	Senior Researchers Group
SVQ	Scottish Vocational Qualification
UK	United Kingdom
WILAW	Ways into Learning and Work
YMCA	Young Men's Christian Association

Index